From Our Own Correspondent

TONY GRANT joined the BBC after working in commercial radio and on newspapers in Merseyside. He was at BBC Radio 1's *Newsbeat* before becoming a foreign news editor and then, in 1992, the producer of *From Our Own Correspondent*. He is married to a political correspondent and they have two children.

From Our Own Correspondent, broadcast on BBC Radio 4 and on the BBC World Service, has been one of BBC Radio's flagship programmes for more than fifty years. Every week more that 100 million people listen in.

From Our Own Correspondent

A Celebration of Fifty Years of the BBC Radio Programme

Edited by Tony Grant

With a Foreword by Kate Adie

PROFILE BOOKS

This paperback edition published in 2006

First published in Great Britain in 2005 by
PROFILE BOOKS LTD
3A Exmouth House
Pine Street
Exmouth Market
London
EC1R 0JH
www.profilebooks.com

By arrangement with the BBC
BBC logo © BBC 1996
The BBC is a registered trade mark of the
British Broadcasting Corporation and is used under licence

1 3 5 7 9 10 8 6 4 2

Typeset in Palatino by MacGuru Ltd
info@macguru.org.uk
Printed and bound in Great Britain by
Bookmarque Ltd, Croydon, Surrey

A CIP catalogue record for this book is available from the British Library.

ISBN-10: 1 86197 747 6
ISBN-13: 978 1 86197 747 2

Contents

THE EARLY YEARS

Correspondents

Introduction

Just occasionally it doesn't seem like the best job you could have. This thought usually occurs to me while trudging into work over a rainswept Waterloo Bridge at dawn on a Saturday, hours before the programme is due to go on air; painfully aware that if those last two pieces don't arrive as planned, there won't be a programme to put out, and the continuity announcers will be reaching for discs marked 'Only to be used in times of crisis'. But invariably, and often at the last minute, the dispatches do come in; they're powerful, thought-provoking, colourful and beautifully written; an excellent programme comes together in the final few moments before transmission, and once again producing *From Our Own Correspondent* seems like a dream job.

I've been working on the programme since the early 1990s, but *From Our Own Correspondent* itself has been going for fifty years. It's one of BBC Radio's longest-running shows. Of course, a great deal has changed since the fifties both in styles of reporting and in advances in technology. In the early years, filing a dispatch for *From Our Own Correspondent* could be an arduous business. If anywhere near a foreign radio station, the correspondent might book a circuit at a specific time of day or night and, amid much line crackling and arguing with international operators, would then be hooked up to the newsdesk in London. If out of town on assignment, there was a faint possibility that a field telephone could be used. But in the unlikely event of the dispatch actually making it to London, the audio quality was usually so appalling, it would have to be read out by an announcer on duty at Broadcasting House.

Today, with 24-hour television and radio, the broadcast beast is insatiable; there are bulletins and programmes demanding reports and interviews night and day and the next deadline is always imminent. The mobile telephone means a correspondent can be reached instantly almost anywhere in the world. The portable satellite phone he or she will be carrying means that they can broadcast in near-studio quality and the portable video phone means they can also do live television interviews.

FOOC, as it's known, goes out on BBC Radio 4 and the BBC World Service several times a week. Our website is read by millions of people. Sometimes the correspondent offers us a dispatch, at other times we will contact him or her and try to persuade them to do a piece for us. The busier the correspondent is, the less likely he or she is to offer a piece; more likely we'll call them up on the mobile, plead for a dispatch for *FOOC*, which is often written late at night in the hours before the programme goes on the air.

Frequently, a journalist on a big story is confined to a hotel room for hour after hour filing voice reports and doing 'two-way' interviews with on-air programmes. The correspondents are sometimes heard complaining that they're so busy going on air that they have little chance to actually go to the scene of the story to see what, in fact, is happening.

I remember asking one of our senior people how he coped while out on a big breaking news story with the torrent of requests, hundreds of them, from the whole range of bulletins and programmes on both BBC radio and television. And how did he ever get any sleep? It was simple, he said. You filed for all of them, did all the two-way interviews, wrote all the dispatches, pondered long and hard on the piece for *FOOC* and made sure everyone was happy, whatever the hour. Big stories didn't happen every day, he said, and were only of interest for a relatively short period. After that, you could relax.

One or two correspondents tell us they knock off the 800-words we require in next to no time. Far more frequently we hear that the dispatch has been re-written over and over again and is still being re-shaped as the words are being spoken down the line to London. We've heard many times that writing for *FOOC* is a cathartic process. The reporter may return to the hotel in the evening bursting to tell more about the story, much more than can be included in a forty-second news clip or in a couple of answers in a live interview. There's the whole context to explain: how history shaped the events being reported on; there are people and places to be described, experiences to be shared.

On the programme, we try to mix the 'stories behind the headlines' with insights into life in different parts of the world. We welcome a great deal of colourful description of faraway places and plenty of humour too, and I hope a similar mix is to be found in these pages. When we came to selecting the chapters for this book, it sadly became apparent that many favourite pieces would have to be left out – I was strongly discouraged from editing a work which stretched to several volumes! As some earlier dispatches have been reproduced elsewhere, it was decided that we would include a larger proportion of contributions from more recent times, in particular the last ten years, a period in which a less formal and more personal style of writing for the programme has developed. The choice was essentially a personal one, although space constraints meant that we could include no more than one offering from each correspondent.

Compiling the book, like putting together the programme each week, involved much consulting of reference works. I suspect that few of my colleagues working in radio news and current affairs are as reliant on these works as we are in the *FOOC* office. We have a full shelf of them here in our office in Bush House in London and often we are reaching for them even as the correspondent is filing his or her piece from some distant location. Battle of Lepanto? What on earth was that all about? Rustle of pages. Ah yes, of course. October 1571, the naval clash between the Christian Holy League and the Ottoman Empire off the coast of Greece. 'Off of?' Surely she can't say that? And what's this 'Paddy' he's on about? Ah yes. From the Malay. Meaning rice in the husk. And 'the mills of God', where is that from? Oh yes. Henry Wadsworth Longfellow; and they do, of course 'grind slowly' and 'exceeding small'. And what about the word 'harass'? Has the time finally come to stop telling the correspondents it should rhyme with 'embarrass' rather than, in the American way,'Madras'? Language is, after all, constantly evolving. And, anyway, is it 'Madras' these days or are we calling it 'Chennai' now?

The pieces included in this book contain plenty of evidence that the foreign correspondent has a dangerous job. The list of journalists who've been beaten up, blown up and shot gets longer every year. Our colleague Kate Peyton died after being shot in Somalia as this manuscript was being prepared. The shooting in Saudi Arabia of Frank Gardner, a frequent contributor to *From Our Own Correspondent*, was another example of the perils of this business. He was left with serious injuries.

Yet the belief persists in some quarters that foreign correspondents lead a life of constant glamour; they shimmer from one exotic location to another, solving mysteries and uncovering international intrigue while becoming intimate with millionaires, film stars and secret agents. The expense account is limitless, the correspondent uses only the world's finest hotels and only rarely will this diet of hedonism have to be interrupted by anything as mundane as covering a story.

The reality, of course, is different. These days editors keep a close watch on what is spent; often they rule out travel altogether on grounds of cost and, when it is deemed essential, the correspondent has to operate within the tightest of budgets. There'll be a meals allocation which might just stretch to a sandwich at lunchtime and a pizza for dinner, and the firm is only likely to sanction treating someone to alcoholic refreshment if the expense claim is accompanied by copious documentary evidence proving that the journalist was lunching a contact of the status and influence at least of a US president and one, of course, who isn't a noted teetotaller!

It may be that there are one or two correspondents operating at the very apex of their profession who do get to stay at smart hotels, but many of those I know stayed in better places when they were impecunious backpackers in the years before they were journalists. Anyway, the dodgy hotels in remote corners of the world prove an invaluable source of anecdote. The Soviet Union used to provide the richest vein of hotel stories: the cockroaches and the lack of bathplugs, the bugged phones and the Mata Haris who came knocking in the middle of the night; the rude waiters and appalling service in the restaurants, the menus where nearly all the items were unavailable and those which weren't were of unspeakable nastiness.

As to the assignments themselves, how glamorous are they? The job involves a great deal of hanging around, often late at night or early in the morning, waiting for people to arrive at airports or to emerge from hospitals or courts clutching statements. Not much in the way of glamorous anecdote there.

One of the biggest news events of recent times was the Indian Ocean tsunami disaster. The correspondents there found themselves facing scenes of such horror they were unable to show them on television, while even the most experienced of journalists found it hard to summon up the words to describe the scenes they were witnessing. Although none had to endure the miseries of those who'd lost families, friends and loved ones to the tidal waves, they did have to work interminable days and nights amid the stink of piles of rotting corpses while short of food and sleep, surrounded by devastated, emotional people. This is about as far from glamour as anyone can imagine.

My thanks are due to Sarah McDermott, my colleague in the *FOOC* office, whose help with the preparation of these pages has been invaluable; to other *FOOC* colleagues past and present, Andrea Protheroe and Mike Popham; to our editors Maria Balinska and Gwyn Williams for their support; to Malcolm Downing and Peter Burdin in the BBC's Foreign News Department, who liaise with the correspondents on a daily and sometimes hourly basis; to the staff of the News Traffic area, who bring in the correspondents' reports night and day; and, of course, to the vast army – no, the golden horde – of BBC foreign correspondents past and present whose professionalism, courage, ability and sense of humour have made *From Our Own Correspondent* one of BBC Radio's most popular programmes these last fifty years.

Tony Grant
Producer of *From Our Own Correspondent*
Bush House
August 2005

Foreword

Kate Adie

Then: written by candlelight, script delivered by canoe, wireless broadcast interrupted by mosquitoes, accompanied by low-flying bombers and the world's inadequate plumbing and the sound of a distant country in tumult.

Now: tapped out on a laptop computer, script lost into electronic ether, satellite radio broadcast interrupted by mosquitoes and a cruise missile launch and the usual plumbing and the sound of a world still noisy with news.

The technology changes, but the desire to describe what it's like to witness history in the making does not, regardless of the hazards and hiccups in a correspondent's life. Not just the great events, but the small details which paint a vivid picture of everyday life.

From Our Own Correspondent is one of those special programmes for which contributors have to indulge in some discreet elbowing to win their place on air. Even in the most fly-blown or shell-shocked environments, after having rattled off countless terse dispatches for the news bulletins, it's a treat to be given five minutes of air-time to reflect on momentous events. Not that it's a heart-on-sleeve outpouring of personal emotion. Rather the sense of what it is like to be present at that notorious 'ringside seat of history'.

It's a seat which isn't always comfortable. However, this is a chance to catch the listener's ear about matters which don't always make the news. It's extraordinary the number of banquets which have to be consumed in pursuit of a story; the hotel bedrooms which double as insect traps; the government minders who confide they want to be poets; the militia roadblocks which turn out to be full of Manchester United fans; the transport arrangements which include camels, mules, dodgy rafts and trucks stuffed with sheep and forty-three of the driver's relatives; the moments when the poorest peasant offers hospitality, the soldiers break into song, the president produces his battered copy of Shakespeare. None of this makes the news, but it paints in the background and makes journalism memorable. And can be shared with others through the programme.

And there is so much else to tell about the world. Admittedly, we now have

24-hour news channels and can receive live pictures from the desert and the Antarctic ice-floe, but much of that news is dictated by convention. The media spotlight is narrow and harsh, excluding the fascinating detail, the reasons and the consequences. Our own correspondents are well-versed in spotting trends, long before the gigantic press horde descends upon a 'breaking story'; and they're also concerned to find what has happened to people, years after the earthquake, the assassination or the war have dropped out of the headlines. There's analysis and reflection, too, always made worthwhile by having the correspondent on the spot, conscious of the people in the local coffee shops or casualty department who have just given their views. And for those listeners who believe we're now becoming one unified and bland global marketplace, there are countless dispatches about the sheer oddities and weird joys which thrive despite cheap travel and television.

As a child, I listened to postwar wireless and was not a particular fan of the 'radio talk', pioneered by the BBC in the thirties – carefully grafted essays which revelled in telling language, backed with experience and shrewd judgement (Jennings and Toytown were more to my taste). But such a talk was intended for grown-ups – and still is. Away from the frenzied instant satellite chats, the simplification of complex conflicts into tit-for-tat action, the three-second soundbites and the numbing effects of dumb political correctness, there is still very much a place for a trenchant and colourful look at life to complement the brief news bulletin dispatches.

Over the years, the enthusiasm and amusement which correspondents bring to the job have been given full reign on the programme. Some have burst into song, others delivered full-throated football chants or political slogans, and many more attempted accents and acting which they'd formerly kept rather quiet about. All backed with a passion for communicating the essence of their experience, whether on the presidential plane over Texas or getting drunk in Mongolia.

But the essence of the dispatch is the personal fascination with both the everyday and the unexpected – and the correspondent's own reaction. And it takes a seasoned observer to find the balance between the egotistical and the mawkish participation which can so easily overtake an observer of high emotions and tumultuous events.

Our Own Correspondents find their balance in the midst of the awful and the awesome. They're part of a long tradition now, but one which responds to change. If this means wrestling with bits of exquisitely tiny computer equipment which has just been colonised by ants, well, that's all part of the fun. The satisfaction is sharing their experience with the listeners.

Europe

1
A Family Affair

Misha Glenny

The BBC's then central Europe correspondent explained how his relationship with his translator father led to a lifelong fascination with Europe and its peoples.
(8 January 1993)

'Here I am in Moscow. It is very cold.' Every time my father travelled abroad, which was frequently, he would dispatch four enormous colour postcards, one to each of his children. They were adorned with his dramatically curly Italic script, which aptly reflected his exaggerated fascination for life. Each sibling's postcard would add to the collective knowledge of where he happened to be. So, having learnt from the postcard sent to younger brother Paddy that Moscow was freezing, I was then informed: 'Here I am in Moscow. Everyone wears furry hats.' Of course, the information became progressively more taxing intellectually until we got to the postcard addressed to his eldest child, my sister Tamara: 'Here I am in Moscow. It is all pretty miserable and there are posters of Lenin all over the place, but there is plenty of vodka and caviar to take my mind off it.'

Lenin was an old acquaintance of mine long before I had heard of the Queen or Jesus Christ. Not that this implied approval of Vladimir Ilich on the part of my father, far from it. But his stern features stared down at us toddlers from every second book in the house, pictured either on his way to the Finland Station or impatiently pacing up and down in the elegant mansion where he passed some of his exile in Zurich.

For me as a child, Lenin was just another magical figure from Russia, my very own fantasy kingdom. He took his place next to the characters we would hear about at bedtime as my father translated Russian fairy tales for us before we went to sleep. Along with Lenin, there was Baba Yaga, the gruesome Russian witch who flew menacingly through the air in her mortar, rowing with her pestle. Few friends from childhood have left such an impression on me as Baba Yaga with her putrid yellow eyes. The shack where she lived deep in the forest stood on human bones and was lit by fire emanating from the skulls of her victims. Fairy-tale witches are not intended to be nice figures, but Baba Yaga's undisguised devotion to torture and cannibalism make the less likeable characters drawn by the Brothers Grimm look positively philanthropic.

On the brighter side, there was Vasilisa Prekrasnaya, Vasilisa the Beautiful, a gullible heroine whose evil stepmother sent her into the woods where she stumbled across said Baba Yaga. Her only salvation was a magic doll who comforted her every night after another miserable day in the service of Baba Yaga with the words: 'Go to sleep, Vasilisa, for morning is wiser than evening.' Of course, the following day brought even greater misery for Vasilisa, but then her doll belonged to that rich tradition of Russian politicians whose advice is better left ignored.

Our house was littered with mementos from Dad's encounters with Russians and other East Europeans. Probably the most valuable of these was his sixteen-stringed Portuguese guitar. He won this in Berlin in the early fifties when, as an officer in the Royal Horse Guards, he was working for military intelligence. Given his unswerving commitment to disseminate liberally even the most uninteresting piece of information, I often wondered as to his suitability for this line of work, especially since he seemed to spend much of his time fraternising with the Russians over a glass or two. That's how he got the Portuguese guitar. One evening he and some other British officers were drinking with the Soviets. As the senior Allied officer, he was challenged by his Russian counterpart. Each had to drink a pint of the other's national spirit. 'Of course,' my father told me with the sonic boom of a laugh which was his most striking hallmark, 'the Sov had to drink a pint of gin whereas I only had to deal with vodka and he was down on the floor before he'd finished the half.'

His tales of Berlin during the Cold War influence my understanding of history to this day. Those people responsible for regulating the Cold War on both sides of the Iron Curtain treated it as a great game. Moves often took a long time to execute in this ultimate ritual of brinkmanship in which ordinary people were pawns to be manipulated, more or less at will. Occasionally, of course, the pawns refused to budge, or worse still started wandering around the board against the wishes of the court pieces. When this happened in the

East, the results were spectacular, beginning with the uprising in East Berlin in 1953 and culminating, via the Hungarian revolution, the Prague Spring and Solidarity, in the revolutions in 1989. The West, however, did not enjoy a monopoly on the truth and its leaders were forced to resort to all sorts of dubious tricks to sustain its nuclear leadership in the game.

If the Cold War had been staged as a medieval morality play, then Duplicity and not Everyman would have been the central character. My father, for example, used to take regular trips into East Germany along the routes which the Allies were allowed to travel. His job was to lose his way on purpose, map the forbidden terrain and then play the absent-minded Englishman when the Russians arrested him, as indeed they did. On one such occasion, he was recognised by a Soviet officer. Would this mean the end of my father's career as master of ceremonies during Portuguese guitar drinking sessions? Not at all. Dad was immediately given lunch, which included thick, black Beluga caviar, and escorted politely back to West Berlin.

But beyond his curious anecdotes, I was fascinated by the baffling contradictions of both Russian and German political cultures which he outlined in his tales. In very different ways, the Russians and Germans were people without mercy and yet at the same time incorrigible romantics. So accustomed were they to shattering historical events that they wallowed in a hopeless fatalism while still dreaming of the essential perfection of the Russian or German soul. Hitler and Stalin forged a demonic alloy from power and violence. With this satanic material, they attempted to imprison history and then mould events in their image. Dad taught me how in the 1930s and 40s they built shrines to their peculiar dystopias which were constructed on mountains of skulls, to borrow a metaphor from the great Russian poet Osip Mandelstam. What was it about their national spirit which enchanted so much and yet appeared to deliver nothing but suffering? Why were Russia and Germany, two countries which my father loved dearly, hopelessly attached to the most ruthless examples of authoritarian rule in Europe this century? Following the revolution of 1989, this is once again more than a matter for idle speculation. Now as then, these two countries cradle the delicate future of the continent and even perhaps the world in their hands and it is to these great empires and cultures that we should be paying the closest attention.

To help me explore that dichotomy which led these tremendously resourceful peoples to autocracy and dictatorship, my father directed me to Russian and German literature. For when it comes to exploring the cruelty and despair engendered by despotism, they know no equals. The prison-camp literature of the Soviet Union is known chiefly through the remarkable work of Alexander Solzhenytsin, pages of which flowed through our house when my father was translating it. But of all the Gulag tales which Dad uncovered and conveyed into English, one stands out above the rest. *Faithful Ruslan* is the tale of a prisoner, known simply as the Shabby Man, who in 1955 is released under Khrushchev's amnesty. But the story is told through the eyes of Ruslan, the guard dog whose job it is to oversee the Shabby Man among others. This expressionistic use of animals is widespread in Russian literature and, in this case, it is used to great effect.

Ruslan views the Shabby Man and all others under his control as well-intentioned children who cannot know what is good for them. From cradle to grave, Russians must be told what to do by those who know better (the state). If that includes suffering, so be it. That, at the very least is what Ruslan, with his sharp teeth, believes.

My father found that his fascination for the subtleties of European life was not really compatible with the frequently mundane pen-pushing required by military intelligence. Not everybody made it to double-O grade and frankly the idea of Dad shimmying over the Berlin Wall at night is ridiculous.

But after leaving the army, he was soon back where he wanted to be, in Europe. My father landed a job as Wedgwood Pottery's European Sales manager. He was dispatched from London around the continent selling china. His remarkable capacity for languages proved a winner. In Stockholm, he needed badly to land a deal with a wholesaler. The latter spoke no Russian, no German, no French, no Italian, no English and no Spanish. No talk, no sale. My father went to the English department at Stockholm University and hired a student to teach him Swedish over the weekend. On the Monday morning, he waltzed back to his customer and in fairly decent Swedish secured the deal.

My father was an exception who proved the rule about the British and foreign languages. On the whole we are hopeless for two reasons. Everything else, such as poor language teaching, follows from them. Firstly as islanders we do not come into contact with other languages with anything like the frequency that other European cultures do. Secondly thanks to the Americans, English is the essential language of popular culture, so there is little incentive for young people to learn new tongues. Young Germans, Poles and Spaniards spend hours poring over the lyrics of Bruce Springsteen in order to be hip. Britons' linguistic incompetence is not just a social embarrassment. It is through knowledge of language that we understand foreign cultures. Only the English have derogatory terms for so many different nationalities. This is partly because our vision of Europeans is two-dimensional; our lack of interest in their languages means we do not know or care how they perceive the world. Instead we cover our insecurity and ignorance by labelling them 'wops', 'krauts', 'dagos' or 'paddys'.

The truth is that with three main Indo-European language groups, the Romance, the Teutonic and the Slav, dominating Europe, it is actually not difficult for the average European to develop enough language to get around the whole continent. The more languages you learn, the easier it becomes. As my father pointed out, you soon get to a stage where you can recognise immediately how the English word 'cheap' evolved from the Teutonic *'kaufen'* or *'koopen'*. The key to language learning is motivation. Once one is motivated, Europe becomes a treasure trove of historical and cultural absurdity begging to be explored.

It was no great surprise that my father began to devote himself full-time to translation. His translations were masterpieces, although he was hopelessly disorganised and slow. It was also evident to the whole family from an early stage that translation of literature is not a lucrative business. On the contrary, having developed champagne tastes on Wedgwood's expense accounts, my father was not able to satisfy these needs and those of a wife and four children on the erratic ginger-beer income of the freelance translator. He was so late with his translation of *August 1914*, the enormous tome by Alexander Solzhenytsin, that the publishers, Bodley Head, ordered him down to London, booked him into a hotel and sent a minder over to ensure that he didn't leave his room until he had finished the job. To rub his face in the dirt, they sent him the hotel bill six weeks later. I, for one, did not regard the demise of Bodley Head a few years ago as a blow to the British publishing trade.

My father's greatest achievement was to retrieve for an English-speaking audience the works of the Russian novelist Mikhail Bulgakov. His best-known work is *The Master and Margarita*, one of the most impressively complex novels of the twentieth century, which exposed the sham of the revolutionary Russian state in the 1920s and 30s by imagining a visit of the devil to Moscow. But there are lesser-known works of Bulgakov which I remember with even greater affection. The most curious of all, entitled *The Fateful Eggs*, was about a professor who during the early days of the Soviet state invents a ray which enlarges eggs, a process resulting in giant chickens and hens. Immediately recognising its economic potential, the Commissar for Agriculture requisitions the ray gun, but it is mistakenly used on a batch of reptile eggs. Soon the young Soviet land is being ravaged by huge reptilian monsters destroying all in their path.

These bloodthirsty leviathans, of which Bulgakov was warning, have regularly laid waste to Russia this century. Elsewhere, they have perpetrated the most despicable crimes against European Jewry and, even as I speak, they are again walking abroad in the Balkans. Sometimes they raise the banner of Slavdom, sometimes the might of the Aryans. They suck blood sometimes in the name of Christianity, sometimes in the name of progress. My father and I had our first falling-out when I was in my early teens. His unflagging liberalism frustrated me as a young socialist and my highly politicised view of life created a rift between us which separated us until his death.

Only then did the political implications of all the cultural work he did dawn on me. The fear and loathing of these totalitarian leviathans who live off human blood and suffering, this is what outraged him and motivated him. He would not, however, allow this outrage to spoil his fun. He was determined to enjoy his life and his friends through literature, through culture, by eating, drinking and laughing his way through adversity. There was enough of that partly thanks to the cruel wheel of history and partly thanks to his legendary inability to manage his financial affairs. It was only after he died, only after the Yugoslav wars began, that I understood how we shared a deep love of Europe and a deep fear of what this insecure continent is capable of.

Even in death, my father was determined to affirm life. He died in Moscow peacefully after an evening of doing what he did best, carousing with his Russian pals, singing songs, drinking vodka and eating zakuski and caviar. I will never be reconciled to his death, but I am comforted to know that he has not had to witness the slide of much of Eastern Europe into economic chaos and fratricidal war. He died believing there was still real hope for his beloved Russia.

2

Agostini Killed my Budgie

Andy Kershaw

*The annual TT motorcycle races on the Isle of Man have a special appeal for bike
fanatics. But it's a controversial event; many feel that the course is too dangerous
for the modern, powerful machines that take part and over the years several riders
have lost their lives. (5 June 1993)*

The old lady was taking the sunshine on the doorstep of her whitewashed
cottage, just along from the butcher's. 'Good afternoon,' she said. 'Grand
day for practice.' Her two-year-old great-grandson jabbed his finger into
the hot engine of my motorcycle. 'Bike! Bike!' he shouted. At this hour of
the day, Kirkmichael is a sleepy, picture-postcard village (you wouldn't be
surprised to meet the cast of *Trumpton* in the post office). But by late afternoon the street outside the cottage that Mrs Keggan has occupied these last
forty-seven years becomes part of the most dramatic motorcycle road-racing
circuit in the world: the last truly white-knuckle spectacle in motor sport.

The Isle of Man Tourist Trophy Races have been run on the 37-mile
mountain course since 1911. They began here to avoid mainland restrictions
on the closing of public roads for motor racing. That first race, on unsur-
faced roads, was won at an average speed of 47 mph. A bend on Snaefell
Mountain, known to this day as Keppel Gate and now a fast left-hander, is
so named because there was a gate there; in the early days of TT racing, the
leading rider was obliged to dismount from his spindly machine and open
it; and it was the duty of the luckless rider at the back of the field to get off
and close the gate behind him.

Top riders in the big event of race week, the six-lap Formula One, will be
averaging 122 mph, fickle Manx weather permitting; and TT fans are hoping
this year that they will see the first 125 mph lap of the island. Some corners on
the course – there are so many no one can agree on the precise number – are

taken at little more than walking pace. So, to be lapping at nearly 125 mph riders are dashing through other sections, between drystone walls, trees, bus shelters and lamp-posts, at a shattering speed. Coming down Kirkmichael High Street this afternoon, past the butcher's, the parish church, Quail's the grocer's and, of course, Mrs Keggan's front door, the 750cc hi-tech Formula One bikes will be touching 170 mph.

It is the sort of disruption that proud villagers in other parts of the British Isles wouldn't tolerate. But most Manx people are irredeemable race fans. Not only do they recognise their world-famous motorcycle races as part of the island's heritage, they also realise the annual boost that 50,000 spectators bring to the otherwise depressed tourist industry. Many of the hotels along Douglas's splendid Edwardian seafront are boarded up, sorry monuments to the cheap package-holiday boom of the late 1960s, from which Manx tourism has never recovered. And though the island needs as many visitors as it can attract, the closure of so many hotels creates an accommodation crisis during TT fortnight. I have already re-booked my ferry crossing and cottage in Kirkmichael for next year.

Park View Cottage, the Kershaw billet, is a race fan's dream, particularly for the early-morning practice sessions, which start at 5 a.m. I need only push my bed to the bay window, switch on the Manx Radio commentary and plump up my pillows to watch the bikes howl through Birkin's Bends, an ultra-quick right- and left-hander at the exit of the village, where the faster riders, using every inch of the road, brush their shoulders against the ivy-covered wall at 140 mph. Birkin's commemorates Sir Tim Birkin, a racer who died at this spot in 1927 after colliding with a fish truck. In those days they didn't bother to close the roads to ordinary traffic during practice.

More than 150 riders have lost their lives on the mountain course since 1911. This grim tally has led to the occasional media outcry, a boycott by several top riders in the 1970s and the loss of Grand Prix World Championship status sixteen years ago. The nine-times winner, Steve Hislop, and the current lap record-holder, Carl Fogarty, are not taking part this year. Neither has anything left to prove on the Isle of Man. Hislop, though careful not to condemn the TT outright, admits with characteristic humility that it was getting too fast for his liking. Two years ago, when he was clocked along the bumpy Sulby straight at nearly 200 mph, he described the experience of rushing between the hedgerows as 'aiming at the piece of light between the green bits'. It was difficult at that speed, he said, to see where he was going. Still, he has not ruled out the possibility of returning to the TT in the future.

The TT races are an anachronism. And they are, undeniably, very dangerous. Falling off a bike at Donington Park, a rider will slide across grass and land in a sand trap. On the Isle of Man, a competitor making a similar mistake would be lucky not to hit a gable-end or a telephone box. But there is one overpowering argument against banning the TT: people race here because they want to; nobody makes them do it. Alan Batson, a carpet-fitter from Aylesbury and a contender for a rostrum place, embodies the easy-going enthusiasm that sets the TT apart from the corporate self-importance of Grand Prix racing. 'The more you enjoy it,' he says, 'the faster you go.'

The second-largest TT entry in history, 530 riders from eighteen countries, including five women and a sixty-one-year-old grandfather, are flinging themselves around the island for the same reason that brought a young New Zealander, Michael Willemsen, to race here for the first time this week. He is going well, coping cheerfully with the biggest challenge of the TT: memorising the wriggling sequence of countless blind bends. 'Michael, why do you do it?' I asked him in the pub after his first practice session. 'It's costing you a fortune, there are no championship points, and tomorrow you might be killed.' He looked at me, still wide-eyed from his first practice session that afternoon. 'I love it,' he smiled. 'I've always wanted to race here, and now I'm doing it.'

But some TT fatalities have had no say in the matter. As I turned to leave her at her cottage door, Mrs Keggan seized my forearm. The first riders were just leaving Douglas, fourteen miles away, and Kirkmichael was waiting, as quiet as the grave. 'Giacomo Agostini was always my favourite,' she said, referring to the magnificent Italian MV Agusta rider of the 1960s. 'But then he killed my budgie.' For once I was lost for words. 'Y'see, his bike was so loud,' she explained, 'when he came down the street, the budgie had a heart attack and dropped dead. I've got another one now,' she added, and nodded at a nervous-looking bird in the cottage window.

'What chance do you give him?' I asked, trying not to laugh.

'Oh, he'll be all right,' she said. 'The bikes aren't as noisy these days.'

3

Tides of History

Kevin Connolly

*The glory days, for Russians living in the remote communities which had been set
up north of the Arctic Circle in the Stalin era to mine minerals and other natural
resources, were long gone. The Soviet Union had treated these people like heroes
and paid them accordingly, but that all changed with the fall of Communism,
when the workers of the far north found themselves increasingly isolated.*

(6 October 1994)

If you ever want to find Norilsk on a map, not that there's any reason why
you should, trace a finger across Russia from Europe towards the Pacific
Ocean. Stop when you're halfway, and look up towards the North Pole. In
other words, start in the middle of nowhere and work outwards. Do not be
deceived by the streams and rivers which appear to radiate prettily away
from Norilsk; this is a landscape which makes you feel as though you are
seeing it on a television set with the colour turned down. It rolls towards
the horizon in dreary shades of grey and brown under a sky the colour of
cigarette ash. And that's in the summer.

This far north inside the Arctic Circle, winter lasts for ten months of every
year. It's dark even during the hour or so a day which is officially described
as daytime and it's so cold that the liquid on the surface of your eyes freezes
between blinks. There are more snowploughs than cars and there's more
snow than they can cope with. In the middle of summer there are 23.5 hours
of sunshine every day.

The local council gives the handful of foreign visitors who make it this
far into the Russian interior a souvenir packet of postcards which includes
a picture of a group of townspeople muffled up like polar explorers struggling to pick up a pensioner who's blown over in a blizzard. She was lucky
they saw her. Pedestrians generally walk backwards during storms to keep

the stinging snow driven by Arctic gales out of their eyes. Norilsk clings to life on the edge of the inhabitable world. A local official summed it up for me with a kind of tragic pride: 'Only Russians would have dared to create a town here,' he said. 'Or wanted to.'

Norilsk survives as a testament to the crazed logic of Stalinist economics. It was built 500 miles inside the Arctic Circle to exploit the world's largest deposits of nickel, copper and uranium. Summer comes and goes as fleetingly as the beam from a lighthouse sweeping across the horizon and the townspeople are experts at making the most of it. Because it was built in such a remote place, Norilsk comes to an abrupt halt. One moment you are walking along a street of apartment blocks, bus stops and telegraph poles, the next you are facing a polar wilderness which stretches for thousands of miles and betrays not a single sign of human habitation. Keep going a little beyond the last building, though, and there, stretched out before you is the world's most godforsaken beach, a miserable scrap of land which you reach by crossing a disused railway track and climbing over a mains sewage pipe the size of an underground railway tunnel.

On the far side of the cold, blue Yenisei river, some curious illusion makes the plumes of smoke billowing from the power stations and the smelters appear absolutely still so they have the appearance of clouds drawn as children draw them. None of the sunbathers appears to notice the faint but mistakable tang of metal which the smoke leaves in the air.

No one speaks of spring, summer or autumn in Norilsk. Better to say that the brief period of the year which isn't actually winter flashes past like one of those speeded-up nature films of a flower blooming and dying. Nowhere on earth do you see such determination to get the most out of sudden good weather. In the shallows, a huge water pipe with holes drilled every ten feet or so provides a series of fountains under which children play, wincing every now and again when their feet slip on to sharp stones.

Further out, in the deeper water, fathers coax older children into swimming their first few faltering strokes. Everything has about it an air of urgency; after all, in some years it snows again in late July and then there'll be no more swimming until the next brief polar summer. Most people, though, are content just to lie in the sun.

There is no high-factor sun block here, no mirror sunglasses, no visors to keep the glare out of anyone's eyes. When the sun appears in Norilsk you do not ponder the distant future prospect of skin cancer or worry that your face will become a mask of unsightly wrinkles in twenty years' time. The first sight of the sun, the first hot day of the year, has always been something to celebrate. Here and there balding pensioners sport paper hats fashioned from old copies of *Polar Pravda*, the local newspaper, but everywhere in this bleak place there is an unfamiliar air of luxurious abandonment.

Ten years ago, before anyone noticed that the fabric of Soviet society was unravelling, summer would have been spent in the Black Sea resorts of Georgia, Ukraine or southern Russia, where the hard-living free-spending tourists from the Arctic were favoured visitors. They reminisce now about how they used to begin sunbathing almost as soon as it got light in the morning, as though their bodies were like rechargeable batteries which would allow them to take some of the warmth back inside them to their homes on the polar ice cap.

But those holidays are a thing of the past now. They were holidays from the Soviet era, when everything was allocated by central government decree, from your subsidised seat on the crowded flight to Moscow to your numbered space on the beach. There was special treatment in this as in all things for the hero Soviet workers of the Arctic metal plants, who were paid twice as much as anyone else in the country and given three times as much annual leave. Young families used to volunteer to come to Norilsk like pioneers of the old West in America to save enough money to buy a home in the south or an apartment in Moscow. The long years in the endless cold and the darkness, they used to say, were worth it.

It is not worth it now. In a few months inflation has destroyed savings which took years to build up and which had been carefully set aside to buy what would pass in Russia, in the old days, for a life of luxury. Now the men who brought their families to this freezing wilderness, who worked for years in the burning, choking darkness of the mines and the smelters, earn about the same as tram drivers or hotel doormen in Moscow.

The Soviet era is already known in Norilsk as the old days and, although no one can quite bring themselves to say it, they leave you with the impression that for them, at least, they were the good old days. They speak of the Soviet era now as Russian aristocrats in exile in France must once have spoken of the late nineteenth century, as a time when they lived as a privileged elite and knew themselves to be the envy of every other worker in the Soviet Union.

A ticket via Moscow to the beaches of the South used to cost about a day's pay. Now it costs as much as most people earn in a year. The beach beside the River Yenisei might not be much of a beach, but it's the only beach that most of the people of Norilsk will ever see now.

The road back to town is cracked and pitted and crumbling, partly because the temperature climbed from minus 40 to plus 30 in a matter of weeks, but mostly because even here in this most extreme of climates the Russian government builds roads with the strength and durability of pie-crust pastry. It winds through a dismal series of housing developments where the occasional flash of decorative gaiety, like a bright red painted hammer and sickle, somehow serves only to make the buildings seem even more despondent.

Walking through the town is like walking through the opening sequence of one of those old black and white science-fiction films where some supernatural force has made time stand still. I feel like an archaeologist sent to identify the very day on which the Soviet system ran out of energy and confidence. If the date-stones on the dilapidated swimming pool, cinema and restaurants are to be believed, it would have been sometime in the mid-1970s, during the period that Russians now refer to as 'the era of obstructionism and foot-dragging'. Up until then, it seems, money could always be found to build; even to build an indoor ice-hockey stadium on the edge of town, surely the only one in the world ever constructed because it gets too cold to play ice-hockey outdoors. But no money was ever found to maintain anything. The cracked window panes, peeling paintwork and potholed car parks are evidence of that. It almost looks as though at some point in, say, 1975, every painter, cleaner, glazier and handyman in the country knocked off for lunch and never came back.

Here and there by the side of the road there are neatly arranged piles of bricks, bundles of sewage piping and piles of concrete blocks with twisted bits of rusty metal sticking out at odd angles. Norilsk looks as though it was built by the kind of do-it-yourself enthusiast who never quite gets round to finishing anything. It's a history of Soviet failure written in crumbling cement; a monument to a system that simply ran out of steam.

It didn't run out of steam early enough to give Tatiana Nikolaevna and thousands like her a normal life. She came to Norilsk in the 1940s from Ukraine, and like many of the people who built this town and made it work for so long, she came as a prisoner. She was a sixteen-year-old schoolgirl in the nationalist west of the Ukraine in 1949, old before her years like many teenagers in the Eastern Europe of those days, when she was arrested. She remembers, vaguely, the men who arrested her. One of them, who'd known her father before the war, was executed himself eight months later.

Her crime, officially, was slandering the Soviet state, a charge related to remarks made in the school playground about the Ukrainian-language nursery rhymes she'd been taught at home. This teenaged enemy of the people was taken down to the local railway station at three o'clock one morning from the local KGB headquarters, having been sentenced to eight years in a labour camp. Tatiana's voice as she described her experience was flat and matter of fact. They knew they were going north, she said, because the geography teacher from her school was on the train as well. She even remembered that she'd been impressed that the teacher was able to work out the direction of travel in a windowless train. And then being less impressed when it turned out that the teacher had simply asked one of the guards who'd once lived next door to her.

They weren't taken in cattle trucks either, she said, as she's often read since in accounts of the period. They went instead in purpose-built prison trains; it is after all a reflection of Soviet economic development that there were more carriages for transporting people behind bars than there were for moving food supplies.

She finds it difficult to talk about her time in the camp now, not because there were individual moments of great horror and fear, but rather because there were not. What she finds impossible to put into words is the relentless grinding misery of it all, the years of eternal drabness, the endless cold, the loneliness and the isolation.

Every now and again something will wake her up at night even now, usually the memory of the day when an old friend died and they had to light fires on the iron-hard frozen ground to make it soft enough even to dig a shallow grave at the back of the hut. It is a familiar and dismal story, the story of millions of prisoners forced into decades of hard labour whose story is the black side of the official heroic history of the Soviet conquest of remote Russian lands in the far east and the far north.

Forty years later, though, Tatiana is still in Norilsk, a free woman now in the city to which she came as a slave. She chose to stay when she was released because she felt in her mid-twenties that somehow she'd already grown old, with thinning hair, rotting teeth and calloused hands from years of captivity. Her parents in Ukraine had died, so she felt no urge to return. And anyway the Soviet authorities, having released her and thousands of other prisoners like her, still had one final misery to inflict. They did not, when you were freed at last, pay your fare home and so you were stranded at the gates of your prison. But in Norilsk it was the whole town that was the prison, not just the guarded compound with the barbed wire, the floodlights and the watchtowers.

She got a job in a local foundry that paid four times the average salary for Soviet workers and began to save, dreaming of the day when she would have enough to pay for a flat in Moscow or St Petersburg, and dreaming of holidays in the sun. Now, after three years of inflation, reform and chaos, her life savings wouldn't even buy a return air ticket to Moscow. She fingered my ticket thoughtfully; having asked to look at it so she could find out how much it cost without asking me directly. She clucked indignantly when she saw the price, then handed it back wistfully. 'You're a very lucky young man,' she said, not looking me in the eye.

She dismissed with an embarrassed shrug the idea that her life story tells you anything about the Soviet system and the people whose lives it ruined and shortened. But she's wrong. As we sat over a final cup of tea with the midnight sun blazing away through the thin curtains of her small apartment, she even put it into words herself.

'I came here,' she said, 'as a slave and I chose to stay for the money, but now, now I know I can never afford to leave, not even for a short break, I feel as though I'm more of a prisoner than ever.'

4
Farewell to War

Martin Bell

Martin Bell reported from many war zones during his career as a BBC correspondent. He decided he'd had enough after being wounded while covering the fighting in Bosnia-Hercegovina which led to the break-up of Yugoslavia.
(4 April 1996)

I have always wanted to be a peace correspondent and to this day I don't know whether the job exists or whether, in the particular case of Bosnia, there is a peace to correspond about. There is at least what we didn't have before, which is a merciful suspension of the war. The snows of winter are melting and this is the first year in four years when they do not presage the opening of the spring campaign. Rather, this spring we are looking for and reporting on the legacy of the war that lies underground. It lies in the land-mines, perhaps three million of them, so recklessly sown across hundreds of miles of front line.

The other day I found myself on the edge of a minefield four miles wide and two and a half miles deep which alone had 5,000 anti-tank mines in it. And there are other minefields of which no records exist, or if they did it was in the memories of the soldiers who laid them and were later killed. The old Yugoslavia, sadly, was one of the leaders in landmine technology and its people will pay the price for a generation and more. A British army mine expert estimates that it will take a thousand men thirty years to clear these mines, or most of them. Children are being killed every day.

The other part of the war's underground legacy is grimmer still: the mass graves where its innocent victims, mostly Muslims but not all, were dumped after being executed. Now, with the melting of the snows, the International War Crimes Tribunal is beginning its judicial excavations at a dozen sites in eastern Bosnia, where thousands of men lie buried. These were victims of the greatest single atrocity of the war: the mass murder of 3,000 inhabitants of the enclave of Srebrenica in July last year. It was supposed to be a UN-protected safe area. The UN abandoned it though the consequences of the abandonment were predictable, for the Serbs held the Muslims of Srebrenica collectively responsible for a massacre of Serbs elsewhere in the early months of the war. They then exacted a terrible revenge.

For one who reported this war from the start and is now attempting to move on to something else, the greatest sadness lies perhaps in these predictabilities; that actions have consequences and so does lack of action, that the withdrawal of the Dutch troops from Srebrenica could have only one consequence in view of the people and the circumstances there. It had that consequence. The world then threw up its hands in horror and asked how this could happen.

Was the press at all influential? We were supposed to be, indeed we were criticised for the so-called CNN factor – I should prefer to call it the BBC factor – which forced the hands of governments through the power of television to take some action to end the war or at least to ease the plight of its victims. So there was a sequence of limited actions and cosmetic solutions like the escorting of humanitarian aid, the safe areas which were not safe and the protection force which did not protect.

Looking back on it now, I would judge that the lesson of the Bosnian war was a simple one. Force prevails, and force prevails especially where diplomacy falters. It was the force of the Serbs that expelled the Muslims from eastern Bosnia in the early weeks of the war and from other areas in the closing months. It was the force of the Croats, main force units of the Croatian army, which rolled back the Serbs from their western strongholds in August and September last year. It was the force of NATO air power and artillery, not symbolic but deep and disproportionate, that finally broke the stalemate and made a kind of peace possible. That and the act of involvement for the first time of the United States.

I leave Bosnia now, after four years, aware that even if I haven't changed it, it has certainly changed me and my ways of working and being in war zones especially. This was not just a reflection of the dangers of the Bosnian war, which were unique, but an effect of being so close, so consistently, to the suffering of so many innocent people. Dispassionate and distant journalism, bystander's journalism I would call it, was simply not an option and the abiding memory that I shall take away with me is not of any particular massacre or atrocity or ruin or traitor or front line, but of hundreds of refugees fleeing on foot down a mined country road all wearing their

Sunday best, formal black suits for the men, ample black dresses for the women. For if all you can take is what you can walk away with, then you walk away in the best clothes that you have and in the pockets you carry the family photographs.

But that is the past, or we must hope it's the past, and what of the present? The Bosnian peace is uncertain, the federation between Muslims and Croats is fragile, the compliance of the Serbs could yet founder on the war crimes issue if either of their leaders, especially their army commander, General Ratko Mladic, is arrested. But this is as near to peace as Bosnia has been since April 1992; this is the best that we have had. The international pressure and sacrifice are actually achieving something.

5

Aunt Natasha

Andrew Harding

Faltering attempts to end years of fighting in Chechnya came too late for one of the residents of the capital, Grozny. (5 October 1996)

It's a strange, disorientating feeling, driving back into Chechnya after a few weeks away. Sometimes it's hard to recognise the place; new checkpoints spring up, familiar buildings are replaced by craters, friends suddenly turn into refugees. But for all the horrors and destruction of the last couple of years, there has, for me at least, been one rock of stability. Her name is Tyotya Natasha, or Aunt Natasha, a tiny, wrinkled, sixty-eight-year-old Russian lady with big, bright eyes, a cackling laugh and bedroom slippers on her feet.

Natasha lives in the centre of the Chechen capital, Grozny. Turn right off Victory Street, follow the giant potholes leading towards the market and hers is the second gate on the left. Inside is a small courtyard, and an even smaller white cottage, speckled with shrapnel scars. Natasha has lived on Griboyedovo Street all her life. 'This is my home, and I can take care of myself,' she says stubbornly every time her son begs her to leave the republic and come and live with him. Somehow Natasha, her house and the big walnut tree next to it have survived the war. They sit, miraculously intact, surrounded by a sea of rubble.

I always try to stay at Natasha's when I'm in Grozny. In all I must have spent a couple of months camped out on her floor, being woken up each morning with a cup of tea, an omelette and another lecture about how I need feeding up. On summer evenings we'd sit on a bench in the courtyard, watching the tracer bullets zipping overhead; Natasha saying how pretty they looked in the dark.

Like so many people in Chechnya, Natasha has lived through hell in the past few years. Sometimes it gets to her, but sometimes she seems quite blasé even hooting with laughter as she tells her latest horror story. There was the time, three years ago, when a bunch of local thugs broke into her house, beat her up and, for want of anything better to steal, ripped out her gold front teeth. Then the occasion last year when she decided to go and collect her pension during a ferocious Russian bombardment. Not surprisingly, there were no buses working, but Natasha, ever resourceful, stowed away in the back of a Russian army truck carrying artillery shells to the front line. She was found, crouching under a tarpaulin, and arrested for a few days, until the commander got bored and let her walk the rest of the way home.

Long before the war, she worked in one of Grozny's giant oil refineries, an administrative job with a good salary. Years before that, when she was a teenager, she had a brief affair with a German prisoner of war; my only true love, she says. Her mother nearly killed her when she found out.

These days, Natasha boasts that she's become an accomplished marauder, scavenging for food all over the city. Bombs and bullets don't seem to worry her at all any more. She doesn't even bother to go to the cellar to hide. 'I'd prefer to die in my own bed,' she says nonchalantly. Besides, it's cold and wet down there. Thieves have stolen her television and destroyed her fridge. A Russian shell landed on her outside lavatory. Shamil Basayev, the legendary Chechen fighter, turned up on her doorstep once asking for directions. She showed him the way through her neighbour's garden, a tiny figure in bedroom slippers leading a column of soldiers. Later, Shamil came back and asked her to peel some potatoes for his men.

Now, finally, Natasha seems to have had enough. She's the only ethnic Russian left on her street and she's started snapping at her Chechen neighbours: 'I don't trust them,' she says. Her neighbours, Zara, Hussein and others, have got used to Natasha's eccentricities and sharp tongue and they tend to leave her alone. It's extraordinary how little ethnic tension there has been throughout Grozny during the war despite the fact that Russian and Chechen soldiers have been killing each other in such huge numbers. 'There's no such thing as a bad nation, only bad people,' the Chechens say. It's a platitude, but it has some truth to it.

As far as Natasha's concerned, though, the time has come to leave Chechnya for good. The last time I saw her, she announced that she was trying to sell her cottage; she's hoping to get the equivalent of £3,000 for it. True to form, Natasha says she wants to depart in style. She's already ordered a new set of teeth from the dentist, and is waiting for him to sober up enough to fit them. She's also getting a wig made. 'You won't recognise me,' she said, curtseying extravagantly. 'I'll be beautiful again.' I don't blame Natasha for leaving Grozny. It's no place to live, and probably won't be for years to come. It's amazing, really, that she's stuck it out for so long. But Chechnya won't be the same without her.

6

Death Homes

Diana Goodman

Tens of thousands of Russian children were living in conditions of squalor and discomfort in institutions which locals called death homes. Many of them were mentally or physically disabled; others were orphans or children who had been abandoned. Western experts say that many of those diagnosed as mentally retarded were in fact perfectly normal. (12 December 1996)

It was the sound of crying which hit me first as I stepped inside the home. It was the sort of heart-wrenching plaintive sobbing that makes any mother instinctively look around for a child in need of comfort, the sound which says a child is cold and hungry or in pain. This time it wasn't one child crying, it was dozens. But the director of the orphanage sat impassively behind a desk, apparently oblivious to the noise. She was a large, portly woman, dressed in a warm coat and a fur hat. When I shivered and commented on the lack of warmth, she laughed merrily and said: 'No, it's not cold at all, I'm only dressed like this because I'm going outside.' She ordered us to take off our coats and sit down.

I'd turned up at the Internat, as these homes are called, with a Russian musician turned lobbyist called Sergei Koloskov. He has a daughter with Down's syndrome and, like all such parents, when she was born he was pressured by the authorities to give her up. He refused and has since become actively involved in helping other parents to keep their children at home. He's also trying to relieve the suffering of children who are in Internats by providing volunteers and equipment. The director was deaf to his suggestions and brushed his photographs away. 'We need finance,' she said, 'not fancy ideas. My priority is to find enough money to pay the staff.'

Sergei gently suggested that the human rights of children had to be defended. The director laughed with contempt and then began shouting about the rights of pensioners. They had to be defended too, she said. All this talk about the special rights of retarded children was ridiculous. Eventually the director got bored and retired to her office in a completely separate building. Before she left she privately told Nadia, the medical worker who was showing us round, not to say anything indiscreet.

But when Nadia opened the door of the so-called lying-down room, home to the children who can't walk, no words were needed. There, in a long narrow room, two rows of children lay marooned on their tiny beds. Some were staring at the ceiling. Others were weeping inconsolably or softly whimpering. Despite the cold, most of the children were dressed only in T-shirts plus the pieces of rag which were used as nappies. One little boy had feet that were blue with cold. All of them were frighteningly pale and their heads were shaved. Some were covered in sores or rashes. The nurses looking after them work twelve-hour shifts. They get paid just £25 a month. Their job is to change, wash and feed the children, nothing more.

It was lunchtime when I was there and the nurses were going round with metal billycans of food. Western experts say that despite their disabilities many of these children could learn to feed themselves, but they're regarded by the authorities and, as a result, by their carers as idiots and imbeciles, and no attempt is made to teach them anything. The nurses went from one bed to another spooning a few mouthfuls of porridge into each of the children. As soon as they turned their heads away, the nurse moved on. Some children eventually die from malnutrition. Just a few days before, a seventeen-year-old girl had died of starvation because she could no longer digest the food. Asked why she had not been taken to hospital, Nadia said: 'They turn our children away; they don't want to waste their resources on kids like these.' A telegram had been sent to the girl's parents, but they didn't come to collect her body. Like most of the children here, she'd never had a visitor.

Nadia quickly rattled through the problems of each child. Closest to the door was Carina, a four-year-old girl who was born with twisted legs because her mother had syphilis. She was the size of a normal one-year-old. As she whimpered, she continually clenched and unclenched her hands. When I lifted the covers on her bed I found she was naked below the waist and was lying on a cold rubber sheet with not even a cloth to catch her excrement. When I stroked her hands, she unclenched her fists and stopped crying. She listened intently as I talked. When I moved away, she was quiet for a moment. Then she realised she was alone once more and started to weep.

Across the aisle was Valyera, an eight-year-old girl with cerebral palsy. She was abandoned at birth and then adopted. When she was three her new parents realised she was disabled and she was abandoned for a second time. 'She can stand up sometimes,' the nurses said. 'And she understands everything.' Valyera squeaked and bellowed as we moved away to another bed. Ninety-five per cent of all handicapped children born in Russia are rejected by their parents and if a mother does decide to keep a child the father will often leave. The social stigma of having a disabled child is too much to bear in a country where handicapped children are seen as freaks who carry the evil eye.

The nurses in the Internats are not unkind. But they're completely untrained and they have no time to provide individual love and attention. They confessed, however, that they do have their favourites and one of the older women rushed over to pick up a frail little girl. 'When I'm alone here at night, I cuddle her and hold her,' she said. 'Sometimes I even try to make her walk.' 'Oh Valya,' said her colleague. 'Don't be so crazy, you mustn't spoil her.' 'I can't help it,' replied Valya, holding the small girl close to her chest as she crooned: 'Don't cry my tiny one, please don't cry.'

As she lifted the child into the air, we saw that the bottom of the girl's spine was covered in weeping bed sores. At that point Nadia insisted it was time to take a break. As we sat in the adjacent office she boiled up a kettle for tea and brought out biscuits and chocolate. None of us was in the mood to eat. Sergei began pressing Nadia to help him establish a connection between this orphanage and his charity group. 'We could help you,' he said. 'We could send doctors and maybe heaters to keep the children warm and all the medicines you need.' But Nadia just shook her head. 'You don't understand,' she said. 'It's pointless.' She looked around and then she whispered: 'The truth is that the director uses this job to make herself rich. She sells everything she can; sometimes even the coal which is supposed to be used for heating.' I protested that she couldn't be serious. Nadia looked at me pityingly. 'You're completely naive,' she said. 'Just like that American missionary who is here at the moment. Last time he went round handing out soft toys and, as soon as he'd gone, the director told me to collect them up immediately. We never saw them again.'

As we drank our tea we could hear bellowing and wailing from the room behind us. I suggested we should go inside. Nadia shrank back in her seat. 'I can't,' she said. 'The director would kill me.' She explained that that was the room for difficult children with psychiatric problems, who needed strong drugs to keep them subdued. She said the drugs were not always available. We sat in silence and listened to the noise of hunger, pain and despair seeping out from behind the locked door.

When the ritual of afternoon tea was over, I went in search of the visiting American. He told me his name was Dan and he was a former insurance underwriter who'd given up his job to help orphans in Russia. He was sitting on the bed of a bright-faced seventeen-year-old who was talking nineteen to the dozen. When Dan lifted back the cover on the boy's bed we saw that his legs were deformed, but his arms appeared to be normal. He's spent seventeen years in homes like this, given idiot status because his legs are bent. How could he still be smiling?

As it began to get dark, we moved into the other half of the orphanage; the place where the so-called 'walking children' are kept. The nurses have painted murals here: of playful foxes and geese and brightly coloured gardens. Some of the children get a token amount of education and they even watch a bit of television, but the misery felt by some of the others is overwhelming. They sit on the floor in the long corridor, their legs pulled up to their chests, rocking silently as they stare into the distance. Are they mad, or are they desperate because they're sane?

Down the hall the children who are considered to be beyond help were wandering aimlessly around starkly empty rooms. Some of them had green blotches on their temples. It was antiseptic lotion, used to cover the wounds caused when they banged their heads against the walls. When we arrived, the children sprang into life and rushed to the door, clamouring for attention. I asked their nurse why they had no toys. 'They would eat them and beat each other up,' she said. 'They're too stupid to know what to do.' In the girls' room one of the children was in a makeshift straitjacket, constructed from a sheet. The nurse explained that on the girl's first day she'd tried to break a window to get out, so from then on she'd been tied up.

Before we left the orphanage I stopped to visit a boy banging his head repeatedly against the end of his bed. I sat down and slowly rubbed his back and muttered the sorts of things that mothers say when they're trying to calm their children. 'Don't worry, it'll be all right,' I found myself saying, and his breathing became calmer. But then I felt like a heel because for him it wasn't all right and it never would be. Retarded children are never even offered for adoption. I knew this boy would be in a home until the day he died.

Volunteers who are trying to help children in Russia face a dilemma: should they send money to the Internats, thereby helping to perpetuate a corrupt system they hate, or should they devote their efforts to supporting groups who are trying to find a new way of caring for children? The Moscow-based Action for Russia's Children, which is manned by expatriate volunteers, has chosen the second course of action and is supporting an imaginative new scheme, run by a saintly former physicist called Maria Ternovskaya. With the help of a Christian group she's opened a small independent orphanage in Moscow. She's also working on trying to change the law to make it easier for children to be adopted or fostered.

The small, cosy orphanage is divided into sections and there's a den mother in charge of each group. As I spoke to one of them, a cheerful woman called Ludmilla, a small dark-haired girl was playing at her feet. Ludmilla explained that the child had been taken away from her drunken parents after they threw her out of a fourth-floor window. If Maria's orphanage didn't exist, she'd now be in a Moscow Internat.

Each night now before I go to sleep I think of the pinched and lonely little faces of the children at the Internat as they lie staring into the darkness in their narrow beds. Sometimes I get up and sit by my own son's bed and pray that nothing similar will ever happen to him. And I remember the smell which hung over the home; the smell of disinfectant, urine and death.

7

Oliver's Gone

Kieran Cooke

*The Republic of Ireland has seen enormous change over recent years: prosperity
has arrived, the standard of living has soared and, thanks in part to the prominent
role it now plays in the European Union, it has become a country to be reckoned
with on the world stage. And yet, some things never change: every Irish town still
has its characters and the death of one of them can have a profound impact on a
small interwoven community. (30 January 1997)*

Oliver Harney was not a particularly famous man. Yet when he died recently
in his small home town of Louisburgh in the west of Ireland, thousands
turned up for the funeral. Oliver was the proprietor of Harney's, the town
garage. As his coffin was carried to the small cemetery, the salty air whipped
in from the nearby Atlantic. Clouds rolled down from Croagh Patrick, Ireland's sacred mountain, just outside the town. From its summit St Patrick
is said to have banished snakes from the soil of Ireland. Louisburgh has
changed little since the 1920s. The butcher's doubles as an off-licence. Two
elderly men stand sentry at the town crossroads, carefully watching every
coming and going. Oliver's funeral cortege meandered slowly up the main
street. His beloved vintage cars, a Model T and a Ford Prefect, were driven
behind. The people of Louisburgh knew they were not only saying goodbye
to a man, they were bidding farewell to an institution.

Harney's, with its bright yellow walls and big green doors, was opened
by Oliver's father in 1923, just about the time the first motorcars started
chugging and wheezing their hazardous way along the rough roads of the
west of Ireland. The clatter and chatter coming from Harney's was as much
part of the rhythm of life in Louisburgh as the tolling of the church bell or the
flow of the river at the bottom of the main street. Now it's likely Harney's
will close. Small garages are disappearing, not only in rural Ireland. These

days they are being overtaken by impersonal main road monoliths, selling everything from tights to tyres.

The west of Ireland can be a lonely place. Ireland's economy is one of the fastest growing in Europe, but there are still few jobs in rural areas. People, particularly the young, leave for Dublin or the cities of England or the United States. Schools and village shops as well as small garages are closing down. But the small garage is also a victim of technology. Gone are the days when a gifted amateur mechanic like Oliver could replace an engine in a morning, when things could be repaired by marrying a bit of this to a bit of that. Now cars, driven more by microchips than motors, are as complicated as the early space rockets. You no longer take your automobile to a mere garage. You make an appointment at a car clinic. Nothing so sophisticated at Harney's. In through its doors was organised chaos. A back axle of a tractor there. A van, minus its front end, here. Country and western music would blare out from the wireless behind a stack of bald tyres in the corner. A pair of overalled legs would protrude from under a battered-looking saloon. 'Be with you shortly,' would come Oliver's voice, straining as he grappled with some particularly intransigent nut.

Eventually he would emerge, beaming an oil-spattered smile. He had a bright red face, topped by a shock of thick, snow-white hair. It was always a surprise to see him scrubbed and clean in a smart tweed suit at Sunday mass or out for his evening pint. He was famous for his enthusiastic but finger-breaking handshake. He always had time for everyone. A trip to Harney's often became a protracted affair, with Oliver being repeatedly called away to do other jobs. A farmer wanted the hitch on his trailer repaired. The baker's van was boiling over. The woman across the road wondered if someone couldn't possibly come and look at the back wheel of her bicycle. In between times the talk would be of the weather, a blow-by-blow account of play in the latest football match or the price of cattle. Local politics was another favourite topic, discussed with plenty of nods and winks, and conspiratorial muttering. There would always be plenty of stories.

An elderly resident of the town once brought a kettle in for repair. Not surprisingly, it became lost among the oil and engine parts. Eventually it was used for storing paint thinner. One morning, unbeknown to Oliver, the kettle's owner came and took it home, and, miracle of miracles, it worked perfectly. Thereafter, there was great speculation as to how the tea tasted in that house.

Harney's ran a breakdown service. Oliver and his badly bruised old jeep would often be out to the rescue in the dead of night. One time he was called to help a man infamous in the district for his lack of skill behind the wheel. Oliver gave a quick lesson on being towed and set off. 'Everything was fine until we started coming down the hill into town,'said Oliver. 'Then I looked in my mirror and there was nothing behind. Next minute I looked over to the right and there's your man trying to overtake and taking a drag on his cigarette at the same time.'

Fittingly enough, Oliver died while serving petrol at the pump outside his garage. His parting might not have made the headlines. Yet it was sadly significant in its own way, marking the disappearance of an important part of life in a small Irish town.

8

The Passing of Don Frank

David Willey

Now it's not often the death of one's landlord makes the news. But when he's the head of one of Rome's most princely families, that's different. Frank Doria-Pamphilj was not an Italian but an Englishman. A former lieutenant commander in the Royal Navy who fell in love with a Roman princess during the Second World War. (10 October 1998)

The great palaces of Renaissance Rome are more than just buildings, they are repositories of history as well as living communities of the present. The Doria-Pamphilj palace where I live and have my office is now divided up into more than 200 apartments occupied by a heterogeneous population of friends and tenants of the Dorias. The palace takes up a whole city block, has seven internal courtyards reached through nine separate entrances and includes an imposing baroque church, a tourist *pensione*, a museum and picture gallery and, at street level, a shoe shop, an artist's studio and a delicatessen run by an English family who import and smoke their own salmon in the Sabine Hills.

The princely family live in some splendour but simply in the state rooms of the palace, furnished, like most houses of the Roman aristocracy, with valuable works of art, paintings, tapestries and sculptures. They have liveried servants and the entrance to their quarters is up a wide white marble staircase with a red carpet running down the centre.

Frank Pogson was the young commander of a British navy minesweeper stationed in the Mediterranean during the Second World War and the circumstances of his meeting his future wife were banal in the extreme. Orietta Doria was a volunteer serving cups of tea and sandwiches in an Allied servicemen's canteen in Ancona when she first met Frank. She said to him: 'By the way, if you ever come to Rome, look me up. I live at number 304 Via del Corso.' Frank had no idea that the uniformed volunteer worker was a princess who lived in a palace, and was amazed to find when he arrived in Rome on leave that number 304 was the entrance to the sprawling family home of a dynasty descended from the famous Genoese Admiral Andrea Doria, soldier of fortune and Italy's foremost naval leader of the sixteenth century. The Dorias also had a Pope in the family, Innocent X, who reigned for eleven years in the mid-seventeenth century.

There was a previous British connection. Prince Filippo, Orietta's father, had wed a Scottish nurse who looked after him after he had been injured in a rowing accident. But the prince, a staunch opponent of Mussolini and Rome's first mayor after the liberation of the city by Allied forces, initially opposed the marriage between his daughter and the English naval officer who was already a convert to Catholicism. It was not until after his death, a decade later, that the couple were able to marry.

Frank Doria (he took over the family name by deed poll) presided over a sea change in the family's fortunes. Another family residence, situated inside a large park on the city outskirts, was sold to the Italian state in order to pay death duties, and the city of Rome expropriated the park, which today is one of Rome's rare areas of green space.

Frank, or rather Don Frank, as he became known in Rome, ordered the dust covers to be taken off the furniture inside the palace and opened up the state rooms to the public just like any English stately home. He was passionately interested in history and had enough material in the family archives to fill many books. He was particularly interested in Queen Victoria. He continued his own and his family's naval traditions by taking the children sailing in the Mediterranean each summer on board their yacht. Two generations of English gentlefolk in Rome found Don Frank a kindly landlord who let out grace and favour apartments to ageing expatriates in reduced circumstances. 'The trouble with my tenants is that they never die,' I remember him telling me once when I was looking around for a new apartment.

Now a new generation of Dorias have taken over the running of their historic palace, which has just been completely rewired with the assistance of a state grant. The upkeep of this important microcosm of European history demands sensitivity in an age of mass tourism. A hundred thousand people a year now admire its art treasures, including the portrait of the Doria Pope, Innocent X, painted in this very building by Velazquez.

Until a short while ago I used to see Princess Orietta cycling around the streets of central Rome on her old-fashioned bicycle. The modern Dorias have never been ones for standing on ceremony. Now they sometimes rent out the state rooms in their palace for society functions to help keep the family fortunes afloat. But I sometimes wonder how much longer this unique Roman palace will maintain its special character with the passing of Don Frank.

9
Villa Villa

John Sweeney

The habits of the British holidaymaker may have changed over the years, with the remotest corners of the earth now easily accessible to everyone. And yet the British tribe like to holiday among familiar sights, sounds and smells; to take a little bit of home away with them, particularly when the traveller concerned is a correspondent who's just back from reporting a brutal war. (11 September 1999)

The epic surreality of modern Majorca became apparent to me on the midnight coach trip back from *'Pirates,'* a swashbuckling show steeped in the history of the Balearic Islands. Well, kind of. To be honest, history had walked the plank very early on in the evening when the audience, split into four groups and soused with sangria, started shouting for their own pirates. The show is a staged battle between four 'goodie' pirates; Sir Francis Drake, Barbarossa, Blackbeard and Captain Scarlett, against the baddie, Jacques La Fitte, who is, of course, French. Our pirate was Barbarossa, a name which is too polysyllabic to shout competitively. One of our party, a sharp wit from Lancashire, brilliantly subbed Barbarossa down to Barbie and we sang lustily: 'Come on Barbie, let's go party,' to the theme tune of the doll of the same name.

Oddly, there was no mention of Admiral Byng, subject of the best joke ever made originating in the Balearics. Two centuries ago he lost the island next door, Menorca, to the French and was tried and shot on his own poop deck for his incompetence. This caused Voltaire to remark that the British shoot an admiral now and then, adding the immortal phrase: *'Pour encourager les autres.'* No Byng, no Voltaire, but plenty of leaping around and thunderflashes, and a play-show of war and inhumanity. Barbie won, or was it Captain Scarlett, not he of the Mysterons but a young woman in tights, against the evil froggie, Jacques La Fitte, while we waved our plastic swords, a snip at 1,000 pesetas each, and sang the *Match of the Day* tune. Very historical.

On the coach back, we were treated to a medley of local Balearic tunes: 'Villa, Villa, Villa …' Oh, all right, the 'Villa' in question was Aston Villa, the other football team in Britain's second city. One of the claims made by their rivals, supporters of Birmingham City FC, you will recall, was that during the reign of one particular Pope, Aston Villa managed to score no points at all! 'Villa, Villa!'

I hadn't meant to come to Majorca, but had booked a holiday at the last minute for myself and my two children. We ended up not in Mallorca, pronounced Mye-orca, you know, the sophisticated island retreat with lots of beautiful walks and splendid vistas. No, we were in Madge-orca. This is a long, riotously ugly coastal strip of hotels, burger caffs, bars and pedalo hire shops, where Spanglish is the lingua franca and paella a daring departure from egg and chips. Bingo was a regular feature at the poolside, and the kids played 'Hunt The German' around the hotel, a game which, I fear, failed to show due respect to our gallant European allies. In short, the English seaside, captured in Donald McGill's saucy postcards and famously defended by George Orwell, has moved to Majorca lock, stock and barrel. But the kids loved it, and, after a while, so did I.

Holidays are dyed the colour of one's own mood. To be honest, my mood at the start was pretty black. I know a man, Qamil Shehu, a Kosovo Albanian, who lost two sons, three brothers – forty members of his extended family in all. They were machine-gunned by a Serb death squad. It was hard to imagine that Qamil lived in the same Europe as the Villa fans, the Lancashire wit, his wife and son, and the others basting in the sun and getting up every now and then for more beer or chips.

Brooding over, the kids finally persuaded me to go in for the Dads' Talent Contest. The first competition involved doing as many press-ups as possible. I did five real ones, if that, then five more broken-backed cheats, then collapsed and lay on the floor like a cod on a fishmonger's slab. No points. The second competition was to find a white bra. Now I was on my own with the children, I am not a transvestite and was completely snookered. No points. Humiliation stared me in the face, and the faces of my kids, and all their friends. The final competition was to drink a pint of lager as quickly as possible. I've been a reporter for twenty years, and that I can do. I drank my pint so quickly the others lagged hopelessly behind. TEN POINTS!!!

This is the New Europe. It's tacky, sybaritic and a little bit moronic. But most of us don't kill each other any more. We only champion our proxy tribalisms. As the man sang: 'Villa, Villa, Villa Villa …'

10

Revolution in Belgrade

Jacky Rowland

There was a revolution in Serbia as hundreds of thousands of people rose up and overthrew the president Slobodan Milosevic. Days earlier, our correspondent had been ordered to leave the country, but she defied the expulsion order, went into hiding and emerged to cover the momentous events there as they happened.
(7 October 2000)

I have got a confession to make. I gave the impression that I had left Belgrade, but I did not. A week ago, late at night, I let the heavy metal door of the BBC office close behind me. I stood in the dark on the landing, my satellite phone in one hand, my laptop in the other, and a small rucksack over my shoulder with enough clothes to keep me going for a few days. The old rickety lift was out of order again, so I walked down the four flights of stairs to the street. I had taken this route numerous times in the past few days, walking to and from the offices of state-run television. But the walk this time was different. At any moment, my friend Milos would pull up alongside me in a borrowed car, I would jump in and we would drive away.

It all happened very quickly. We drove off, past the Yugoslav parliament building with its splendid horse statues, then turned right. Milos decided to take a circuitous route, through the rich residential district of Dedinje. These leafy, discreet streets were home to President Slobodan Milosevic as well as foreign diplomats and newly rich businessmen. By now it became clear that we were not being tailed. We made our way to the suburb where I would be hiding. For the next four days I spent most of the time sleeping, and working out my explanation if and when the police came to arrest me.

'My expulsion was illegal,' I would protest. 'It was a political decision taken by people who are no longer the legitimate authorities in Yugoslavia.' But I did not think it would wash.

I finally decided to venture out of the flat on Thursday, when the opposition had called a mass protest to coincide with its deadline for Mr Milosevic to resign. I went incognito, of course. Milos and his girlfriend, Irena, gave me a pair of dark glasses and a black hat, which I pulled low to cover my hair. My face had become quite well known in Belgrade in recent days as I reported on events for BBC World television.

The three of us hitched a lift to Slavija Square, which was as far as we could go by car. Demonstrators had set up roadblocks and were turning back the traffic. As we started walking in the direction of the parliament building, my black hat was pulled down firmly over my ears. Within moments I felt a tap on my shoulder. It was my friend Vlad, smiling at me. 'Shhh!' I hissed. 'I'm under cover!' With the parliament building just round the corner, I caught the first whiff of tear gas. People ahead of us were turning back, but we carried on. Then we saw two clouds of smoke: one white, that was the tear gas; the other black. Something was on fire. We turned the corner and there it was, the parliament building surrounded in billowing smoke. It was only then that I realised I was witnessing history in the making.

It was time to break cover; I needed to get to a phone. I ran through the streets with Milos and Irena, the crackle of gunfire somewhere not far away. We turned another corner and saw a row of armoured vehicles crossing Slavija Square. We dived into a doorway, but the tanks were not heading in our direction. They were going up towards the main boulevard, the parliament building and state-run television. We came to some offices of the United Nations. Milos talked his way past the security guard and I dashed into an empty room. Within moments I was back on air, much to the surprise of colleagues in London, who thought I had left the country.

Then we went back on to the streets. I ran ahead of Milos and Irena and found myself right in front of the television building, which by now was an inferno. Through the broken windows I could see chairs and tables on fire. People were running away from the building, carrying off computer equipment. 'It's a trophy,' one man cried, a video recorder tucked under his arm. And the trophies got better. In the park opposite the burning parliament building, I met a man carrying a ceremonial chair over his head. Was it from the parliament? You bet it was.

Running down a side street thick with black smoke, we passed the main police station. It was besieged by protesters, about a hundred of them. They were kicking at the doors and windows. Some people emerged carrying police helmets and riot shields. Finally we made it to my office. For the next three hours I barely moved from my desk, the phone clamped to my ear and people running in and out of the room with information. We left the office late at night and started the long walk back to the flat. At the corner we passed Scandal, a vulgar perfume shop belonging to Mr Milosevic's son, Marko.

There wasn't a shard of glass left in the window, or a bottle of perfume left in the shop. The place was trashed. I the impartial and objective reporter surprised myself, punching a fist into the air and shouting 'Yes!' Irena was dancing along beside me. I have lived in Belgrade for two years. This is my city and the people around me on the streets were, in a way, my people. That night I shared their joy, their emotion and their hopes for the future.

11
Ships Below Ground

Malcolm Billings

Medieval shipwrecks were being found in forests and fields in the Netherlands.
Large areas of this country were once under the sea and its farmers have become
used to unearthing fragments of the region's maritime past. (6 January 2001)

If an archaeologist claimed to find medieval shipwrecks in forests and cornfields, you might well be sceptical. Shipwrecks, in the normal course of events, are rarely found by farmers. But the plough has become a major archaeological tool in the Netherlands. Many of the ships discovered by farmers in this country have V-shaped slices taken out of their sides. This is where the plough has taken a bite just under the surface.

More than 400 wrecks have been found like this and more turn up every year. It only made sense to me when I realised that I was on reclaimed land and that the cornfields and forests were about three metres below sea level. I was on the bed of the former Zuider Zee, what was once a large inland sea in the centre of the Netherlands. Since the 1930s the Dutch have systematically established a unique landscape by reclaiming large parts of the sea for farmland. Whole new provinces have been created by pushing back the water and new towns, industrial areas and much-needed agricultural land have emerged from the sea bed.

In some cases ancient fishing ports, which were on islands in the sea, have survived as part of this new landscape with their harbours and seafronts stranded in hectares of arable crops and market gardens, and miles from the new coast line. It is in this landscape that the shipwrecks turn up. Many are well preserved, having been deeply buried, and it is not unusual to find all or most of their cargo still on board, along with the personal possessions of the crew.

I could see some of these wrecks a long way off as I drove across the flatter than flat landscape. They stick up out of the fields like prehistoric burial mounds. These are wrecks that were discovered and which are now being protected with plastic sheeting under and over the ships' timbers. Looking a bit like ships in squidgy bottles, they are then covered with sods of earth and the top left open so that the rain can get in and keep the timbers from drying out. The farmers then plough around the wrecks which, in theory, can stay where they are until time and money are available to investigate them further or conserve them as museum objects.

Some remarkable ships have been discovered. There was one medieval ferry that sank in a storm in the 1440s. A passenger must have been carrying some eggs, and you can imagine the surprise of archaeologists when they found them with their shells in perfect condition. Their insides, however, had been replaced by sea water. Unusually there was a skeleton left in that wreck. The bones were scarred in a way that suggests the man may have been a leper. In medieval times they were obliged to carry a warning device that gave out a clackety-clack sound a bit like castanets. Such a thing was found by archaeologists when the wreck was excavated. The device had a handle carved in the shape of St Katherine, the patron saint of lepers. We know that ships did carry lepers and that ship-owners of the time could not refuse a leper passage. But from the evidence it looks as though there was no obligation on anyone to get the leper ashore when the ship got into trouble.

Some of the wrecks are dug up and carefully transported to a museum and conservation centre specially set up to deal with them at Lelystad, a new town on one of the biggest tracts of reclaimed land. The National Institute for Ship and Underwater Archaeology is a long tunnel of a building, like a huge Nissan hut. I walked into a climate that was like that of a tropical rainforest, with a mist of water sprayed from nozzles in the roof to stop the timbers from drying and cracking into dusty piles. The ship, or parts of it, can then be dismantled and the individual timbers soaked and washed in large tanks of water that are kept clean by shoals of small fish. The timbers then embark on months or even years of soaking in vats of hot liquid wax. This soaks into the eroded wood, replaces the water in the cells and gives the timber back its strength. After that the ships can be reassembled and put on display further along the museum tunnel.

One very well-preserved vessel from the early seventeenth century was a fish transporter. Part of its main deck has survived along with much of the hull and many of the interior divisions. The ship's stove in the galley was intact and in the hold there were large tanks that could be flooded. There was no fishing gear on board and archaeologists soon realised that they were dealing with another unique find, a medieval fish transporter: a fast vessel with tanks full of live fish that could be landed at the fish markets ashore, while the fleet pursued the herring or the cod at sea.

But the most extraordinary ship was a mid-nineteenth century cargo vessel. I had to hike into a forest with an archaeologist from the museum to find the site. We followed a path through birch trees and oaks. The grasses and brambles on either side of us were waist high and impenetrable. It was almost impossible to imagine that just fifty years ago all this was at the bottom of the sea.

We came across a sizeable coaster about thirty metres long and with high sides that needed a viewing platform to see into the hull. It was sitting on its keel under a shelter, exactly where it was found in the 1960s. A plough had located the top of it and the rest was three or four metres under the ground. They had to excavate a very wide and deep trench to get under the keel. They found that an entire hull was there and at one point the pumps could not keep up with the seepage of water into the trench and a small lake began to surround the vessel.

Then something extraordinary happened, unique in the history of maritime archaeology. As the water rose the ship bobbed up like a cork and floated as if nothing had happened to interrupt her voyage.

12
Cruel Winter

Caroline Wyatt

The north and east of Russia were suffering their harshest weather in fifty years. Hospitals around the Siberian city of Irkutsk were running out of anaesthetic because of the number of amputations being performed on frostbite casualties. But people were not counting on any assistance from the central government in Moscow. They had learnt to fend for themselves. (20 January 2001)

It was only minus 28 degrees centigrade when we landed in Irkutsk. But that was cold enough to make breathing an effort, the air felt like ice as it scraped the back of my throat. Five minutes later, I needed a second pair of gloves and pulled my scarf tight over my nose and mouth. I was obviously a beginner at this.

At the petrol station, Mikhail the attendant laughed when we asked if he wasn't freezing. He'd spent the whole day outside with no more than his fur hat and a sheepskin coat for warmth. It was mid-afternoon and icicles were hanging from his moustache like Dracula's fangs. He said he never drank to stay warm, unlike many others. There's a belief in Siberia that enough vodka will insulate you from the cold. It's been proved tragically wrong in the past few weeks. Dozens of bodies of the homeless or men walking drunkenly back from the pub have been hauled out of the snowdrifts, frozen or so badly frost-bitten that many will never walk again.

The local hospital in Irkutsk is overwhelmed. Ironically, it's the burns unit that's taken all the frostbite victims, 200 of them in just two weeks. Even here, icicles are hanging down on the inside of the windows, though the heating is on full power. The doctor was too busy performing amputations to talk to us. But we could hear the screams from the operating room. They'd run out of anaesthetic after performing sixty amputations that week. The other patients could hear it too, and one girl in the corridor, clinging to her mother for support, was near to tears.

Nastya is only sixteen years old. Last week she missed her last bus home, so she walked instead; five miles through the snow, in temperatures of minus 40. She had no gloves. Now her hands are bandaged and hang down uselessly. She'll find out soon if they need to be amputated. She was far from the worst case. In one bed Nikolai Dobtsov lay quietly, staring at the ceiling. Underneath the sheets, blood was seeping through his bandages from where his feet and hands had been amputated the day before. He was a truck driver, he explained, with a good job delivering wood; and recently there'd been a lot of demand. So he'd set out to deliver a last load up-country.

The weather forecast, just minus 25 in Irkutsk, seemed to suggest that the journey was safe. It wasn't. His truck broke down miles from anywhere, and for six desperate hours he fought to repair the axle. He even greased his hands for pr-fection and finally managed to get the truck going again. Somehow he found the strength to drive himself back and straight to hospital, but it was already too late. I asked Nikolai what would happen to him now. He just laughed and shrugged. Nikolai has no wife or family in Irkutsk, and invalidity benefit is a pittance. Life in an institution may be the best he can hope for, and he'll almost certainly never work again.

That incredible stoicism is everywhere. In Irkutsk at least, people seem simply to accept that winter is harsh and this one especially so. It is without doubt the cruellest Siberian winter in living memory. Yet outdoors everything appears to function normally; even schools reopened as the temperature rose briefly to minus 25. The trams and buses are back on the roads, though everyone drives slowly to avoid skidding on the layers of ice below the grit. The main street bustles with people wrapped in layers against the cold.

But even indoors, the chill is inescapable. After her shift as a tram conductor, Natasha Fillipova comes home to a freezing house. She shows us the bedroom where ice has built up on the inside walls. She scrapes it off with her fingers, but that has little effect. One night, Natasha says, she washed her hair before going to bed. When she woke up, it was frozen solid to the wall. The children are doing their homework in the bathroom, the only room warm enough to sit in. Natasha doesn't want to complain. But she is angry with the state and the architects for building shoddy houses. The flats here are supposed to withstand up to minus 40 degrees. They don't, and her children are ill with coughs and colds.

Natasha's anger is brief and she seems faintly embarrassed about it. Siberians are used to cold weather, she explains. Here, she tells us, people prefer to rely on themselves and the knowledge that, eventually, spring will come.

13

Race Against Time

Tim Whewell

*Yiddish was once the language of millions of East European Jews, but not many
speakers survived the Nazi holocaust in the language's original heartland, on the
western fringes of the Soviet Union. But, as the region opened up to outsiders
following the end of Communism, an American linguist, Dovid Katz, began
travelling through the villages of Lithuania and neighbouring Belarus, tracking
down elderly Jews and recording their native speech. (7 April 2001)*

'And this, what did you call this?' demands the apparition across the table,
tapping his paunch to indicate what he's asking about. There's a moment
of silence in the old Soviet apartment with its stern family photos, its faded
wallpaper and dark cabinets. The clock ticks. '*Boykh* or *beykh*? *Boykh* or
beykh?' The old woman, Eshke Fyodorova, screws up her eyes, determined to
recover the Yiddish word she would have used sixty years before for tummy.
'*Boykh* or *beykh*?' The questioner waits, his face framed in the tangled hair
and beard of an ancient sage. '*Boykh*!' she says suddenly 'You're sure?' His
pen still hovers over the two variants listed on his questionnaire. 'Yes. *Beykh*.
Beykh was how we pronounced it.' And with a sigh of satisfaction, Dr Dovid
Katz circles her choice and moves on down the list. Thus the borders of a
now almost extinct country, Jewish Lithuania, which had its own customs
and its own Yiddish dialect, are defined just that little bit more precisely. A
civilisation is gone, but its vowels will be recorded.

For ten years Professor Katz, my old teacher and friend, has been rattling
from one such meeting to another, down the long straight roads that run
from the sandy spits of the Baltic coast to the Pripet marshes, across the flat,
melancholy fields of Belarus. This is a region where boundaries changed constantly, a convenient fighting space for the empires of Europe. But because
the land belonged to no one doesn't mean no one belonged to the land, and

for 600 years the Jews belonged so profoundly that each town had not only its own Yiddish name, but even its own biblical etymology.

Modern Grodna, where we begin our trip, was Horodne, supposedly from Har Adonai, the Mountain of the Lord. A landscape shared by many peoples had parallel geographies, Jewish and non-Jewish, so that settlements which appeared on ordinary maps as anonymous market towns, where even many locals saw only a few streets of crooked houses around a muddy square, were famed throughout the Jewish world for the quality of their learning, for their rabbis, their poets or their religious academies. Even rivers had parallel existences. Halfway across Belarus, our minibus hits the Nieman, where Napoleon's army and Hitler's were briefly stopped in their tracks. Rafts of ice are jostling downstream in the spring thaw. Once it would have been rafts of timber jostling down to the Baltic, pushed apart by Jewish lumberjacks as rough-hewn as the logs themselves.

But there's more to the Nieman than that. Suddenly, Dovid is declaiming from the Book of Ecclesiastes 'Kol ha-n'kholim hoylkhim el ha-yam': 'All the rivers run into the sea', the words the ancient rabbis used to link all the waters of the world, and all the sages who ever lived by them. The hamlet where we've stopped, Selets on the Nieman, was the birthplace in the early 1700s of the Vilner Gaon, the greatest Talmudic scholar of modern times, and the icy water that flowed by his home had also lapped, a millennium and a half earlier, the great academies of Babylonia, where the Talmud was created. For a moment the bare willows along the Nieman might almost be the date palms of the Tigris and Euphrates.

We open our eyes again. The forest closes in all around. An icicle drips from the eaves of a mouldering cottage. Stick a calf or two in the sky and this becomes a canvas by Chagall. Only one old woman is moving in the snowbound street. We ask, as we always do, if any Jews live here and if she's ever heard of the great rabbi who came from her village. She'd be delighted to help, she says, but the answer to both questions is no.

A civilisation that's almost dead but not quite. Asking in village squares, we do find Yiddish speakers, like Fyodorova, many of them using their mother tongue, with us, for the first time in years. And even when there's only one Jew left in a town, that's enough for Dovid to hear the dialect changing from place to place. Every interview begins with individual words 'boykh or beykh', for to begin with memories, with songs, would be too painful; these survivors still live at the scene of the crime; the pits where their families lie are just at the end of the village. But as they talk on, back through the war into their childhoods, we glimpse the richness of the culture they were born into. And if, as the rabbis say, to kill one person is to kill a whole world, it follows in reverse that while one person survives, a world is still there. We're racing against time, Dovid repeats again and again, the youngest of these informants is eighty, many are over a hundred. But the parallel Jewish geography of Eastern Europe isn't yet just a ghostly one. Hopefully, he says as we set off for the next village, I've got a few years left.

14
Migrants

David Shukman

With the news full of stories about asylum seekers and economic migrants, our correspondent was looking at the parallels between some of today's migrants and what happened to his own grandparents, who fled from Russia nearly a hundred years ago. (8 September 2001)

I'm sitting on a bus looking into the exhausted eyes of a young Albanian couple from Kosovo. Their faces are taut, and their smiles uneasy. The sun is hot through the windows. I offer to share my bottle of water, but they're nervous about accepting it. They're bewildered. Kadrush says his house was burnt by the Serbs. His wife Shkendie says she knew the victims of a massacre. They've just made it to Britain and claimed asylum. They paid a very high price, £2,000, to the people-smuggler who brought them into the country. Add to that the emotional strain, the leap of faith and the tangle of guilt about those left behind. I hand them my mobile phone and watch Shkendie stifling a sob at the sound of her sister's voice back home.

They had crossed Europe hidden inside a secret compartment in a truck. Their food lasted four days, but the journey went on for seven. When the rhythm of the truck changed from the bumps of a motorway to the swell of the Channel, they knew England was close. Being caught by the police was a relief. Now they are waiting to see if they can stay. 'Are you scared?' I ask. 'No,' they say. 'We're happy to be here, alive.'

As we talk I feel that age-old tingling on the neck. I realise that what I'm witnessing, with this edgy young couple, wide-eyed in a new land, is a part of the history of my own family. Only two generations ago my father's parents were in exactly the same position. The year was 1913 and they were among hundreds of Jews from Russia shuffling down a gangplank and on to British soil at Tilbury. For them it was salvation. They wouldn't have had the new rucksacks of the Albanian couple. Instead they carried a cardboard suitcase and a large, neatly tied bundle of eiderdowns; bedding was too valuable to leave behind. And tucked away was my uncle, then a baby of three months, smuggled in a less sophisticated version of the secret compartment used by the Albanians.

The luggage was different, but the motives may have been similar. Life in Russia a century back must have been appalling. Jews were only allowed to travel in certain areas, most professions were closed to them and every so often there'd be the pogroms, when Jewish communities were attacked. There were waves of emigration: to London, Paris or, along with millions from Ireland and Italy, to Manhattan. As I listen now to the couple from Kosovo, or hear the stories of Iraqis fleeing from Saddam, I try to picture what my grandparents went through faced with the same threat, the same lack of hope.

History has seen tides of people crossing borders and oceans, but how desperate must my grandparents have been, a young David Shukman and my grandmother Maria, to take that fateful step of fleeing? At some point, at their home in the Crimea, amid the poverty and uncertainty, there must have been a decisive moment, perhaps with others over a meal or stepping outside their shared flat away from the in laws, to weigh the pros and cons. There were enough roubles for the tickets, but would that leave anything for food? My grandfather had a Russian army pass, but would it do? He had an aunt in London, but would he find her? There wouldn't have been a BBC man offering a mobile phone.

I assume there were plenty of friends and family telling them not to be crazy, that the risks are huge. Many on the move now must have heard the same warnings. Even more, in refugee camps and villages and cities around the world, must be agonising right now over whether to risk everything or stay put.

There's no family record of my grandparents' journey. We assume they took trains across Russia to the Baltic Sea. There must have been bribes; to get an exit stamp, to board the ship, to keep the harbour guards at bay. Many Jews, who for whatever reason failed to get out by boat, paid smugglers – yes, they were in business back then – to get them into Germany. At sea the poorest passengers had to cook for themselves on deck. Tilbury, though unknown, would have been a welcome sight.

As refugees, my grandparents were registered as aliens, allowed to work, but not allowed to vote; outcasts, but left to live in peace. Before the First World War, Britain took in more than 200,000 Russian Jews. I wonder whether they would have got in now. If they couldn't prove their lives were in danger, they would be refused asylum. If the Home Office were to decide they were only here to avoid poverty, they would be sent back. My grandfather had no money to his name and his trade as a tailor was hardly a privileged one.

The balance between acceptance and refusal is so fine, yet each decision about who can stay and who can't shapes generations to come, like my own. My grandparents did get in, and their grandchildren are leading lives they could only dream of. No wonder so many try.

15

The Last Executioner

Hugh Schofield

Among the residents of the beautiful village of Fontaine-de-Vaucluse in Provence is France's last surviving executioner, Fernand Meyssonnier. He's written a book about his career, most of which he pursued in Algeria before and during its war of independence. (26 September 2002)

The first thing you notice in Fernand Meyssonnier's living room is an exquisitely constructed miniature replica of a guillotine – the mechanical version, he notes, like the one we had in Algiers. He made it in 1946, the year before he attended his first beheading. He was fifteen and he gave it to his father, the chief executioner, who was delighted. It sits in a glass box, and every detail is perfect. In the little coffin-basket there is even a pair of spectacles, which belonged to one of Monsieur Meyssonnier's 200 victims. It is all very macabre in its way, but then on top of the box there is something that makes you want to laugh out loud at the utter unlikeliness of it: it is one of those gimmicks that went on sale a couple of years ago and which someone once gave to the Queen, a Billy the Bass singing fish.

He is gruff, burly, the classic tough former colonial, but Fernand Meyssonnier, France's last executioner, is clearly not without a sense of the surreal. Why else ten years ago would he have chosen this bucolic spot of all places, a beautiful Provençal village made famous by the love-poet Petrarch, to set up his Museum of Justice and Punishments. The museum failed, of course; the tourists, it seemed, were interested in loftier things than devices of medieval torture, but still today in his basement he keeps his treasures packed up in crates: a full-scale guillotine, a preserved head and the notebooks of Albert Pierrepoint, Britain's last hangman.

And then there are the parrots. Two of them, grey, in a cage in the living room. Periodically they start whistling the *Marseillaise*, and then one squawks: '*Tout condamné à mort aura la tête tranché. Vive Meyssonnier!*', which means: 'Everyone condemned to die will have his head cut off, long live Meyssonnier!' And then the other one shouts: '*Vive Papon, ils sont tous des cons.*' 'Long live Maurice Papon [the convicted Nazi collaborator], they are all ...' Well, I probably shouldn't translate that last word.

It is all most bizarre. But then humour and death have always had a strange but close relationship. And when it comes to death, to killing, Fernand Meyssonnier knows his stuff. He began in 1947 as a junior assistant. He tied the convicts' ankles and thighs with fishing wire, before they were bundled on to the plank and dispatched. But later he was promoted to first assistant. His job then was to stand behind the guillotine and look at the convict approaching through the wooden hole known as the *demi-lunette*, or half-lens, and then tug the head through and hold it as the blade came down. Because he was looking through the *demi-lunette*, the first assistant was known in the trade as the 'photographer'.

'You had to be very careful,' he told me. 'Especially with the model we had in Algiers, which was getting old. Later they sent one from Paris which was much better. But if you held the man's head too close to the neck you could get your fingers chopped off. And if you didn't hold his head firmly enough, he could wriggle round and the blade would end up slicing through his jaw. My father had a butcher's knife in case that happened.'

There is plenty more detail if you have the stomach for it. The blood spurts, he says, like two glasses of wine thrown three metres. He gives a quick double-flick with his wrist. There are nervous tics on the face for some seconds, but he scoffs at those who say there is any actual life. He was curious and undid the ties on the legs, but there was never any movement. They didn't kick like some people said. The heart ran down slowly, he said, like a bicycle after the last pedal.

Fernand Meyssonnier is ill now. He has liver cancer, which is why he has decided to talk for the first time about his job. He is bringing out a book which he hopes will dispel the image of the bloody axe-man. He was the arm of justice, he explains. He got through what he did by concentrating on the technical aspects of the job and by thinking of the hideous nature of the crimes that were being punished. As for the guillotine, it was simply the quickest and most humane form of execution. From leaving the guardroom, it was round the corner, up the steps and 'Crack!' Four seconds later the head was off.

What a strange sensation to meet a man who practised what we now instinctively regard with such horror! But, as he points out, in all of human history it is only in the last fifty years or so that societies have dispensed with the services of the judicial killer. Pity, he says, is such a recent thing!

16
Borderlands

Chris Bowlby

There was excitement in some parts of the Czech Republic at the prospect of joining the European Union. But the enthusiasm was mixed with anxiety in the west of the country, close to the border with Germany. This part of the world used to be known as the Sudetenland. In the notorious Munich Agreement of 1938, Britain and others agreed to hand the territory over to Hitler. After the war, the Czechs took their revenge by forcibly expelling the entire German population which had been there for centuries. The people who live there now were worried that joining the EU could bring the past back to haunt them. (27 September 2003)

The café in the small Czech town of Jachymov was rough and ready. Garish fizzy drinks, soggy cream cakes and a hearty chef in a brewery T-shirt dispensing three sorts of tripe soup. But propped up against the cash till was something altogether unexpected. A faded photograph of rows of well-scrubbed smiling children, dated 1901, with inscriptions in German and the name of their school: Sankt Joachimsthal.

The chef explained that he'd been replastering his bedroom ceiling when this photo had suddenly come floating down from in between the rafters. He realised it had belonged to one of his home's former owners, Germans who'd lived here a century or so ago when virtually this whole town had been German. Until recently most Czechs would have ruthlessly destroyed such traces of this area's alien past. But now he'd decided to display it as a curiosity for Czechs and visiting Germans who pass through this area on the Czech Republic's western edge.

And as I walked through this old mining town I saw how, if you know what to look for, you can begin to read a hidden history emerging from nooks and crannies, layers beneath layers. There on the grimy façade of one hotel building was the Olympic symbol of interlocking rings and a date: 1936. It had been put up to celebrate the Berlin Olympics, a showcase for Nazi prestige, an impressive event for many Sudeten Germans then living here, who aspired to join the Third Reich and abandon multinational Czechoslovakia.

Nearby was the cemetery, its modern graves with Czech names, but an older area full of German memorials and full, too, of the misery that followed once this town was annexed by Hitler and sucked into Nazi expansion. There were several imposing tombs of soldiers recruited from the town who'd fallen for the Reich during the invasion of the Soviet Union. I wondered how many of those fresh-faced boys in the 1901 photograph I'd seen in the café had ended up as Nazi cannon fodder. And there was also a memorial to the victims of a so-called death march that passed through here as the Nazis emptied their concentration camps at the end of the war.

And then no more recent German graves, because the people of what was Sankt Joachimsthal were driven out in 1945 and this became Jachymov, a Czech town. Whereas some German settlements near here were simply abandoned, and are now virtually untraceable beneath the fields and forests, here a new population was imported. And for decades, when this town was in Communist Czechoslovakia, the Iron Curtain kept away most of the town's former inhabitants, who'd settled in West Germany. Now, with borders evaporating, things have changed. Today's mayor of Jachymov, Zdenka Fiedlerova, sitting in the imposing town hall built by local German burghers in the sixteenth century, told me that lots of Germans come ancestor-hunting at the weekends. There's a knock at the door as they cry out: 'Here's where grandma was born!' The Czechs who live here, she told me, receive them politely but not warmly, as they're always wondering whether the first visit will be followed by a legal claim for compensation or restitution of property. Joining the EU, say local Czechs, opens up the borders, but maybe makes them vulnerable to foreign law. And the legal rights and wrongs of the Sudeten Germans' expulsion in 1945 formed a delicate part of Czech negotiations to join the EU.

Whatever the lawyers may decide, there's little chance of large numbers of Germans coming back to live here. But the ghostly presences are real enough, as are the tensions. The chef's old photo in his café displays perhaps the best approach; a disarming openness, a sense of shared inheritance going back centuries which serves as a happier model for the future than the horrors of the mid-twentieth century. Smiling schoolchildren on yellowing paper will continue to haunt the buildings of what was the Sudetenland, watching the latest chapter in the old story of Czechs and Germans trying to live together in one of Europe's most sensitive borderlands.

17
Dinner for One

William Horsley

A feature of New Year's Eve in Germany and some other nations on the continent is the screening of a short television comedy sketch called Dinner for One. *It's forty years since this cultural transplant first crossed the North Sea from Britain, where it was made but is now little-known, to Germany, where it's taken on a life of its own. (8 January 2004)*

It's like an initiation ceremony, spending New Year's Eve in Germany. The first time I did, I could hardly believe I was really watching the madcap piece of British music-hall comedy that popped up on my television set. Soon afterwards I found out that many Germans know by heart the names of all the characters in *Dinner for One*. It is not surprising, really, as they watch the same piece every year. It is a cult, a ritual, a piece of quintessential English humour that has now become immortal abroad.

This year, as every year, I've heard Germans laughing out loud as they recite the refrain spoken time after time in *Dinner for One*. 'The same procedure as last year, Miss Sophie?' the butler asks the genteel elderly lady. And then Miss Sophie's reply: 'The same procedure as every year, James.' Those simple lines are also, I have found, a sure way of breaking the ice with strangers in Germany, or Austria, or Switzerland, or the other countries where it has taken root in the hearts of many millions of people. It's a shared joke on a continental scale.

So each year, on New Year's Eve in homes across Europe, the curtain rises on the same stage scene, a country house with a table lavishly set for a dinner party. And it is a stage. Because forty years ago a German television station, Norddeutsche Rundfunk, signed up the British comedian Freddie Frinton to perform his popular stage version of *Dinner for One*, in English, in a Hamburg studio. What people see now is the black and white recording made then. Freddie Frinton plays the part of an elderly butler, James, who is serving the lady of the house, Miss Sophie, played by May Warden, at her ninetieth birthday party. Four other places are set for her male friends, Sir Toby, Admiral von Schneider, Mr Pomeroy and Mr Winterbottom. But the chairs are empty, because sadly they all passed away long ago. Hence the title *Dinner for One*.

James is immaculate in his black tie and tails, and the very model of an English butler. But he is frail and unsteady on his feet, and he gets more and more drunk as the evening goes on because Miss Sophie, all dressed up for the big occasion, insists that her butler should fill, and then drink down, the glasses of all the guests. First he goes round pouring out the sherry to go with the mulligatawny soup; then the white wine, with the North Sea haddock; next champagne, with the chicken, and finally the port. Each time James has to serve another round of drinks, he asks his high-spirited lady employer if he should follow 'the same procedure as last year, Miss Sophie?' And each time the answer comes back: 'The same procedure as every year, James.'

The barely fifteen minutes of *Dinner for One* are a crescendo of laughs. There's the tiger-skin rug, which James duly trips over on each of his journeys between the table and the sideboard. And the routine each time James has to impersonate the absent guests. For Admiral von Schneider he clicks his heels in the old Prussian way and barks 'Skol' each time he downs another drink. As Sir Toby, the bluff Englishman, he shouts 'Cheerio'. The laughter of the live studio audience who watched the performance all those years ago is still infectious.

At last Miss Sophie announces meaningfully that she's tired, so 'I think I'll retire.' 'Are you going to bed?' her loyal butler asks. And then: 'The same procedure as last year, Miss Sophie?' Back comes her reply: 'The same procedure as every year, James.' And the two of them run arm in arm up the stairs towards the bedroom.

A day or two after my first experience of this New Year ritual, I found myself in a bank in Berlin, on a second visit to open a bank account. The lady behind the counter was looking very strict, and handed over several forms in German for me to fill in. I looked over one of them and asked innocently: 'The same procedure as last year?' At once the stern bank lady unfroze. She glanced at me and said: 'The same procedure as EVERY year, Herr Horsley!' And we both laughed.

The behind-the-scenes story of *Dinner for One* is more bittersweet. To the end of his life, Freddie Frinton heartily disliked Germany and the Germans, thanks to his own wartime experience. He refused to allow a German-language version to be made. That is what has led to the extraordinary fact that today the Germans as a nation have embraced a trifling one-act play in English as their all-time favourite entertainment. Equally odd is the fact that this piece of comic acting of pure genius, which delighted British audiences in seaside resorts for many years, has so far been spurned by British television, including the BBC, as something unfamiliar that probably wouldn't catch on.

Nonsense, I say. It's sheer stardust. Cheerio!

18

Plain Speaking

Barnaby Mason

However serious the international crisis, diplomats and their staff will be discussing how the resolution should be worded. One of the skills required of the diplomatic correspondent is the ability to read between the lines of the official communiqué. (29 May 2004)

In May 1994 I found myself in New York covering the Security Council for a few weeks. It was the height of the genocide in Rwanda; unspeakable massacres were taking place every day. 'It's so awful, we must do something,' an aide to the Secretary General, Boutros Boutros-Ghali said to me. Instead, the members of the Security Council argued about something called the concept of operations for an expanded UN mission. A senior American official said it had to be a do-able operation; expectations of what the UN could achieve shouldn't be exaggerated. Scarred by the painful experience of Somalia the previous year, the Clinton administration delayed a vote on a resolution to send 5,500 troops, even though there was no question of American soldiers taking part. 'Everyone is very conscious of the urgency of the matter,' said a British representative, but the dry-as-dust haggling went on.

Strikingly, the big powers, especially the United States, resisted the use of the word 'genocide' to describe what was going on in Rwanda. So the resolution eventually passed talked instead of mindless violence and carnage, the death of many thousands of innocent civilians; there was only one oblique reference recalling that the killing of members of an ethnic group with the intention of destroying it was a crime under international law. Using the word itself, calling a spade a spade, would have mattered, because if it was genocide, how could you not act, however difficult it was?

In a similar way, British officials in the early nineties tended to describe the fighting in Bosnia as civil war rather than Serb aggression: the phrase implied that all the parties were as bad as each other and weakened the demand for intervention.

In the end, the pretence over Rwanda at the UN was swept aside. Mr Boutros-Ghali appeared before the media to declare: 'Genocide has been committed, and we're still discussing what is to be done. I've begged them to send troops; I failed. It's a scandal.' It was a rare instance of emotion bursting its diplomatic bonds, the kind of moment that diplomatic correspondents relish as compensation for the amount of time they spend studying ambiguous phrases to find out what lurks beneath them.

I can remember others: Boris Yeltsin, for example, ailing but still larger than life, at a summit of more than fifty leaders in Istanbul in 1999, angrily rejecting Western criticism of the behaviour of Russian forces in Chechnya as interference in an internal matter. Bill Clinton publicly turned the tables on him by recalling Mr Yeltsin's stand for freedom on a tank in Moscow: 'If they'd put you in jail,' he said, 'I hope every leader round this table would have stood up for you and not dismissed it as an internal Russian affair.'

Then there was the British Foreign Secretary Robin Cook the previous year visiting a Jewish settlement site at Har Homa outside Jerusalem in torrential rain. The Israeli government accused him of breaking an agreement not to meet Palestinians there; demonstrators called him an anti-Semite and the prime minister, Binyamin Netanyahu, cancelled a dinner with him. Mr Cook proclaimed: 'I did not submit to Israeli pressure.' His officials, for once, were just as undiplomatic, accusing the Israelis of a fantastic overreaction, of being in an ugly and defensive mood.

Those were moments of plain speaking. Usually words are carefully chosen as instruments of policy. The leaders of the big powers try by constant repetition to get their terms adopted by everyone, because they carry with them value judgements and a particular view of the world. The most obvious example is the word 'terrorist'. When President Bush calls someone a terrorist, he thinks that's all that needs to be said. The word is intended to close off argument, ignoring the disagreement across the world about who is a terrorist and who is not. It's become just a term of abuse. There are similar objections to the label 'war on terrorism', but it still flourishes. Can you have a war on a technique, since that's what terrorism is? Can the war ever end? The attraction for Mr Bush is that Iraq can be verbally neutralised as the central front in the war on terror. Diplomatic correspondents worry about this sort of thing.

American and British politicians, and the media, now talk of transferring sovereignty to an interim Iraqi government at the end of June. Pedants object that they can't do that because they don't possess the sovereignty in the first place. All right, then, they're going to hand over power. Are they? Really? Perhaps a transfer of 'limited administrative authority' would be more accurate. But that doesn't have the right ring to it; it certainly doesn't sound like a clear end to the occupation. So you see, words do matter, even if facts on the ground matter more.

A Lost Generation

Emma Jane Kirby

A third of the population of Moldova, Europe's poorest country, had decided that life abroad was better than life at home. With average income lower than in parts of Africa and corruption rife, an entire middle generation had gone, leaving just the elderly and the very young at home to tend the animals and the crops. Moldova became the source of much of the continent's trafficking in human beings. Tens of thousands of its women were sold into prostitution abroad. And the local police seemed unable to stop the trade. (26 June 2004)

Florica's blunt fingers moved her knitting needles inexpertly. Occasionally, she scowled and put her hand to her stomach. She was eight months pregnant and clearly uncomfortable. And no wonder, because Florica had not planned this pregnancy; she was carrying the child of the man who'd raped her and who'd then sold her into prostitution in Russia. Today was her seventeenth birthday.

'Happy Birthday, dear!' cooed Lilia, a big, homely-looking woman who was sitting beside the sisters. Lilia was the local psychiatrist and she gave me the rough outline of Florica's story. Rejected by their mother, the girls had found themselves on the streets. Easy prey then for the 'traffickers', the criminal gangs who seek out vulnerable women and con them into believing they can offer them great jobs abroad before forcing them to work as prostitutes. When Florica was told she and her sisters would be working in an office in Paris, she had no hesitation in boarding the bus for Romania, from where she expected to make the long journey to France. It didn't happen, of course. The sisters were brutally beaten and bundled into a car bound for Moscow, where for the next six months they were chained to beds and forced to have sex with hundreds of men.

I looked over again at Florica, who was still knitting mechanically, staring into space with dull eyes. Lilia seemed to know what I was thinking. 'She's not quite alive, is she?' she whispered. 'Once, I asked her how she felt, being raped by all those men, and she told me that at first it was so cruel she was sure she had gone to hell, and then after a few days it just didn't matter any more, because she had ceased to matter.' And the most frightening thing is that to many people in Moldova, Florica really doesn't matter. Or at least they can't afford for her to matter. Moldova is Europe's poorest country. In the capital city, Chisinau, the average wage is not much more than a pound a day; in the countryside, it's half that.

And that's what prompts so many people to look for work abroad. One in three Moldovans now lives outside the country. The hope of a more prosperous future means risk is embraced almost blindly. Tell a desperate girl like Florica a fairy tale about France and she'll believe you because she wants and needs perhaps to believe you.

Teaching young women the art of reading between the lines is the goal of one of the charity groups working in Moldova, the International Organisation for Migration. It's sponsoring the screening of a special film, *Lilia Forever*, in all Moldovan secondary schools. *Lilia Forever* is a gritty, frightening movie which Western European parents might well object to their teenage daughters seeing. Sixteen-year-old Lilia, abandoned by her mother, is left to fend for herself until she meets a man in a bar who promises her a flashy job in Sweden. When she arrives in Stockholm, of course, that flashy job turns out to be prostitution and there are graphic scenes as Lilia is shown being brutalised by scores of old and dirty men.

Watching the film in a Chisinau high school one afternoon, I was embarrassed to find I was crying. The actress playing Lilia was a slender blonde and she shared no physical resemblance with Florica, but there was something about her eyes which was all too familiar. Dead eyes which reflected nothing and which entertained no hope. I shouldn't have been self-conscious about the tears; all around me the students were sobbing. Many of them would have had older sisters or friends who'd gone abroad and who had then mysteriously failed to write home ever again. 'However much we need money,' instructed their teacher after the film was finished, 'we mustn't be tempted to take risks.'

Money is needed everywhere including, I discovered, at the local police station. Superintendent Ion Bejan had kindly agreed to talk to us about the Moldovan police force's efforts to crack down on the trafficking gangs who were targeting girls like Florica. He was embarrassed as he showed us into his office at Chisinau police station; he didn't have much furniture, he said, and he apologised for the room being a bit dark, but not all the light fittings had bulbs in them. On his spacious desk there were a few neat piles of paper folders which he tapped proudly. 'All our solved cases,' he said. 'The Moldovan police force is really cracking down on the trafficking gangs.'

But I know that Florica's case notes were not among those triumphant papers. The police haven't even begun an investigation into what happened to her. It's not that they don't care; they simply don't have the funding for yet another case. When I'd telephoned the Chisinau police station and asked one of the officers if we could drive to the Romanian border with them to film their work at the crossing point, the spot where Florica had been sold, there had been an awkward silence on the line before a strained voice responded: 'Well, could you possibly pay for our petrol? You see, we only get a limited amount for the week.'

Superintendent Bejan is a proud man and he doesn't like it when I mention money. As soon as I say I want to start filming him, he excuses himself, goes to a cupboard in the corner and pulls out a beautifully pressed uniform, carefully preserved in plastic sheets, so that he might, as he tells me a little self-consciously, 'look more the part'. Once dressed, he sits down again behind his vast desk. And then suddenly I realise why the desk looks so big. The chief of the Moldovan police force doesn't even have a computer.

'No, we don't have much,' he agrees miserably. 'It's pretty hard to keep track of cases when you only have paper records; it makes sharing information across different districts a bit difficult.' He looks down at his paper folders and becomes more animated. 'We don't have enough patrol cars, we can't afford enough officers, our weapons are old and well ...' He points to my chair. I'm sitting on an old car seat which has been glued to two lumps of metal.

It's a known fact that where there's abject poverty in a society, there's usually overt corruption too. Superintendent Bejan acknowledges the problem, but says he is confident things are improving. 'It used to be really bad,' he says. 'But now the officers are committed to stopping trafficking. Once you meet a girl who has been sold into the sex trade and you've seen for yourself the terrible injuries she's received, well, you want to get the man that did it to her; you want him brought to justice.'

I thought of Florica back in her hostel, silently knitting baby clothes for her rapist's child, and I knew that she'd long given up any hope that justice would come her way. 'But people ARE caught,' insisted the superintendent, and perhaps to drive home the point he suggested I go down to the police cells to meet someone he'd arrested the previous week on suspicion of trafficking.

The jail was in the basement. It was a dungeon, a place of childhood nightmares; damp, dark corners with peeling paint, and the fusty air was filled with the sound of strange, muffled shouts and cries. 'She's in here,' said Bejan. 'She?' I asked incredulously. 'Oh yes,' he smiled. 'Svetlana is a woman and a family doctor. In Moldova, many people will do anything for a few dollars.' Svetlana's cell was tiny and it contained nothing but a filthy double bed which she shared with another woman. Along the corridor, a radio was blasting out a maddening football chant. It couldn't be switched off, I was told. It was there to stop prisoners talking to each other.

Svetlana was a fat woman whose face was dripping with perspiration and tears. She stank of old meat. 'I was just the go-between,' she kept saying. 'I told you I didn't know the girl was going to be sold to the traffickers. I just got the papers for her so she could go abroad.' 'I know you're lying,' said Bejan. 'It was the girl herself who told us about you.' Svetlana began to sob. 'I wasn't even paid,' she insisted. 'I wasn't even paid.'

Superintendent Bejan asked if I had any questions for Svetlana. I asked her if she knew what had happened to the girl she'd arranged the papers for. 'She thought she was going to be a dancer in Germany,' she said softly. 'But she was made to work as a prostitute in Saudi Arabia.' I asked her if she felt bad about the part she had played in bringing the girl such unimaginable misery. Svetlana covered her face with her hands and wept. Later, after she'd been taken back to her cell, I became curious about the sentence she'd receive if found guilty at her trial. Superintendent Bejan smiled.

'She'll probably get away scot-free,' he said. 'We'll get her to court and then she'll probably just walk away at the end of it.' I looked at him incredulously and felt my face flush red with anger. 'We have talked about poverty and corruption in the Moldovan police force,' he said politely. 'What makes you think the Moldovan justice system is in any better shape?'

It's sometimes difficult to remember that Moldova is a European country, but if Romania succeeds in its bid to join the European Union, then Moldova will form the EU's external border. With African levels of poverty, no one is exactly on tenterhooks waiting for Moldova's accession date to be announced. In fact, few people see any future in staying in the country. Day after day the bus stations, thick with diesel fumes, are packed with impatient people buying tickets for the battered blue minibuses that will take them over the Romanian border. I met one of the buses at the crossing point and talked to some of the young women on board, who were jittery with excitement. One of them, Elena, was about nineteen and was dressed from head to toe in fake Gucci, from her pink tinted sunglasses to her synthetic leather miniskirt.

'I'm not really going to Romania,' she confided. 'I have a friend in Italy, he's my boyfriend. Well, I haven't seen him for three years, but he says if I meet him in Romania, he can get me a job in a fashion house in Rome!' I asked Elena if she was sure she could trust this 'boyfriend' she hadn't seen for so long? 'He loves me!' she laughed. 'It's a great chance for me.' An immigration officer stamped her passport and slipped a leaflet inside it. 'Can you be sure you're not the victim of a trafficking scam?' asked the leaflet, printed by an international charity organisation. 'If you are worried and want to talk to someone in confidence, call our hotline.'

I felt a ridiculous urge to run after the bus, thump on its windows and yell at Elena and her young friends to get off, to turn around, to go back. But to go back to what? A pound a day? A pound a day when you know that just over the border is the real Europe, the Europe where people go to college, find jobs and can afford to buy nice clothes? There was a chance, as Elena said, just a chance that it might work out okay. But as I watched the bus recede into the distance, with Elena's grinning face beaming at me through the back window, I couldn't help wondering if that's how Florica had looked when, six months before, she'd boarded a bus she thought was taking her on the first leg of her journey to Paris.

20

Love Actually

Thomas Kielinger

*All the world seems fascinated by a royal wedding and there was considerable
interest when, after much speculation, the heir to the British throne Prince
Charles married Camilla Parker-Bowles. Correspondents, including this German
journalist, travelled from far and wide to the town of Windsor where the ceremony
took place. (9 April 2005)*

It is a strange sensation for me to be actually standing at the foot of the statue
of Queen Victoria, with Windsor Castle's imposing structure right behind
it, and muse about the event that has captured the world's attention for
weeks and months, if not years: the marriage of one Charles Philip Arthur
George Windsor to his bride, Mrs Camilla Parker-Bowles. So inured are we
to the constant drip-feed of salacious news from the production line of the
Windsor saga that I, for one, am having a hard time liberating myself from
the mass of media coverage and developing something of a coherent view of
what this event might betoken for the monarchy and its subjects.

Pondering my plight I chance into a souvenir shop on Windsor High
Street, where I browse around the bric-à-brac of royal memorabilia to knock
my thoughts into shape. The first thing that strikes me is that nowhere is
there a single item with Camilla Parker-Bowles alone on display. She is on
sale only in conjunction with her new husband, never on her own. Whereas
Diana Spencer, unforgettable Princess of Wales, beams at you from hundreds
of items sparkling with her uniquely iconic lustre.

Thus, for starters, I can't help asking myself if the British people will ever
forgive Charles and Camilla for the role they played, willingly or unwilling-
ly, in Diana's sad undoing. Can people ever be comfortable with Charles
III and Queen Camilla when someone with far more glamour and charisma
might still have been commanding the nation's rapt attention?

It doesn't take long before the lady at the till in the souvenir shop dispatches my doubts with a vengeance. 'They are so well-matched, aren't they?' Mrs Dillon divines, in true vox-pop fashion. Not a word of remonstration or backward-looking does she utter as we descend into a proper psychoanalysis of the royal couple. I feel both humbled and enlightened at the hands of my guide. As a media person I am congenitally wedded to the view that newsworthiness comes mostly from things that go wrong, rarely the other way around. This wedding in particular lurching as it did from mishap to mishap right up to the last days of the preparations, when a ghastly security breach at Windsor Castle was exposed by a tabloid newspaper; well, I have rarely seen such malicious glee on display in the British newspapers.

But Mrs Dillon, bless her, is totally unfazed by all this negative hullaba-loo. After all, it is people like her who determine the way ahead for even an ancient institution such as the monarchy. And what is the demotic password my goodly lady has come up with? 'Love Actually', as in the eponymous film starring Hugh Grant, Kiera Knightley and other screen luminaries. Love, actually, also seems to save the day for Charles and Camilla in the eyes of other people I talked to once I had emerged from my education lesson at the hands of Mrs Dillon.

Quite a paradox, when you come to think about it. It has been said that the royal family is mired in dysfunctionality and that the only person really up to the 'top job' is its current holder, the Queen, who has stayed the course with exemplary stoicism, albeit at times somewhat inflexibly. After her the deluge, more or less; Charles's erratic curriculum vitae did not bode well for the future of the monarchy.

Well, what do you know? Now steadfastness rules the day, the very elevating spectacle of a couple true to their love over many a decade. Dysfunctional? Let the media learn to adjust their radar screens. Here is one story that has, against all odds, come right, through the slings and arrows of outrageous missteps, blind alleys and cruel misjudgements. Yes, of course, Diana was a victim, by her own machinations as well as at the hands of others, including these two happy enders. But as a legend in their own right Charles and Camilla have emerged with the paradoxical virtue of long-lasting fidelity. Dysfunctional? I should think not. Anything but.

In Germany, to where I report, the royals are sometimes adored beyond all reason, just as in Britain they are often unreasonably debunked for their remoteness from ordinary life and their own higgledy-piggledy lives. Well, at least with this couple you can forget about both fawning and debunking.

Camilla seems a supremely natural and down-to-earth woman, a boon for the monarchy because of the very absence of that double-edged attribute, celebrity, which so overwhelmingly characterised Diana Spencer. In turn, I see in Charles the contours of a man finally at peace with himself. Love, actually, may be the greatest strength of this much-maligned prince.

Asia / Pacific

1

The Ayatollah's Funeral

Alex Brodie

Huge crowds paying their last respects to Ayatollah Khomeini, the architect of the Iranian revolution, took to the streets of the capital on the day he was buried.
(10 June 1989)

The millions who swamped Tehran on Tuesday were almost to a man and woman dressed in black. From the air it appeared as if a black lake in the foothills of the mountains had disgorged into rivers which flowed south through the city of Tehran to a black sea fifteen miles away. The innumerable mourners poured out of the hundreds of acres of waste ground where the Ayatollah's body had lain in state, through the streets of the city to the Behesht e-Zahra graveyard, where the Ayatollah was to be buried.

It was not a stately progress. There was no pomp and circumstance, and the austere old man who ruled Iran for a decade of turbulent, continuing revolution died and was buried as he had lived, in a manner which contrasted starkly with the flamboyance and profligacy of the ruler who came before him, the Shah.

The body of Ayatollah Khomeini lay in state in the middle of dust and gravel, a half-built tower block and an electricity sub-station. The refrigerated glass of the Perspex case in which the body lay was raised above the waste ground, which will now become the capital's new prayer ground, on a pile of cargo containers and guarded not by a braided palace guard but by members of the green-fatigued, bearded or unshaven Revolutionary Guard corps, created by Khomeini to be a ubiquitous presence throughout the life of the new Iran, to make permanent his revolution and to police the morals and behaviour of his flock.

The body was carried from the prayer ground on a simple wooden structure and manhandled into a refrigerated lorry which was then swamped by the frantic crowd. The Ayatollah's son, Ahmed, had to be carried out, passed from hand to hand across the heads of the throng. It would have taken days for the lorry to reach the cemetery had not a helicopter been brought down to spread the mourners and to airlift the body. But when the helicopter landed at the cemetery those waiting, in a frenzy, dragged the body out. It was enveloped in the crowd and fell to the ground; hastily retrieved, it was flown away.

Later, this time encased in a metal box, the sort in which air cargo is carried, the body was brought back and the Revolutionary Guard escort just managed to take out the remains of Ayatollah Khomeini and partly bury him in a simple hole in the ground before the frenzied mourners broke through and, howling in anguish, fell on the grave. A cargo container was winched in and placed over the grave to protect it.

Those who made up the sea of black which took over the capital were largely the poor of the slums and the villages; those who see the black-turbaned, white-bearded Ayatollah as a holy man. To the embattled middle class, Khomeini's revolution is anathema, but even those who did not mourn the passing of the Ayatollah watched, riveted on their television screens at home, as the whole bizarre spectacle unfolded. 'Iranians love mourning,' said one. 'All our main religious holidays are mourning days.' But no matter how much he tried to make light of it, he knew that what he was seeing was evidence of the hold Ayatollah Khomeini had over the poor and ill-educated. No matter how much they want to, few of his enemies believe the Ayatollah's revolution will crumble. The funeral showed them that, as it was surely intended to.

2

Nehru Dynasty

Mark Tully

Election campaigning in India was brought to an abrupt halt when the leader of the Congress I Party, Rajiv Gandhi, was assassinated. Rajiv was the grandson of India's first prime minister, Jawaharlal Nehru. His mother, Indira Gandhi, was killed by her own bodyguards six years before, and Rajiv was immediately chosen to succeed her. Anxious to continue the Nehru dynasty, the Congress Party immediately elected his Italian-born wife, Sonia, as the party's president, an offer she declined. (25 May 1991)

The King is dead. Long live the Queen. Thus spoke the frightened men and women who had made their political careers out of being courtiers of Indira and Rajiv Gandhi. They had, as one friend of mine put it, become political. That was why they attempted a coup in the Congress Party by starting an immediate move to make Rajiv's widow, Sonia Gandhi, the party's president. It was all too easy because once her name was proposed, even those congressmen who did have political stature of their own were reluctant to oppose her, for fear of being accused of disloyalty to the Nehru family.

Nevertheless, it was quite extraordinary for a party in the middle of a general election, and facing a determined onslaught from a Hindu nationalist party, to choose a woman who was Italian by birth and a Roman Catholic by baptism as their new leader. Sonia issued a dignified statement rejecting the offer. But the efforts to persuade her continue. It all just goes to show the extent to which India's only national party has become the fief of the Nehru family.

How have the Nehrus developed into a dynasty? When Nehru became prime minister, he was a stickler for democratic nicety, but leadership is lonely and he was a widower, and so he fell back more and more on the company of his only child, Indira. It would be wrong to say that Nehru deliberately groomed Indira as his successor. After all, there was a brief interregnum when he died. But he certainly pushed her into prominence in the Congress Party. After the death of Nehru's successor, Lal Bahadur Shashtri, there was an unseemly scramble for power and Indira was chosen by a group of senior politicians who wanted to keep out their rivals and thought she would be like clay in their hands.

That was where the transformation into a dynasty started. Indira Gandhi never forgot the humiliations heaped on her during the early years of her prime ministership and was determined she should never again be *prima inter pares*, or first among equals. But, like her father, Indira found her pre-eminence lonely. And like him, too, she fell back on her family. First on her son, Sanjay, and then, when he was killed doing aeronautical stunts over the centre of Delhi, on Rajiv.

Indira's refusal to tolerate rivals led to a cult of sycophancy in the Congress Party. When she was returned to power, after being punished by the electorate for her Emergency, I asked a senior member of the party what role he would play. He replied: 'Oh Mr Tully, don't ask me that, I'm just a sepoy of Madam.'

It was almost inevitable, therefore, that when Indira Gandhi was shot the party should automatically turn to Rajiv. Although one of Rajiv's most outstanding qualities was his charm, within the Congress Party he was even more regal than his mother. A few days before his death, I was discussing the election campaign with a member of the committee running it and I noticed that he never referred to Rajiv by name but spoke only of the Congress president.

Towards the end of his life Rajiv himself realised that the awe in which he was held within the party was cutting him off from the people. That was why he changed his whole style of campaigning in this election, brushing aside the security and the sycophants who surrounded him last time round and allowing himself to be mobbed wherever he went. A close friend of his who travelled with him throughout the campaign told me that his last day had been a particularly happy one because the reaction of the crowds, wherever he went, had been so warm.

Rajiv Gandhi paid for that democratic decision with his life.

Obviously the Nehrus could not have been so successful if the Indian people regarded dynasticism with distaste. Perhaps one reason why they don't is that India has an old tradition of dynasticism which is different from the West. It's the tradition of the king as a servant of the people. The god Ram is regarded as the model of the perfect king and he and his faithful lieutenant, Hanuman, are the two most popular gods in India now, at least in the politically crucial north.

And that must be reinforcing fanaticism. It would therefore be very dangerous to write off the Nehru dynasty, whatever the outcome of the present power struggle in the Congress Party; a struggle I foresee not being finally resolved, at least not until the results of the general election are known next month.

3

Australian Christmas

Red Harrison

For Britons accustomed to images of snow and holly, sledging and skating,
Yuletide Australian-style might seem a little bizarre. To those enjoying the holiday
in blazing sunshine, at barbies and beach parties, the frozen parts of northern
Europe must also seem a long way away. But, whatever the season, the foreign
correspondent remains forever on call.
(23 December 1995)

There's something about Christmas in Australia that tends to put journalists just a little on edge. It's not the heat, though that can certainly melt away a lot of seasonal goodwill, especially for anyone silly enough to eat a vast and piping hot Christmas dinner when the temperature is more than a hundred degrees. No jingle bells for them: if they don't become diabolically dyspeptic, it's only because they've fallen down unconscious. No, what makes people in the news industry a little apprehensive, a little more alert, is that Christmas is a time when everyone is relaxed and suddenly something startling, something entirely unexpected, shatters the holiday mood. Only rarely is anyone ready for it. There are lots of examples.

A few Christmases ago I was sitting at a small grand piano tying knots in my fingers when all at once the other end of the piano reared into the air. Now pianos don't normally jump like kangaroos, no matter who's playing! But this one did. I saw it happen. And in the next moment I became aware of a tremendous silence. All the birds had stopped singing. Even the trees seemed to be still. And then, because I remembered something similar in New Zealand many years ago, I realised what had happened: earthquake.

In minutes the radio confirmed that an earthquake had struck the city of Newcastle, about a hundred miles away, a tremor strong enough to destroy buildings of stone and send a shock wave rippling into my home to toss the piano into the air. It was on a Christmas morning that Australia woke up to discover that the northern city of Darwin had been flattened by the most ferocious cyclone in the country's history. The prime minister then was Gough Whitlam, later to be sacked by the Governor-General. Mr Whitlam was spending Christmas in Greece, and the ruins of Darwin brought him hurrying home from the ruins of ancient Europe. He was luckier, however, than Prime Minister Harold Holt, who went swimming in his Christmas holidays and has never been seen since.

It's astonishing how the traditionally British ways of observing Christmas have travelled to all kinds of unlikely places. One year, the BBC sent me to Fiji to look at what had happened since an army colonel overthrew the government there. I'd been in the islands about a week, intending to return home on Christmas Eve, when the airline advised that all planes were full. And there were no planes on Christmas Day. So I was stuck in Suva. Early on Christmas morning, the Fijian kitchen staff told me cheerfully how they were going to cook a wonderful English Christmas dinner. 'Please,' I begged them, 'don't do it.' Apart from the absurdity of being in the Tropics in the middle of summer, I was the only guest in the hotel! That evening, while I was dining alone on tropical fruit and regretting that the hotel bar was closed on this religious day, a Fijian waiter told me the staff had all been looking forward to a big slap-up Christmas feast. But because I didn't want it, because I was Scrooge, no one got it.

Christmas in Australia is a time of great and dangerous beauty; a time for man-eating sharks and poisonous jellyfish in the sea, deadly snakes and spiders in the garden, a time when people drown in the holiday surf or absorb enough skin cancer on Bondi Beach to kill them. This is when flying insects are at their most vicious; cicadas and cockroaches on the streets, clouds of mosquitoes buzzing and biting around the barbecue. And when evening skies turn blood red and the air has a sharp tang of smoke and gum trees, it is fire that comes to everyone's mind. Only two Christmases ago, when bushfires destroyed many houses in Sydney, whole trees exploded in the heat. Elsewhere in the country, it's the time for monsoonal rains, and that means sudden and violent floods. This year, for those who insist on enjoying themselves, lawyers say that new laws on sexual harassment and anti-discrimination mean that employers who hold Christmas parties face significant risks if they forget to invite someone, or somebody tells a racist or sexist joke. And if anyone drinks too much and gets hurt, even after the office party, well, that's the employer's fault, too, and he can be sued for having condoned such indulgence. What a Merry Australian Christmas!

4

Letter to Daniel

Fergal Keane

This dispatch, a letter from a foreign correspondent to his newborn son, became the best-known and perhaps the best-loved piece ever aired on From Our Own Correspondent. *(15 February 1996)*

My dear son,

It is six o'clock in the morning on the island of Hong Kong. You are asleep, cradled in my left arm, and I am learning the art of one-handed typing. Your mother, more tired yet more happy than I have ever known her, is sound asleep in the room next door and there is soft quiet in our apartment. Since you've arrived days have melted into night and back again and we are learning a new grammar, a long sentence whose punctuation marks are feeding and winding and nappy-changing and these occasional moments of quiet. When you are older, we will tell you that you were born in Britain's last Asian colony in the Lunar Year of the Pig, and that when we brought you home the staff of our apartment block gathered to wish you well.

'It is a boy, so lucky, so lucky. We Chinese love boys,' they told us.

One man said you were the first baby to be born in the block in the Year of the Pig. This, he told us, was Feng Shui, in other words a positive sign for the building and everyone who lived there. Naturally your mother and I were only too happy to believe that; we had wanted you and waited for you, imagined you and dreamed about you, and now that you were here, no dream could do justice to you.

Outside the window, below us on the harbour, the ferries are ploughing back and forth to Kowloon; millions are already up and moving about and the sun is slanting through the tower blocks and out on to the flat silver waters of the South China Sea. I can see the contrail of a jet over Lamma

Island and somewhere out there the last star is flickering towards the other side of the world.

We have called you Daniel Patrick, but I have been told by my Chinese friends that you should have a Chinese name as well and this glorious dawn sky makes me think we will call you 'Son of the Eastern Star'. So that later, when you and I are far from Asia, perhaps standing on a beach some evening, I can point to the sky and tell you of the Orient and the times and people we knew there in the last years of the twentieth century.

Your coming has turned me upside down and inside out. So much that seemed essential to me has, in the past few days, taken on a different colour. Like many foreign correspondents I know, I have lived a life that on occasion has veered along the edge; war zones, natural disasters, darkness in all its shapes and forms. In a world of insecurity and ambition and ego, it is easy to be drawn in, to take chances with our lives, to believe that what we do, and what people say about us, is reason enough to gamble with death.

Now looking at your sleeping face, inches away from me, listening to your occasional sigh and gurgle, I wonder how I could ever have thought glory and prizes and praise were sweeter than life. And it is also true that I am pained, perhaps haunted is a better word, by the memory, suddenly so vivid now, of each suffering child I have come across on my journeys. To tell the truth, it is nearly too much to bear at this moment, to think of children being hurt and abused and killed.

And yet, looking at you, the images come flooding back. Ten-year-old Ande Mikail dying from napalm burns on a hillside in Eritrea; how his voice cried out, growing ever more faint, when the wind blew dust on to his wounds; the two brothers Domingo and Juste in Menongue, southern Angola: Juste three years old and blind, dying from malnutrition, being carried on ten-year-old Domingo's back and Domingo's words to me: 'He was so nice before, but now he has the hunger.'

Last October in Afghanistan, when you were growing inside your mother, I met Sharja, aged twelve, motherless, fatherless, guiding me through the grey ruins of her home. Everything was gone, she told me. And I knew that for all her tender years she had learnt more about loss than I would likely understand in a lifetime. There is one last memory. Of Rwanda and the churchyard of the parish of Nyarabuye, where in a ransacked classroom I found a mother and her three young children, huddled together where they had been beaten to death. The children had died holding on to their mother, that instinct we all learn from birth, and in one way or another cling to until we die.

Daniel, these memories explain some of the fierce protectiveness I feel for you, the tenderness and the occasional moments of blind terror when I imagine anything happening to you. But there is something more, a story from long ago that I will tell you face to face, father to son, when you are older. It has to do with the long lines of blood and family, about our lives and how we can get lost in them, and if we are lucky find our way out again into the sunlight.

It begins thirty-five years ago in London, on a January morning, with snow on the ground and a woman walking to hospital to have her first baby. She is in her early twenties and the city is still strange to her, bigger and noisier than the easy streets and gentle hills of her distant home. She is walking because there is no money, and everything of value has been pawned to pay for the alcohol to which her husband is becoming addicted.

On the way a taxi driver notices her sitting, exhausted and cold, in the doorway of Marks & Spencer, and he takes her to hospital for free. Later that day she gives birth to a baby boy and, like you are to me, he is the best thing she has ever seen. Her husband comes that night and weeps with joy when he sees his son; he is truly happy. Hungover, broke, but in his own way happy. For they were both young and in love with each other and their son. But Daniel, time had some bad surprises in store for them, the cancer of alcoholism ate away at the man and he lost his family; this was not something he meant to do or wanted to do. It just was. When you are older, my son, you will learn about how complicated life becomes; how we lose our way and how people get hurt inside and out. By the time his son had grown up, the man lived away from his family, on his own in a one-roomed flat, living and dying for the bottle.

He died on the fifth of January, one day before the anniversary of his son's birth, all those years before in snowbound London. But his son was too far away to hear his last words, his final breath. And all the things they might have wished to say to one another were left unspoken.

Yet now, Daniel, I must tell you that when you let out your first powerful cry in the delivery room of the Adventist Hospital and I became a father, I thought of your grandfather, and, foolish though it may seem, hoped that in some way he could hear, across the infinity between the living and the dead, your proud statement of arrival. For if he could hear, he would have recognised the distinct, immutable voice of family, the sound of hope, of new beginnings that you, in all your innocence and freshness, have brought to the world.

5

China Waltz

Matt Frei

*China's long march towards a market economy was bringing surprising changes
to the world's most populous country. (26 April 1997)*

When I first visited China fourteen years ago I was struck, like every other
visitor, by the extraordinary uniformity of such a vast country. The population then hovered somewhere near the one billion mark. Almost everyone
wore the blue Mao suit, which has now been replaced by the mud-coloured
double breasted suit, with the designer label still worn on the sleeve. Then,
bicycles far outnumbered cars; now Beijing is as congested and smogged-
out as any other Asian capital. Patriotic posters with square-jawed proletar-
ians trumpeted the party's commandments. Foreigners were a novelty. In
one village in Yunnan province in the south-west I found myself eating a
bowl of noodles at a roadside stall while several dozen people gathered to
watch me with an unnerving intensity. I was travelling on my own. A young
boy sat right in front of me, mesmerised as I clumsily wielded my chopsticks
and slurped the thick noodles up through my pursed lips. I felt truly alien.

At the time it seemed the entire country was learning English with the
BBC series *Follow Me*, which was broadcast nightly on national television.
That week one billion people were getting to grips with lesson seven. From
Urumchi in the far west to Harbin in the north-east, conversation in English
at least focused almost exclusively on buying groceries.

I arrived in one small town after a long and bone-rattling bus journey to
find the streets deserted. Suddenly I could hear the Queen's clipped and
disembodied English. 'I would like six apples and three oranges, please.'
'But of course!' replied a male voice. There was no one in sight. As I walked
round the corner I came across dozens of people sitting on stools, watching
a single television set, a crude form of drive-in cinema. I had walked in on

lesson seven, and since I was carrying an umbrella and wore a hat my arrival from nowhere must have seemed like a virtual reality teaching aid.

Back to the noodles in Yunnan. I was finishing my bowl when a man pushed himself to the front of the audience and showed me a crumpled piece of paper. On it were drawn what looked like a series of footprints with arrows. I was baffled. Suddenly the man started to sway as if in a trance. He swivelled clumsily on one foot and then jumped. Everyone laughed. The man grabbed my arms and tried to swing me round. I was getting anxious. Other people got out their pieces of paper with hand-drawn footprints and arrows. They pointed at them, clearly excited. Verbal communication was impossible. My Mandarin extended to asking the directions for the nearest loo and these were clearly not model students of *Follow Me*.

Finally I realised that the villagers wanted to recruit me as their dance teacher. On closer inspection, the footsteps on the pieces of paper revealed the outlines of a waltz. The man and I waltzed, badly. The villagers couldn't stop laughing. A month later I was in Hohhot, the dusty capital of Inner Mongolia. My friends and I decided to go to a discotheque. The band played Elvis Presley and the *Blue Danube* on traditional Chinese instruments that sounded like a litter of cats on heat.

Suddenly I was cornered by a man with extraordinarily high cheekbones. He showed me a piece of paper with footprints and arrows. The same waltz, 2,000 miles away at the other end of China. As I discovered later, I had chosen to visit China in the very summer that the government decided to legalise Western dancing. Within weeks tens, perhaps hundreds of millions of people were scribbling footprints on pieces of paper and waltzing, fox-trotting or tangoing up and down the Middle Kingdom. My dancing experience was capped when I walked into the Beijing Hotel, then the grandest in China, to find a ballroom-dancing competition in full swing in one of the ornate function rooms.

Last week I returned to Beijing for the first time since 1983. We were filming a story about the gender gap. China is perhaps the only country in the world where men outnumber women. In fact, sociologists working for the United Nations believe that there are as many as forty million men of marrying age who cannot find a wife, because the country has run out of wives. The reasons for this imbalance are threefold. The first is the one child per family policy. The second is the traditional preference for sons, especially in rural areas. And the third is the ultrasound machine which has enabled pregnant Chinese women to choose. Although there are no real statistics, it is thought that millions of abortions are performed every year because women discover that their only child will be a girl.

This would have far-reaching social consequences in any country, but in a nation of 1.2 billion it creates social upheaval on a massive scale. Even in the official *China Daily*, which likes to paint a rosy picture, there have been 12,000 reported cases of abducted women in the last two years alone. There is supposed to be a veritable slave market for eligible women shipped to rural areas, starved of females.

In Beijing we visited the Number One Dating Agency. The place was full of men, clicking anxiously through the database for suitable and available wives. One of the men, a good-looking computer engineer with a respectable income, had been looking in vain for six months.

What has all this got to do with dancing, you may ask? Simple. It explained the fact that the dance floor of the Nightman disco, where we were filming part of our feature, was packed with men, swarming around a handful of women in latex microskirts. The waltz, the tango and the foxtrot had been replaced by the pogo. You don't need a partner to dance the pogo.

6

The Bauls' Festival

Frances Harrison

The Bauls are mystic vagabonds who travel through Bengal trying to earn money with their songs. It's a lonely life, but every year they gather at the shrine of their founder to celebrate the anniversary of his death. (23 October 1997)

_____

Hundreds of the most zany-looking people in Asia assemble once a year in the small provincial town of Kushtia, near the Bangladeshi border with India. Some are dressed like Hindu sadhus or holy men, in red turbans and robes with sceptres and giant silver pendants. Others are more austere, shaven heads, dressed in coarse white cloth with only some shells and beads for decoration, or ragged shirts hardly visible under vast beards and Rastafarian-type hair coils. The only thing that seems to be standard issue is a miniature wooden chopping board for cutting marijuana and a pipe for smoking it.

It is full moon and we are here to celebrate the 107th anniversary of the death of the emperor of the Bauls, Lalon. Nobody even knows whether Lalon was a Hindu or a Muslim, but he gave birth to a cult of tolerance followed by Bengalis of all religions. Amid the clouds of marijuana smoke and the bodies stretched on the ground in stupor, I search for a definition of what a Baul is. Their songs refer to the numbers six and nine, which are supposed to represent parts of the body, but nobody is in the mood to explain things. All I get is advice about how I should live my life; no children until twelve years after marriage is recommended practice. It's all right to go to prostitutes, though when I asked the man who told me this whether his wife wouldn't get upset, he was a bit evasive. Actually Bauls don't believe in the institution of marriage, but this couple were married before they renounced the material world to go on their mystic journey.

Interviewing Bauls is tricky; many belong to another world in which my questions are puzzling. I ask whether they suffer harassment from Islamic fundamentalists, who must consider their way of life abhorrent. Enigmatic pronouncements follow, such as we all follow God along different paths, but no real answer. Meanwhile a mad man is following me, periodically touching my muddy shoes as a sign of respect. In a valiant attempt to communicate with a limited English vocabulary he repeats a few words in almost every permutation, saying God is mother, mother is all, all in all is God. At first I think I know what he's getting at, then I wonder if he knows.

I buy one of the musical instruments, the ektara of the Bauls. Made out of the dried shell of a gourd with a bamboo frame, it has one string that reverberates with an eccentric twang. Plucking the string is addictive and soon I have a vast following behind me; like the Pied Piper I lead them backwards and forwards and round in circles. I cannot shake off my vast tail of spectators; police officers try to help, but they end up following me, too, sucked into the chain. It seems the lure of a foreign woman with a camera exceeds even the most exotic-looking guru. I am wondering what is so strange about me in my checked shirt and jeans. All around are faces wrinkled with age and eyes moist with marijuana smoke, men with patchwork coats and dark glasses juggling trident sticks with bells on them.

Then people come up to me, asking for my autograph and the familiar question, Madam what country, what village? Never has London been so often reduced to the status of a village. Normally I attract curious glances, but in this setting it is a bit disturbing to be the centre of attraction, upstaging even wild bohemian mystics. Rather charmingly, the Bauls deduce I must have a spiritual power to pull such a crowd. Eventually the truth emerges: a series of rumours are circulating as to my identity. The best is that I am Princess Diana's sister and have come on a humanitarian mission to Bangladesh. Why Princess Diana's sister would want to go to the Baul festival is a question no one thought to ask. Nor did they wonder why I came without any security personnel or the razzmatazz that accompanies a dignitary's visit. Most of all, I assure you I do not look anything like the late Princess.

Oblivious to my new-found status of minor royal celebrity, I continue to try to get some sense out of the Bauls. One man tells me there is no difference between a conventional life and the life of a Baul. We are all mad, he says; you are mad, I am mad, mad to be sitting on the earth under this tree. He points to the crowd of royal watchers and we agree they are definitely very mad to have nothing better to do. But there is a sting in the tail; apparently I am the maddest of them all because I have come all the way from what he calls BBC London to see the Bauls. I had to concede he had a point.

7

Washed Away

Juliet Hindell

The Japanese take bathing very seriously; the practice has its roots in the country's religious purification. (5 March 1998)

My bath is Japanese-style, square and deep enough to sit up to my shoulders in hot water. It is also run by computer. Just press the button on a small control panel and it fills itself to the perfect depth and perfect temperature in about fifteen minutes. The control panel shows a picture of a happy bather when it's ready. I confess to a love affair with my bath. But I only realised how deeply immersed I had become in Japanese bathing culture when it broke down the other day. I was forced to renew my acquaintance with Japan's other bathing possibilities.

Many Japanese have a serious approach to washing. The ritual goes something like this: scrub thoroughly with soap outside the tub. Rinse off and only then climb into the tub. The idea behind this is that all the family can use the same water. My Japanese bath has a function for this, too. It will reheat the water from the night before. The other day I pressed the button with confidence and left the bath to fill itself. Fifteen minutes later I returned only to find a boiling cauldron close to overflowing. I pressed the stop button, but to no avail.

I called my landlady, who lives upstairs. But she didn't know how the bath worked. She called my neighbour, who has the same bath but couldn't stop the flow. They called the architect of the building, who installed the bath. He at least knew where the mains tap was and switched the water off altogether. It was by now eleven at night and my landlady offered me her bath. A fraught evening ended in a fragrant bathe in what looks like a big box made of cedar wood. The hot water releases the scent of the wood. Many Japanese used to have wooden baths, but now they are an expensive luxury. Not in possession of a cedar bath myself, I sometimes perfume my bathwater Japanese-style with iris leaves or the skins of citrus fruits. These not only smell nice, but are good for rubbing on your skin.

The next day the repair man came. 'Your bath has gone berserk,' he said. Worse, it would take five days to get the necessary part. I decided I couldn't impose on my landlady every night, so I resorted to the public bath. Enough people still have no bath at home to mean there are communal bath houses in most Tokyo neighbourhoods. Some have baths filled with herbs, saunas and even some dubious ones with electric currents flowing through them. But a large hot pool where the bathers can sit together is standard. My local has a mural of Mount Fuji and a clientele of friendly old ladies who offered to scrub my back. I was left pink and squeaky clean. The public bath got me through to the weekend, but then I decided to go to Japan's ultimate answer to bath breakdowns, a hot-spring resort.

There are thousands across the country, from tiny rustic inns to huge glitzy hotels. I took the rustic option and soaked all weekend in a rock pool on a snowy mountainside. The inn has baths both inside and outside, mixed and single sex. Before you get the wrong idea I should explain the rigorous hot-spring etiquette. Bathing suits are not allowed, at least not in authentic inns. Instead, bathers are provided with a tiny towel smaller than a tea towel but bigger than a face flannel. It's supposed to preserve the bather's modesty when entering and exiting the water. I can testify that it requires extreme dexterity of movement to come anywhere near keeping it in place, and woe betide anyone who puts it in the bath water.

Japanese often fold them up and put them on their heads. They also sometimes bring bottles of sake, Japanese rice wine, into the bath and warm it in the hot-spring water. Drinking warm sake when you are already warmed by the spring water can lead to a very merry bathe.

There were almost no other guests at the inn I chose. Foreigners, especially women, can get some very curious stares from Japanese bathers both male and female. Some may be worrying that the foreigner may pollute the water by washing with soap in the communal bath, a definite taboo, or worse, try to cool the temperature by adding cold water to the bath. Despite these strict rules, there is nothing more relaxing than sitting back in the natural steam of a hot spring, perfectly warm even though snow is falling all around you. It was almost with regret I pressed the button on my new improved bath computer. The inconvenience of having no hot water had been washed away by a tour of Japan's delightful baths.

8

Finding Shangri-La

Colin Blane

The Chinese authorities said they had identified the remote area which inspired the story of Shangri-La, the utopia set in a hidden valley untouched by the troubles of the outside world. (29 August 1998)

The story of China's claim to Shangri-La begins in an upstairs room in an elegant wooden house in the old town of Lijiang. The man reaching up to the top shelf of the bookcase is Xuan Ke, a musician and amateur historian of Yunnan province. He's convinced that it was this south-west corner of China which inspired the legend of Shangri-La, even though the author, James Hilton, never came here. At sixty-nine, Xuan Ke is a man of energy and enthusiasm and soon magazines and books are scattered across the table of his attic study in support of his theory. Mr Xuan says James Hilton derived all the detail he needed from the writings of an eccentric American adventurer, Joseph Rock, who roamed south-west China throughout the period when Hilton was researching his book.

Over the last couple of years, the Yunnan provincial authorities have started to pay attention to the legend of Shangri-La. Hilton's novel *Lost Horizon* places the mountain paradise somewhere in eastern Tibet, but that doesn't deter Yunnan's claim. A Shangri-La research committee's been set up, local beauty spots have been renamed and, as myth merges with reality, an elderly woman has been identified as the living relative of a fictional character in James Hilton's tale.

There is a growing Shangri-La industry in Yunnan and driving it all, of course, is tourism. This part of China wasn't always so welcoming, as Joseph Rock once observed when he described how a local bandit chieftain used to ambush travellers, hang them by their thumbs from a tree and leave them dangling above a roaring bonfire. Nowadays, Yunnan offers an altogether friendlier face as well as some of the most spectacular, unspoiled country-side in China. But what of the evidence for Shangri-La? In *Lost Horizon*, it was a haven of serenity in an increasingly materialistic world. It was a green valley hidden in the eastern Himalayas and dominated by a single snow-capped peak. It was also a place of religious tolerance between Buddhists and Christians and, most astonishing of all, a place where time passed so slowly, it was possible to live for hundreds of years.

That is the legend of Shangri-La. I set out from Xuan Ke's sunlit courtyard to track down China's version of it. I took the bus 350 miles along a bumpy single-track road which pushes north-west along China's border with Burma and climbs to 4,500 metres beneath the icy ramparts of the White Horse Mountains. At three miles high the air's so thin the slightest effort makes it difficult to breathe, just as Hilton's characters discovered in their Shangri-La. For much of the way, the road is cut into the steep slope of the hillside, with no barriers and a dizzying drop below. During the summer rains, ava-lanches of mud crash down, leaving tear-shaped scars on the mountainside. At one point we came upon two trucks wedged side by side in the mire, blocking the traffic in both directions. We abandoned our bus, shouldered our luggage and squelched our way past the obstruction; then hired another vehicle on the far side.

Our destination was the village of Zitong, still in Yunnan but not far from Tibet. According to our Chinese guides, this was the inspiration for *Lost Horizon*. On the last leg of the journey the road, previously difficult, became even narrower. We drove on through forests of pine and oak, still more than 3,000 metres up. We inched past herds of goats, nudging them to the brink of the precipice, then the road petered out and we were there, in a tiny village about to feel the full weight of China's tourist industry, a village so quiet it was almost comatose. At the centre of the community, there was an old Catholic church with an ornate tower, built by the French ninety years ago. Across the lane, a timber homestead flying Buddhist prayer flags from its roof. And, sloping down to the river, there were bright green terraces of rice and rows of maize. In the village itself, there were walnut trees and grapes. Without question it could have passed for James Hilton's 'enclosed paradise of amazing fertility'.

Zitong is a small Tibetan-speaking community of about sixty people. Christians and Buddhists work in the fields together. I sought out some of the oldest residents to ask about Shangri-La. They hadn't heard of the story until two years ago, when some officials told them. One woman, Roanna, had been instructed to tell visitors she was the grand-daughter of Chang, a character in the book. She smiled when I asked her about the legend of long life and contentedness. The village was healthy and peaceful enough, she agreed, but she told me: 'It's a poor place and the young people are leaving.'

So the villagers co-operate with the Shangri-La Research Committee in the hope of attracting visitors and development. Back down the road at the town of Deqin, the promotion of Shangri-La is even more determined. It's a shabby place, a centre for the logging industry, busy with trucks and traders. But Deqin is hitching its wagon to the Shangri-La star. New hotels are being built and posters up and down the street urge residents to pay their taxes to ensure the prosperity of Shangri-La.

In his attic study hundreds of miles away, historian Xuan Ke is having second thoughts. He says he's worried China's newly discovered Shangri-La is already in danger, threatened by the rush to develop the area. Next year, a new airport is to open 160 miles closer to Zitong village.

It's hard not to feel sorry for the unworldly residents of China's Shangri-La. It could be another year or so before tourism brings them the progress they think they need, shattering their tranquillity in the process. But the road can be widened and the bridges strengthened. Already, the holidaymakers' minibuses are clattering round the mountain. It won't be long before there are traffic jams and karaoke bars in Shangri-La.

9

Military Coup

Owen Bennett-Jones

Relations between Pakistan's army and the country's civilian administration had been growing increasingly tense. When the government announced it was sacking army chief General Pervez Musharraf, the military's response was immediate.
(16 October 1999)

I was standing outside the television headquarters when the troops arrived. At first the soldiers asked to be allowed in, but officials on the other side of a high iron gate had their orders. 'No,' they said. 'You can't come in.' The troops reported back to their headquarters on the radio: 'They won't let us in.' The response crackled back immediately: 'Take control, take control!' Seconds later the soldiers were clambering over the gate. The prime minister's elite force was inside to protect the building on behalf of the civilian government. But it seemed to acknowledge that it was outgunned. The elite force saw the army coming and the men simply sat down and put their weapons on the ground in front of them. The army had scored its first victory and the coup was under way.

It all began about a couple of hours earlier, when Pakistan television broadcast a news flash saying that the army chief, General Pervez Musharraf, had been sacked. Within minutes the army had dispatched a major to the television building with a simple order: 'Stop the broadcast going out again.' And the major did have a go. He marched into the newsroom and told them not to transmit the news item. Recognising a superior force when it saw one, the newsroom complied. But within minutes the government got wind of what was going on and it dispatched its own man to the newsroom. This one was a brigadier from Prime Minister Nawaz Sharif's elite force.

'Play the message,' he ordered. 'Broadcast it.'

'Don't,' the major insisted. 'Pull it.'

Deadlock. The brigadier upped the ante. He took out his pistol from its holster and repeated his demand: 'Play it!' The major responded in kind. He pulled out his pistol: 'Don't play it!' We now had two military officers, pacing the corridors of Pakistan Television, pointing guns at each other. The stakes were high. Was the general sacked or not? Would the government's will be done? At the time, the prime minister's man, the brigadier, prevailed. The news of the sacking was played on a couple of extra occasions, but the army had the final say. Once the major had told his superiors about his failure to get the news blocked, the army dispatched the troops who I witnessed taking the building. Within twenty minutes of them clambering over that gate, PTV was off air.

The signal did come back a few hours later, but by that time the news it was broadcasting was very different. This time it said the prime minister, Nawaz Sharif, had been dismissed. The chief of army staff, it said, would make a statement shortly.

But if I thought I was seeing high drama, it was nothing compared to what was happening in the skies above the city of Karachi. Whilst his troops were securing the television station, the chief of army staff, General Pervez Musharraf, was returning from an official trip to Sri Lanka. The prime minister had chosen this moment to sack the general and it was done with care; since the general was airborne, he wouldn't be able to do much about it.

The government's plan went like this: they'd get the general's plane diverted from its intended destination of Karachi to Nawab Shah, a small rural airport in Sind. The general would then be taken into custody to make sure he couldn't organise any resistance to his sacking. But the plan went wrong. As the general's plane approached Nawab Shah, the crew noticed that there were a lot of vehicles near the runway. That was unusual. The airport was so small that it was normally absolutely empty. They told the army chief and, perhaps realising what was up, he ordered the plane to return to Karachi. But when it reached Karachi there was another problem; the runway had been blocked by civilian aviation vehicles and the control tower was refusing the plane permission to land.

General Musharraf took over on the radio. 'This is the army chief,' he shouted. 'Let me land.' 'No,' the reply came back. 'You cannot land. You can land at a foreign airport, but not in Pakistan. You cannot land here.' This was a remarkable statement for a number of reasons. It wasn't just a question of refusing General Musharraf permission to land. He was on a commercial flight. There were 268 other passengers on board the aircraft and it was fast running out of fuel. The general tried to argue, but to no avail. Eventually he managed to make radio contact with his corps commander in Karachi.

Troops were rushed to the airport. They took over the control tower, cleared the runway and the plane managed to land. It had just six or seven minutes' worth of fuel left on board. As soon as the general got off the plane, he took command of the coup. The government of Nawaz Sharif was toppled within a matter of hours and Pakistan's latest period of military rule had begun.

10
A New Era

Jill McGivering

Hong Kong had embarked upon a new era; after 150 years as a British colony, it had returned to Chinese rule. (18 March 2000)

I arrived in Hong Kong as the great handover party ended. The coloured lights and luminous plastic decorations were being packed away. The Chinese had replaced the British, and I would spend the next two and a half years answering the question: 'Has Hong Kong changed since the handover?'

The first year erupted like a biblical plague. An outbreak of bird flu caused the slaughter of more than a million chickens in a flurry of feathers and clucking. A deadly tide left hundreds of thousands of fish floating, bloated and staring, in local waters. A multibillion-dollar airport opened with a drum roll, only to go spectacularly wrong in its first weeks. And then, the economy; property prices tumbled, the stock market went into free fall and unemployment soared as Hong Kong started to nosedive into recession. It's yet to recover.

Danna Chan is a cheerful middle-aged Hong Kong estate agent with heavy make-up and large trendy glasses. When I met her, soon after the handover, she was using a felt-tip pen to slash the prices in her shop window. 'Business is terrible,' she told me, close to tears. 'I may go bankrupt.' That wasn't all. Her savings were all in the stock market. They'd lost seven-eighths of their value overnight.

In a remote and rundown housing estate, I had a secret meeting with middle-aged factory workers, all women. I could sense their fear as soon as I walked in. Their boss had just cut their wages by a quarter. Take it or leave it. They felt exploited but helpless, their fingers fretting at their clothes, as they begged: 'Isn't there anything you can do?' Rising suicide figures suggested their hard-luck stories were not the only ones.

These failures, an unexpected blip after decades of success, have sparked an acute identity crisis. This is, after all, the home of the American dream gone right, a city where everyone is an entrepreneur and it's better to clean the streets than accept welfare.

The sheer audacity of the architecture says it all. From my desk on the eleventh floor I'm looking out now over Hong Kong's central district, at a tight pack of dozens of skyscrapers jostling for a better view of the harbour beyond. The older generation of buildings is squat and solid, the new is a blaze of multistorey chrome and glass whose polished surfaces spin the daylight into a kaleidoscope of patterns.

Then the harbour, from the giant dredgers and cruisers to the small working sampans. In the midst of it all the *Star Ferry* picks her way regally back and forth, a stately old lady now a hundred years old whose rhythm has become the city's pulse. The only sound to reach me up here is the never-ending rumble of traffic and the drilling from an unseen building site below.

In the last few years, I've hung on this scene's every mood. I've seen the thick threatening clouds of monsoon turn the city black, and, best of all, the warm flush of sunset turn it rose-coloured, as the day dies fighting only to be replaced by the brashness of neon. To me, this dense concentration of people and buildings is everything I love most about Hong Kong, the intensity, the drive, the faith in the future. The vision that carved a metropolis out of a barren rock.

I know, because I owe this city everything. I first came here twelve years ago. I'd spent the previous months being turned down for jobs in London. I didn't have the connections, I kept being told. I didn't have enough experience. I didn't have the right background. In Hong Kong they judged my future, not my family. I found a job on the main English language newspaper within a week, and stayed nearly four years before joining the BBC.

It taught me a lesson England never did: that dreams should be cherished, not ridiculed, and, to use those terribly English phrases, that someone who gets ideas above their station, who gets too big for their boots, doesn't need to be put in their place.

In some ways little's changed since those days. I can still wander through Wanchai's street market with its pungent Chinese herbs and bamboo baskets and the stickiness underfoot of blood and innards. I can still drink bitter-tasting tea at the old Chinese medicine shops next to rosewood cabinets full of shrivelled animal parts. When I walk home late at night past night-clubs featuring topless dancers, I can still see the rising plumes of incense and neatly arranged offerings of fruit on pavement shrines outside. And although Hong Kong's ego has been badly dented by the recession, I can already see the powerful 'can do' mentality at work again.

Remember Danna Chan, the estate agent on the verge of bankruptcy? I met her again a few weeks ago. Her money had recovered about half its value, her business had suffered but survived. 'Plenty of hard work,' she told me brightly. I asked her if she was avoiding the stock market now. She looked amazed. 'Of course not!' I emerged into the chaos of the street with her parting words: 'Sometimes you lose, other times you win.'

As well as all these dramas, a battle has raged since the handover for hearts and minds. The Chinese flag has been heaved up flagpoles everywhere. Schoolchildren are taught their lessons in Chinese now, not English, and encouraged to sing the Chinese national anthem. Chinese medicine is moving from the backstreets to the hospitals. In a top Hong Kong university I met Ellen, a straight-A student who clearly had her pick of university subjects and had chosen a new course, a blend of Western and Chinese medicine. She crouched over her classmate's wrist, learning the secrets of pulse diagnosis from a mainland Chinese master. 'I'm Chinese,' Ellen told me earnestly. 'This is my culture.' Her professor beamed.

And what about politics? I found the British colonial government elitist, even pompous, serving the interests of a small minority. Not much has changed. The new government, loyal to Beijing, is dominated by powerful Hong Kong businessmen; the economy run by a handful of tycoons. Democracy is the ghost at their lavish Chinese banquet.

Its time will come. Last year saw the tenth anniversary of the massacre of pro-democracy students in Beijing's Tiananmen Square. Hong Kong's leader called on local people to put the past behind them. It was a not-so-subtle hint to stay away from the annual memorial service and stop embarrassing Beijing. As darkness gathered across the park where the memorials are held each year, I watched to see how local people would respond. They were soon streaming through the gates in force, from offices and shops, factories and classrooms, old and young from all walks of life. Before long there were 40,000 people sitting together in the darkness, their faces softened by the light from candles in paper cones, singing about democracy. Students who'd been in primary school when the Chinese army opened fire in Tiananmen Square, young families with sleepy children mesmerised by the flames.

So when people ask me: 'Has Hong Kong changed since the handover?' I try not to think about the national flags and the patriotic speeches. I think instead of the entrepreneurs and their faith in the future and of a carpet of candlelight stretching as far as the eye can see, and answer: 'No, not really.'

11
The Vineyard

Robert Parsons

In the eighties, nineties and beyond, bookshops were full of volumes by Britons who'd opted to migrate to warmer climes to create their own farms or vineyards. Usually these were in Mediterranean spots like Tuscany, Provence or Andalucia, but our correspondent had his sights set on the Caucasus. (25 October 2000)

In the Alazani valley, it had been a summer like no other. Not a drop of rainfall between June and September and a sun that burnt with a relentless, blinding dazzle. The valley shimmered in a troubling, enervating heat, a furnace that sucked the moisture from the soil and turned villages into clouds of dust. In the village of Kisiskhevi, the men sat beneath their walnut trees and waited, the languid stillness of midday broken by the rattle of dice on a backgammon board and the crackle of desiccated leaves. In the distance, the mountains of the Caucasus quivered green and liquid, playing tricks with my imagination. I followed the flight of a hawk, its wings outstretched to catch the uplift from the heat spirals.

It had been twenty years since I first came to Georgia, carried south from Moscow for two sweltering days on a Soviet train, twenty years since an idea had first formed in my mind. I blame it all on Stalin's barber, the man who once shaved the greying whiskers of the fearsome dictator. It was a chance encounter in the forested hills north of Kutaisi in western Georgia. The memory is clouded now by the passing of time and the cluttered accumulation of experience, but it still lingers, a moment of magic and poetry in my first Georgian vineyard.

It was early March. The winter snow had melted and a herd of pigs was snorting and sifting through the sodden leaves at the side of the mud track. Our car rolled and slithered into a village. Temuri and Maia met me at the station. Friends of friends, they were about to teach me a mind-numbing lesson in Georgian hospitality. We stopped outside a large stone house, its wooden balcony coiled with vines. I had no idea at the time, but this was to be the first stop on a bacchanalian tour of their relatives' kitchens, no small venture in a village where everybody shared the same family name.

The table heaved with food, the air reeked of spices and wood smoke, and I found myself the object of the curious gaze of a small gathering of very large men. They had the stubby fingers of those who have always worked the soil, bellies that boasted of a bucolic wealth and the red glowing noses of men who think nothing of downing several litres of wine a day. I have a vague recollection of a series of introductory toasts and the terrifying appearance of a gigantic drinking horn that made its way inexorably around the table. I felt my brain go numb long before I reached the bottom. The surroundings span into an incoherent whirl. Time was concertinaed until, through the mists of alcohol, I found myself in a vineyard in the chill of early evening.

I believe, and given the state I was in I cannot be absolutely sure, that I was being introduced to Stalin's barber, a man with remarkably steady hands. He led the way through an orchard towards a group of curious mounds, which I first took for molehills. An old man now, he stooped at the first mound, looked up at me and said: 'Let's try this one.' I was nonplussed. Did he intend to drag the mole out by its tail? No, he explained, this was the traditional Georgian way of making wine, unchanged for thousands of years. The juice from the grapes and their skins are poured into a giant amphora, what the Georgians call a *kvevri*. It's then buried in the soil up to its narrow neck. The top is covered with an oak lid, sealed with clay and covered by an earthen mound. And then it's left alone, out among the flowers, to ferment and turn to wine.

There was a moment of hush as Stalin's barber cleared away the topsoil and scraped off the clay. He paused like a priest about to confer the sacraments. Only the lid remained. He stood and, so as to underline the drama of the occasion, trod deliberately around its circumference. I edged closer and willed him to take the final step. As the lid came away, a raspberry haze rose from the ground and was swept away on the breeze. A crimson mirror reflected the scudding clouds, 400 litres of fresh young wine. The barber took his ladle and scooped out the first glass and handed it to me. I raised it to my mouth and drank. It was a moment of magical intensity. 'It's Saperavi,' he said, referring to the grape, which in Georgian means pigment. It was densely red and cool and stained my lips like blood. Georgia and its vineyards had taken over a corner of my mind.

Twenty years on, the memory of that day wafted back across time, conjured by an association of ideas. I had been gazing absent-mindedly at a row of Saperavi vines, my own Saperavi vines, when the image of the barber reassembled itself in my thoughts. 'It's Saperavi,' he said, and I saw myself raising that glass to my lips. A vague wish made then, to own my own vineyard, had been fulfilled.

The house I have built with my friends sits on the southern slopes of the Alazani valley in the province of Kakheti, the heartland of the Georgian grape. It is surrounded by vines: Saperavi, of course, and Rkatsiteli, Georgia's white grape of choice. Looking north from the balcony, across the tops of the walnut trees that mark the end of our property, I can see the Caucasus erupting, magnificent and perpendicular, from the valley floor. In the early morning heat, the mountain range appears to stir and move like a great awakening beast. Mist rolls off its back and tendrils of steam rise from its crevices and canyons. Beneath, spread out for mile after mile, the vast abundant Alazani valley shimmers liquid green and gold.

Archaeological evidence suggests Georgians have been cultivating the grape here and making wine, or '*ghvino*' as the Georgians call it, for more than 5,000 years. The valley is the cradle of Georgian wine, perhaps of all wine. When the Arabs invaded in the seventh century, this is the way they came, hacking and burning the vineyards as they went. Later, the Mongols followed in their footsteps and then the Persians, time after time again. But to no avail; whoever destroyed the vines, the people of Kakheti simply grew them back again, nurturing not just a plant but a culture and a way of life. For Georgians, the vine has evolved into a symbol of their Christian faith and of resistance.

Our house forms part of the village of Kisiskhevi, a place of such somnolent charm it is hard to imagine that until quite recent times danger hung over the valley as heavy as the fruit on the ripening mulberry trees. In 1854, the Muslim tribesmen of the mountains carried out a raid so daring it has entered into the legends of the Caucasus. In the blistering heat of early July, just a short walk from where our house now stands, the wife and daughters of the Georgian prince Tchavatchavdze and their French governess were settling into their country retreat. But as they languished in the shade, watching the peacocks strut about the gardens of Tsinandali, their nemesis was descending in a cloud of dust from the mountains.

Shamil, the commander of the Muslim tribes, who had defied the might of Nicholas II's armies for thirty years, wanted the princesses as ransom for the release of his son, held prisoner by the Russians since childhood. The kidnappers burst with fury upon the estate, clattering across the gorge that marks the end of our village. The princesses were tied across their saddles and driven high into the mountains. Some were never to return.

Generations on, the threat from the mountains has receded, but the rituals of Kakhetian life remain unchanged. It is the start of autumn, but the sun still burns with a ferocity that has filled the grapes with hot juice and split their skins. We know it is time for the *rtveli*, the harvest, to begin. Tomorrow the pickers will come. We drive out into the vast bowl of the Alazani valley, Levan, Vano, Karlo, Niko and a small group of friends. A power cut has switched off the lights right across impoverished Georgia. Outside, beyond the headlights of our rickety car, the infinite darkness of the Kakhetian night is heavy with the thick sweet scent of grapes.

We stop by the banks of a river in a pool of light. At a small taverna, village musicians are locked in a demented battle with a roaring generator. At the table next to ours, two men are deep in conversation. But now they rise as if in a trance. Two brawny peasants, faces blackened by the summer sun, arms spread out like eagles, flick their fingers to the music. They whirl with an ungainly grace that belies their rustic appearance. They snap their legs and stamp their feet, throw back their shoulders and circle each other like lovers. Their cries of exultation fill the room and rebound from the walls. And then, just as suddenly as they had begun, the two men sink back into their seats, clutching their glasses of amber wine.

I woke to the snorting of pigs. Hundreds of them advancing in a hairy black tide up the road that leads past our gate, snuffling out the fallen walnuts and sniffing the air. I rushed to shut the gate to keep them from the vineyard. Kisiskhevi had sprung to unaccustomed life. Horses and carts clattered through avenues of walnut trees, laden with baskets piled high with fruit. In the vineyard, our grapes glistened in the morning dew. The sun had risen and vapour curled in wisps from the steaming ground.

The vine in Georgia has an iconic significance unmatched anywhere else in the world. It is a symbol of regeneration, of wealth and plenty, and of the country's Christian faith in a sea of Islam and of resistance. Perhaps because of this, the grape harvest in Georgia is more than just a Dionysian celebration. It is existential. It is a reaffirmation of survival, a statement of identity and attachment to the land. The *rtveli* also marks the end of the agricultural cycle; it is the last of the harvests. When it is over, preparation for the winter must begin.

Our pickers arrived not by horse and cart but on the back of a swaying lorry. They disgorged into the vineyard, wicker baskets on their backs, and the picking began. We worked all morning, plucking the swollen sticky fruit from their straining stems. By midday the job was done, 300 kilogrammes of grapes. Not a big crop this year, but the fruit was good. Enough perhaps for 150 litres of wine.

That night we celebrated the end of the old and the beginning of a new cycle of life. We roasted kebabs on a bed of vine cinders and quaffed great draughts of last year's wine to an endless stream of toasts. Georgians don't sip their wine like Europeans. They throw it back with gusto, one glass at a time.

I stepped outside on to the balcony and into the great amphitheatre of the Alazani valley. Another power cut had plunged the whole of Kakheti into darkness. Inside, the revellers were in full flow: 'What enmity has destroyed,' they sang, 'love will rebuild,' their words drifting out across the valley. The vineyard was illuminated by the light of the stars alone, glimmering in the inky night in all their unrivalled glory. The bed of vine cinders still glowed, but a crust of ash had already formed.

By morning the landscape had changed. Thick clouds scudded along the ragged edge of the Caucasus, disgorging their entrails along the mountain tops. The fire had died and a fine rain drizzled on the vineyard. The grapes were gone and the vine leaves were turned to gold and red. In the orchard, rain-varnished persimmons hung like perfect orange globes.

12
Expelled

Kate Clark

Afghanistan's Taliban rulers, angered by coverage of their destruction of the famous Buddha statues at Bamiyan, closed down the BBC bureau in the capital, Kabul, and ordered our correspondent there to leave the country. (17 March 2001)

'I'm a refugee from Afghanistan,' I said to the Pakistani officials at the border. 'No, you're a distinguished journalist and our honoured guest,' they said. They gave me sweet tea as well as the kind words. I'd just said goodbye to my translator and driver, all of us trying not to cry. The driver, Haji, a white-bearded veteran, has crossed frontlines and dodged rockets with seven correspondents. This is the first time he's seen one expelled. Azam, the translator, has only been in the job two months. He's keen, intelligent, hungry to learn, and now faces an uncertain future.

Unpredictability is the nature of life in Afghanistan. I've always known I could have to leave at a moment's notice, always tried not to get too attached. But still, the order to leave was a huge shock. At nine o'clock on Wednesday morning I was in the Taliban Foreign Ministry being given a six-month visa. Two hours later, I returned for a press conference, only for officials to beckon me over and tell me they thought it would be better for me to leave the country for a while.

If Afghans want to break the news that your father has died, they will say at first that he is a bit poorly. In true Afghan fashion, the real truth of my position came out slowly, that I had no options, that I was being expelled, that the BBC office was going to be sealed. I joked with the officials. Again Afghans always joke about disaster; it makes it a little easier. Twenty-four hours later, I left the office. No time to say goodbyes, no time to sleep, no time to react, barely enough time to pile everything into the car and race for the border before nightfall.

Reporting in Afghanistan may be the toughest news job in the world.

I don't know, it was my first posting. Certainly, I have agonised over every word I have written. Upwards of seventy per cent of the population listen to the BBC and you want to get the news right for them. That is an immense responsibility for the correspondent and an ever-present source of pressure.

My words are monitored, mulled over and criticised by both sides in the war, although as I've been living in a Taliban-controlled area, the pressure comes mainly from them. And as the only foreign correspondent in the country, I also know that I'm one of the few channels for the voices of Afghans to reach the outside world. I've been careful, too, that my coverage of the Taliban, one of the most despised and condemned governments in the world, is fair. But even tougher than the striving after accuracy and balance is the constant fear that my reporting might endanger an Afghan interviewee or source. Thank God, the worst the Taliban could do to me, a foreigner, was to expel me.

This expulsion has been a huge shock but not really a surprise. My job is to report what is going on, even issues which I knew the Taliban would hate me for revealing, namely violent crime in Kabul, which continues despite Taliban claims to have cleaned up the country; the presence of Arab and Pakistani militants in training camps despite official denials, and the massacre of civilians by the Taliban in January.

And this time, my assertion that it was difficult to find an Afghan who agreed with the Taliban's destruction of the two ancient Buddhas of Bamiyan. The Taliban have had to put up with near-universal condemnation of this action, but my report that even their own people didn't agree with them was too much, it seems. That, along with an Afghan-American professor who in a BBC interview called them '*Jaahil*'.

The term is a huge insult. It means ignorant, but the sort of ignorance which Muslims believe the world suffered before the coming of Islam. The Taliban were furious and I was the obvious target for their anger. Several Afghans have said to me that the destruction of the Buddhas and the closure of the BBC office are similar actions.

Despite drought, bereavement and the ruination of their country, most Afghans seem to have been touched by the destruction of the colossal statues at Bamiyan. It would be like the destruction of somewhere like Stonehenge in Britain. They are symbols of the nation, for many people symbols of a more tolerant past, when the rulers of Afghanistan accepted different religions and points of view, where cultures mixed along the great trading routes and the Buddha, a man of the East, could be depicted. The destruction of the statues has felt like an attempt to wipe out history. And for a country that has seen so much destruction, this deliberate demolition of something ancient and irreplaceable felt obscene.

For Afghans, the BBC is also a deeply honoured national institution. That sounds strange, but Afghans do seem to feel they own us. Whatever their politics, ethnic background or level of education, they listen to the BBC. I know that is mainly because there are few other choices in a country without television or newspapers, but still it's always moving: the small child in an orphanage who confesses the children club together in secret to buy batteries to listen to the BBC soap opera; the shy smile that breaks out on the face of a tough Taliban soldier when he discovers I'm the correspondent.

The toughness of this job has always been rewarded by the generosity of Afghans. Even in the short time since my expulsion, people have spoken of the shame that they feel because I've been ordered out. 'You were our guest,' they said.

One friend quoted lines from an Urdu poet:

> Speak, because your lips are free, speak because you still have a tongue
> See in the blacksmith's shop, the flame is fierce, the iron is red hot, the mouth of
>   every lock has started open
> Only a few more days are we obliged to rest in the shadow of oppression

After I crossed the border into Pakistan, I spoke to another old friend. 'Cheer up, Kate,' he said. 'Don't be too upset. You've become a hero of the Afghan people overnight.' It was infinitely reassuring. My commitment to Afghanistan is undimmed.

13

Lost in the Outback

Dominic Hughes

This correspondent told the programme how Australians had become scared of the great outdoors. He talked of the dangers lurking in the bush and explained the dire consequences which could befall careless hikers who found themselves hopelessly lost. A week or two later, he found himself in that position, lost in a cold, wet forest; scared, hungry and without shelter. And throughout a long night, the words he'd written for this programme came back to haunt him. (10 October 2001)

It all started well enough: a pleasant weekend of camping and walking with my friend Kevin, four hours south of Sydney in a wilderness area of thick eucalyptus forest and stunning mountain ranges. I never imagined my Saturday night would be spent standing in a forest clearing, desperately hugging another man for warmth, all the time hoping I wasn't about to become a news story in my own right.

Our problems began with the rain; on the morning we planned to spend a day exploring the wild Monolith Valley, the autumn weather changed from mild and sunny to wet and windy. But we thought we were fairly well equipped, so off we set, carrying with us some dry clothes and a fuel stove on which to cook lunch and make a cup of tea. My legs were soon soaked and my feet went the same way. But not to worry, I told myself, we're only going to be out for a few hours. And the scenery was stunning. It's a prehistoric landscape of domed rocks and sandstone cliffs, with deep gorges and thick pockets of rainforest.

It was after lunch that things started to go wrong. We missed a path and found ourselves in a slow climb up a ravine. More time was wasted as we slithered down the other side before it became impassable, followed by a treacherous scramble up a cliff face to the top of a mountain. By this time we had about an hour of sunlight left. Kev, an experienced hiker, was looking more and more concerned, but I was still naively confident. Then the weather closed in. We just couldn't see where we were meant to go. We had to get off the mountain, that much was clear. We slid down a gully and on to a path, or at least what could have been a path but might have been a random collection of leaf litter, or an old wombat trail. By this point, for the first time in years, I was beginning to feel scared. I could feel panic bubbling up through my stomach. I had a strange urge to start crying. Kev was also looking very worried.

It was now getting seriously dark and we had to face the prospect of spending the night out in the open. By six o'clock we'd taken the decision; we found a clearing and, rather than risk breaking a leg in the dark, we would stay put. We were wet, cold and hungry and faced twelve hours of standing around waiting for sunrise. Hypothermia was our biggest worry. The ground was too damp to sit on, and a fire was not an option. The last of our food had been eaten three hours earlier. So, we started talking.

Kev, an engineer by profession, told me how to make sweets like jelly babies. I told Kev every family anecdote I could remember. We debated the likelihood of Crystal Palace getting relegated that weekend. But mostly we talked about how we had got into this situation, and how we could get out of it in one piece. After a few hours it got colder. We both knew what we had to do; the best way to conserve heat is through bodily contact, so we overcame our inhibitions and started hugging.

At first it was a sort of polite hug. But after ten minutes the benefits became obvious and we'd progressed to a full-on bear hug, legs pressed together, arms wrapped tight around each other. And so we stood, leaning against a tree, hugging each other, for the rest of the night. At midnight we tried to celebrate the halfway mark with a cup of tea, but the cooker had run out of fuel. At about two o'clock in the morning, we began to fall asleep on our feet; our knees would buckle, waking us up again.

The hours dragged on and then, just after six, the sky began to brighten. In a few minutes we could see enough to retrace our steps back up the mountain. In the end, it turned out we were only a short distance from the correct path, but in the dark there had been no way of knowing. Four hours later we staggered back into our campground, for a welcome bowl of porridge, a cup of tea and chocolate, lots of chocolate.

The thought that haunted me throughout the night was that we would have to be rescued. There was no way I wanted to end up on the evening news as another British backpacker lost in the Australian bush. And the slightly smug tone of my last piece for *From Our Own Correspondent* also kept echoing in my head: 'Almost every summer', I'd written, 'someone goes for a walk in the mountains, takes a wrong turn and gets lost.' And there I was, cold, wet and most definitely lost. I shall be very careful what I write about in future lest it once again becomes my reality.

14
Polish Cemetery

Monica Whitlock

There's a cemetery in the Iranian capital, Tehran, which contains the graves of some 2,000 Polish people. They had been among a large group of Poles who had sailed across the Caspian Sea to Persia during the Second World War, after their release from Soviet labour camps. (23 June 2001)

Mrs Rezai shoved at the iron door in the graveyard wall. 'It's jammed,' she said. 'No one has been here for ages.' Mr Rezai put his shoulder to it and with a screech and a groan it swung open. On the far side lay rows and rows of stones, each marked with a Polish name: Jan, Wanda, Joseph, Jan again, and with a date of death between the 28th and 30th of August 1942. These were the days when a great flotilla put in at the port of Bandar Anzali. The townspeople came out to watch as the ships disgorged more than 100,000 Polish men, women and children on to the jetty. The fishermen who now drink tea and play dominoes on the dockside at Anzali were boys then. 'The soldiers took them up to the wash house and burnt their clothes,' said one. 'I was standing right here where I'm standing now and I saw it. They were lousy with typhus and starving. We brought them milk and they gave us money. It wasn't Iranian money, but we took it. It was Soviet money.'

The Poles had started their journey to Bandar Anzali in 1939, when Poland was divided under the Molotov–Ribbentrop Pact. Stalin, in the midst of deporting Soviet peoples he thought potentially disloyal, sent the Poles into exile as well. Most of the two million or so Poles got twenty minutes to pack before they were put into wagons and taken to labour camps along the Arctic Circle in Siberia and Kazakhstan. Two years later, however, Germany invaded the USSR and the order came that most Poles were to be freed so that the men could fight under Allied command. The mustering point was to be Iran, occupied at that time by Russian and British troops.

And so began the Polish odyssey; begging rides from herdsmen, crammed into trains, walking sometimes, they set out across the Soviet Union from its northernmost edges 700 miles or so south through central Asia, where they're still remembered with affection and where their route is marked by a string of burial grounds. Just outside Tashkent, they assembled for an open-air mass under a scorching sun to bring blessings on the voyage ahead.

By the time they reached Krasnovodsk on the Caspian coast, about half were dead. But the rest made it across the sea and to the jetty at Anzali. 'Where did they go next?' I asked the fishermen. 'Well, we buried the ones who died at sea, and the British put the rest into camps with barbed wire round them and every few yards an Indian soldier with a gun. They'd put uniforms on them, yellow British ones. I remember the British: "Hajib-Bangbang-Singapore", we used to call them. I was only ten,' said one man, straightening his face. And then, they took them away to Tehran. Very many of the Polish men joined a special army core under General Anders and went to fight in Sicily. Others moved on with the British around the Middle East, to Lebanon, Egypt and Palestine. There some stayed put, especially the Jews, who had left quietly with the rest, despite Stalin's order that Jewish and Ukrainian Poles should be kept in the camps.

The late prime minister of Israel, Menachem Begin, was one such who survived the march through central Asia and the crossing to Anzali. Many, mainly women, stayed on. 'Oh, Iran was like heaven,' one survivor told me. 'There was so much food, we ate until we were sick. And the people were so kind; they liked us and we liked them too. Isfahan was a beautiful city.' She, like thousands of others, boarded in a children's home there. Little by little, the Poles picked up their lives, learnt Persian, first stumbling then fluent, but always accented, and married. Some opened pastry shops and brought the *piroshki* dumpling to Tehran, where it's still popular, though few Iranians know where it came from.

It was when we passed back through the iron door that I realised that not only was Bandar Anzali part of the remarkable passage of the Poles, but the Poles were a thread in the story of Anzali. There were all manner of other graves: Italian, Greek, Armenian, Assyrian, Georgian, all kept neat and tidy by Mr and Mrs Rezai, who were Muslims like practically everyone in Anzali nowadays. Anzali clearly was, or had been, home to really foreign foreigners.

This is not a feeling one often gets in Iran. Tehran may be a megalopolis, but it's one in which more or less everyone is drawn from similar roots, speaks the same language, and goes home to dinners familiar to almost every kitchen. Bandar Anzali was something quite different.

The salt wind off the harbour, thick with the smell of fish and diesel, was thick, too, with the outside world. Behind the fishermen sitting on crates loomed the hulls of foreign ships, marked in Cyrillic, which had put in from Azerbaijan. Russian wooden spoons and toy dancing bears from Baku fill the market stalls. Were one to sail north, one would reach Astrakhan; to the east lie the deserts of Turkmenistan. Anzali, like a little Naples or Karachi, was full of the promise of otherness.

Bandar Anzali comes into its own in the evening, when frying falafel adds its scent to the jetty and the bean stew vendors shout their wares; families stroll along the promenade with ice creams; local boys, their hair slicked back, show off on motorbikes on their way to see *Ricochet*, now playing at Anzali's dock cinema. Tough young sardine fishermen set out for a night's work to the cheers and catcalls of friends gathered on the bridge to watch the speedboats bounce over the waves and out to sea. One Polish couple stayed on in Anzali, long after the other foreigners had moved on. They saw the war end, the Russians leave, the British leave, the coming of another Shah, who left a palace here on the front. One can still look around the dusty debris inside, a couple of warheads in the hall, a huge stuffed crocodile.

In 1979, they saw revolution come to Bandar Anzali, and then they died. This was their landfall and the last land they knew, said Mrs Rezai, without sentimentality. Naturally, she couldn't read the names in foreign script on the hundreds of gravestones in her care, but she kept them well. And, like everyone else I met in Bandar Anzali, was more than kind to strangers.

15

General Dostum's Cavalry

Alan Johnston

As the years of Taliban rule drew to a close in Afghanistan, our correspondent met a general who was determined to play a major role in his country's future.
(3 November 2001)

Early one morning in the spring of 1997, I was standing on the Soviet-made airstrip outside Mazar-i-Sharif. Beyond the tarmac the flat steppe land of central Asia gave way to a line of mountains, a spur of the Hindu Kush range. Off to the left sat a dilapidated old military helicopter that looked badly in need of repair. I asked a militia officer where the helicopter was that was supposed to take me to the front line. Disturbingly, he just pointed at the machine that looked badly in need of repair.

Eventually, the pilot coaxed the clattering, shuddering contraption into the air and we were off, low over the steppe on our way to the battleground and an appointment with General Abdul Rashid Dostum. The general started his career on the Communist side of the war, as a security officer in a factory during the Soviet occupation of Afghanistan. But he quickly expanded his horizons. He transformed his security unit into a fighting force drawn from his own Uzbek ethnic group, which dominates this part of northern Afghanistan. Soon his men were being used by the Communist government as shock troops against the Mujaheddin guerrillas. They were sent to do their brutal business in areas where the hold of the regime was most tenuous. And when General Dostum eventually switched sides and allied himself with the guerrillas, it spelt the end for the Kabul government.

By the time that I'd climbed aboard that helicopter in 1997, the war had brought the army of the Taliban movement to the borders of General Dostum's northern stronghold. But that spring morning, the word was that his militia had made some advances on the long front line in the rolling hills of Badghis province.

The helicopter put us down close to the front. The place bustled with General Dostum's fighters, many in traditional Uzbek dress: tightly bound turbans and long padded coats for keeping out the icy winds of the steppe. Far away, across a plain, a column of armed horsemen was making its way down a hillside. They hit the flat ground and broke into a canter. This was Uzbek cavalry, perhaps a hundred strong, surging towards us, dust rising from the pounding hooves. And there at the centre of the line, on a white charger, rode General Dostum himself.

As the riders reached us they reined in hard. There was a great neighing of horses and stamping of hooves. We were engulfed in dust, and the gathered soldiers roared in salute of their commander-in-chief. The general dismounted and strode towards me, a huge man in a turban, his Uzbek jacket reaching down to his riding boots, and in his hand he carried a whip. He was orchestrating what amounted to a grandiose photo opportunity. His fighters had had some success, and he wanted to make sure that the BBC and the outside world knew about it. In his deep, booming voice he joked with his troops and gave a running commentary as he strode down a line of captured Taliban vehicles. The general glowered briefly at a forlorn group of six Taliban prisoners of war.

He lined up his senior officers and introduced them to me one by one. He'd been angered by some report in the media that his generals had been absent from the front. He wanted to make the point that they were, in fact, all there putting in a good day's work. Next a string of jeeps took us rocketing up a hillside. At the summit, arrangements had been made for a picnic like no other. There were carpets and cushions spread on the grass, and there was chicken and rice and fruit and nuts. The guns on the front line were silent, and as we ate and drank we gazed at the hills that turned blue in the distance as they rose and fell towards Iran. The general talked of politics and war, and at one stage he pointed with a chicken bone at a peak off to the left and said: 'See that mountain, the one with the snow on it? Well, I captured it three days ago.'

As it turned out, one of the commanders lounging on the cushions at that picnic betrayed General Dostum a few months later. It was the kind of act of grand treachery that is very much a part of Afghan warfare. General Dostum lost his front line in the hills of Badghis and soon the whole of his northern stronghold was gone. The general endured a brief exile in Turkey, but stormed back within months to retake his lands. In another stunning reversal he lost them once more to the Taliban the next year. And Mazar-i-Sharif could be about to fall yet again. General Dostum is back in the north, and he is determined to drive the Taliban from Mazar one last time. He has complained that he lacks heavy weaponry. He is reported to be using riders armed with Kalashnikovs, just like the cavalry that I saw four years ago before that picnic on the Badghis front.

So here we are, at the start of the twenty-first century and Mazar-i-Sharif is still locked in a scene that could be drawn from the darkest passages in central Asia's history. Armed horsemen laying siege to a city on the steppe; it is a drama in which Genghis Khan would have felt at home

16

Going Nuclear

Humphrey Hawksley

*As India and Pakistan edged towards war over the disputed region of Kashmir,
there were fears the two nations could become involved in a nuclear conflict.*
(3 January 2002)

It was a crisp, glorious spring day in Islamabad, with the cries of street traders
and the erratic blaring of horns reaching us from over the high garden fence.
We were kneeling on the drawing-room floor, cups of tea drunk and forgotten, and poring over maps of Pakistan and India. My host was a retired
civil servant; his career, he thought then, ended, and he was all too happy
to spend an afternoon brainstorming over a book I was writing about what
would lead to a nuclear war in Asia.

At first, with a map of Islamabad, we had plotted a coup, deciding
where to park the armoured vehicles, how to take the television and radio
stations and, trickiest of all, writing the speech of a new military leader,
one which would be accepted, at least in part, by Western democracies.
Then we moved on to the nuclear bomb. This was March 1999, less than
a year since India and Pakistan had carried out back-to-back nuclear tests
which have made their present confrontation so overridingly different and
dangerous.

'You see, what would happen in reality,' said my host, 'is that, although
we say the use of the bomb would be our last resort, it would in fact be our
first resort.'

'You mean you have plans ...' I began to ask.

He interrupted. 'We would have no choice. India would completely over-
power us in a conventional war. The only way to save our nation would be
by going nuclear.'

Perhaps he had said more than he meant to, because suddenly there was a strange tension, as if we had never been talking about a fictional scenario and we were both staring into the abyss of Pakistan's own future.

Back in London, I emailed the first draft of the manuscript to him and he meticulously corrected it and added details. Then, in October, he fell silent. The coup we had envisaged had happened. And my host had been called to high office in the new military government.

People tend to talk more when you tell them you're writing a book, when there are no deadlines, no cumbersome television cameras, and publication is only at an indeterminate date far in the future. I heard how India and Pakistan played games with each other by NOT answering the hotlines specially set up to deflate crises. How Pakistani pilots were trained in toss-bomb tactical nuclear attacks, which allowed the pilot to live while delivering a precision battlefield airburst; that, to dampen international condemnation, Pakistan's first nuclear strike would be against Indian armoured columns actually on Pakistani soil, and that China would guarantee whatever weapons Pakistan needed for its survival.

'China is the most reliable ally any nation could ask for,' a former army chief of staff told me, going on to describe the fascinating train journey he took from underneath Tiananmen Square, through tunnels housing columns of tanks and troops, to the massive nuclear command and control bunker west of Beijing. Pakistan was building one along the same lines.

Both China and Russia have high stakes in any Indian–Pakistan confrontation. Put simply, without Russian supplies India's military would collapse. Without Chinese, including missile technology, Pakistan's would collapse as well. Right now, both governments are getting guarantees from Moscow and Beijing that if war does break out, new tanks, aircraft and weapons will be quickly available. Just as US officials are offering carrots in trade and political deals for Russia and China to turn off their taps, which they are unlikely to do.

My research bounced back and forth between Pakistan and India, with flickering impressions. Pakistan was a nation obsessed with war. The fate of Kashmir was the fate of Pakistan. As its economy and democracy failed, so war with India had become its very lifeblood. For India, the prospect of war was one topic among many: rising property prices, the success of Bollywood, TV soap operas and political scandals. It had an impact similar to Northern Ireland on everyday life in Britain, or today's War against Terror. It was there, but it was not everything.

Yet India was no altar boy itself. My book hit such a nerve there that it became a bestseller. Throughout the first draft, India, a mature democracy, constantly tried to avoid conflict and backed off from a city-for-city nuclear exchange. Such was the successful Cold War principle of Mutually Assured Destruction. But I got a wake-up call. That doesn't apply on the subcontinent. My first draft ending was too pragmatic. And in Delhi, I was given an authoritative list of cities in Pakistan and China which India would destroy and those cities it was prepared to sacrifice in exchange. After publication, the India military still said I was being too doveish. The days ahead could be the closest the world has come to nuclear war. They could also be the best chance yet of making sure it never happens.

17
Mr Computer

William Reeve

Much of Afghanistan's cultural heritage had been lost in years of fighting; but the country's radio archive was preserved, thanks to the efforts of a man they call Mr Computer. (11 May 2002)

I was walking down a corridor at Afghanistan's Radio and Television Centre in Kabul with BBC colleagues also involved with the journalist-training programme. The walls looked as though they hadn't been painted for decades. Signs of decay were everywhere. A pane of glass in a swing door was still missing, no doubt years after a nearby explosion had smashed much else besides. We were being shown around the centre by one of the Afghan radio editors. He politely motioned for us to enter yet another drab room. I really didn't want to bother, thinking there was little more to see in the centre. But we were in for a big surprise, the beginning of a wonderful unfolding tale of guile and sheer devotion. We were introduced to Mohammad Siddiq, who's in charge of looking after Afghanistan's radio archive. With a broad smile, white beard and a brocaded skullcap, he was winding a pile of archive radio tapes forwards then back again on an ancient but sturdy reel-to-reel tape recorder.

'I've been doing this for thirty years,' he said. 'Even when all the bombs were landing in this area before the Taliban arrived, I still came every day.' He explained there were 50,000 radio tapes in the archive and that they all needed to be wound forwards and backwards once a year to prevent them from getting too brittle. His colleagues nodded in agreement, with expressions of awe. 'We call him Mr Computer,' said one. 'He's listened to the tapes so often he knows them all off by heart.'

I asked Mr Computer to show me his treasure trove. This is a country where just about everything else of value has been destroyed in more than two decades of conflict: the ancient stone Buddhas of Bamiyan last year by the Taliban, and Kabul Museum, one of the world's finest, by the warlords before them. In room after room there were endless shelves of radio tapes, all neatly catalogued on the spines of their boxes. One section was the historical archive, including speeches of former Afghan leaders: King Zahir Shah, who's just returned to Afghanistan, and his cousin President Mohammad Daoud, who deposed the monarchy in a coup in 1973, paving the way for the years of chaos that have followed. Another large section had Afghan drama, and there were even more tapes of Afghan music, played and sung by favourite stars of the past. Incongruously, there was one shelf of Mozart recordings.

'But, Mr Computer, how on earth did you save all these tapes from the Taliban?' I asked. The Taliban had banned as un-Islamic all music with instruments, and they had no love for former secular leaders. Mr Computer explained he'd removed all the markings from each box, covered the shelves with blankets, and firmly but very discreetly bolted all the doors. When the Taliban arrived in Kabul they had indeed destroyed what they thought was the archive; one unlocked room full of Iranian and Indian music. Thinking their job done, they never bothered again. After the Taliban fled Kabul in November last year, Mr Computer neatly stuck back all the markings on his 50,000 boxes, and got back to his work.

With me that day was Meena Bakhtash of the BBC World Service Persian Section. She began her career in Kabul and became a well-known Afghan television and radio presenter, but fled Afghanistan a decade ago. This was her first visit back to Kabul since then, and to the radio and television studios. For Meena it was an emotional trip back in time. 'Mr Computer, can you find any recordings of Meena?' I asked. In a flash he found a tape not far away, and lovingly spooled it on to the tape recorder. Before long we sat and listened to Meena's beautiful voice from a recording of seventeen years ago in a programme about classical literature.

Most of the transmitters and much other equipment of Afghan Radio and Television around the country have been destroyed. American bombs at the end of last year caused much of the damage. It's not just the hardware that needs to be rebuilt. Editors in Afghanistan are crying out for training of their journalists to put new life into the media, destroyed by Soviet ideology, followed by the anarchy of the warlords and the constrictions of the Taliban. We were at the Radio and Television Centre that day to discuss in detail what they really wanted, but Mr Computer somewhat stole the show.

It's clear the Afghan radio archive needs preserving. Indiana University in the United States saved Somalia's archive by recording it all on digital tape. It paid for the recordings of two copies, one for itself and one for Somalia. Hopefully another university will recognise the value of Afghanistan's archive. Mr Computer would be delighted. It would vindicate his life's work.

18

Black Wrist Dance

Jonathan Fryer

The most remote of the five former Soviet central Asian republics, Kyrgyzstan, was trying to distance itself from the region's reputation for instability and Islamic fundamentalism. The end of Communism was an economic as well as a cultural shock for a nation that now had to redefine its identity. (31 August 2002)

On Sunday mornings, long before dawn, there's an odd shuffling sound in the streets of Karakul, the provincial capital at the eastern end of Lake Issyk-Kul. There are no street-lamps, so only the moon illuminates the flocks of sheep being driven to market. These are not the cuddly white creatures of the north of England moors that I knew in my childhood but hulking great brown things with flabby backsides. In fact, the flabbier the backside the better. When they reach the market, in a walled enclosure on the outskirts of town, the animals aren't just subject to the stares of prospective buyers; they also have their hindquarters hoisted into the air every few minutes to check just how much fat they've got. The sheep seem completely unperturbed by this procedure, which has presumably been going on since they were lambs.

By the time the first rays of sun are hitting the snow-capped Tien Shan mountains that rear up behind the town, there's hardly room to move in the market. Crowds of sellers and buyers surround the sheep and goats and cattle and horses, ogling and haggling. This happens under the watchful eye of two soldiers, who squat on their haunches on top of the concrete perimeter fence. How they're able to sit there motionless for hours without falling off is only one of several mysteries to an outsider.

Many of the people in the market have walked for hours, some maybe for days, to get there. Most have wild, weather-beaten Mongoloid faces, fierce and canny. On horseback, the Kyrgyz men are particularly impressive. Families tend to opt for low, broad horse-drawn carts. Very few people have cars, those who do are mainly Russians. They occupy a corner of the market out of view of the Muslim Kyrgyz, their car boots full of squirming piglets for sale.

The weekly livestock market is the one moment of animation in Karakul's otherwise sleepy existence. The Soviet-era factories have all closed down, and motor vehicles are few and far between. Life has gone back to the style of a bygone era. Though by far the most important settlement in the area, Karakul gives the impression of an overgrown village. It was settled by the Russians over a century ago. And there are still neat rows of Slavic villas and cottages off the main street, their gardens a riot of giant hollyhocks.

During Stalin's time, Karakul was known as Przhevalsky, in honour of the great Russian explorer Nikolai Mikhailovich Przhevalsky, whose intrepid exploits thrilled his fellow soldiers and the tzar's court. While investigating Lake Issyk-Kul's shores, Przhevalsky foolishly drank from a stream and died of typhoid. He is buried just outside of town, in the grounds of a rather charming museum that commemorates his travels. After the collapse of the Soviet Union, and Kyrgyz independence, the town was given back its old, local name. Karakul, or 'Black Wrist'.

Not far from the Przhevalsky Museum, on the shores of the lake, there's a cluster of upmarket dachas and a sandy beach. Until a few months ago, this was a no-go area for foreigners, as it's a place where bigwigs come to play. But under Kyrgyzstan's new liberal policies, it's been opened up to the masses, which, on the day I went, meant about a dozen Kyrgyz families and me. There's no shade, no multicoloured umbrellas, no beach bars – just an old Russian babushka with a plastic shopping basket, selling delicious home-made pasties at the equivalent of a few pence a time.

Old Russian women like her pop up everywhere, hovering on the edge of markets selling whatever they've managed to grow in their gardens. They are the flotsam and jetsam of the old Soviet Union that were left behind when the Communist tide ebbed away. Their faces are lined and it's rare to see them smile. As their pensions are virtually worthless, it's not hard to understand why.

Feeling dehydrated after a spell on the beach, I found a discotheque in a nearby village. The doors were open, as a young engineer was fixing a new sound system, and the staff were more than happy to serve me with cold beer. But when a blast of music started, suddenly another old Russian woman, in a faded floral dress, headscarf, brown cardigan and rubber boots, came whirling in from the street. She danced crazily in the centre of the empty disco floor, before making a beeline for me. She thrust her face right into mine, flashing her one remaining tooth in anger.

'Stalin sent me here when I was twenty-four!' she screamed. 'Twenty-four!'

I couldn't make out what had happened to her then, but it didn't sound very pleasant.

She ranted on for several minutes. Then, her bile spent, she span back on to the dance floor, boogieing to the sound of Boy George, as I discreetly slunk out.

19
Cross-border Connections

Adam Mynott

After going to war three times in a half-century of hostility, India and Pakistan tried to make friends again. Transport links were to be restored, a decision which was widely welcomed. (17 May 2003)

In the stifling Indian summer heat, the paint from Vishnu's brush dries almost as soon it touches the roof of the Delhi Transport Corporation bus. Vishnu is splattered with white spots. He works with intense concentration as he shuffles barefoot across the roof of the bus, applying a thick layer of paint as he goes. Occasionally, he wipes off a smear with a rag clutched in his left hand. The bus is getting a thorough overhaul at Delhi Bus Station; an engineer is under the bonnet poking away at the engine with a spanner and a pair of pliers. No one will confirm it, but everyone knows that two buses, the air-conditioned pride of the fleet, are being prepared for a route which was closed suddenly nearly eighteen months ago: Delhi to Lahore in Pakistan. It went via Haryana to the north of Delhi, across into the Punjab to Amritsar and then on to the border crossing point and into Pakistan. The journey took twelve hours.

It's about five minutes' drive through Old Delhi from the bus terminal past the seventeenth-century Red Fort to the railway station. Hundreds of passengers heaving suitcases, with bundles wedged under their arms, are struggling towards the platforms. Some are clutching the hands of young children as they peer up at the train timetables. Men with wiry, muscular arms dressed in their uniform of dirty red shirts shout 'Porter, porter' loudly, clustering around as the travellers pull into the station car park. I make my way to the station master's office. He is not available, I am told, and there is no comment about renewed train services to Pakistan.

'That is a decision for the government,' a sub-station master tells me. 'And, anyway, there will be no direct service from Delhi. You will have to change at Amritsar and then at Attari station to catch the Samjhauta Express.' The Samjhauta Express summons up the image of a mighty engine thundering through the barren spaces of the subcontinent. But this express chugs just three kilometres between Attari and Wagah just over the border in Pakistan. The service started in 1976, but for the past eighteen months not one single item of rolling stock has moved though Attari. Inactivity has allowed virulent weeds to push their roots deep into the gravel on which the rails sit. The sun and wind have loosened large flakes of paint, which have fluttered down on to the platform from the boarded roof above. There is thick dust everywhere.

But now there is a buzz at Attari once more. Without any official instruction, railway staff are back, sweeping, checking electrical junction boards, greasing the points and painting white lines on the platform. It is almost as though preparations on the ground are racing to get ahead of the diplomacy. There's a feeling among many Indians and Pakistanis that while they remain deeply divided on a solution to the Kashmir issue, they've had enough of fifty years of squabbling. The diplomatic omens are good. In the highly charged atmosphere between Delhi and Islamabad, a phrase out of place or an ill-considered reaction can put the process of rapprochement back to square one. But, so far, it has been well and delicately handled.

It's all come too late, though, for Maqbool Ahmad. 'My life was ruined,' he says, 'by the attack on the parliament building in Delhi in 2001.' He lives at Qadian near the border, and in 2001 he had become engaged to Tahira who lives in Faisalabad in Pakistan. They knew the trans-national marriage would present difficulties, but this was a love match and, though he is Indian and she Pakistani, they are both Punjabis.

The closure of the border, the cancellation of the Samjhauta Express, put a sudden halt to contact between the two young lovers. 'It became impossible to telephone her,' he said, 'because they blocked phone calls between here and Pakistan as well.' As relations last summer between the two countries worsened and war looked more and more likely, Maqbool thought their relationship was doomed and he travelled to England to speak to members of Tahira's family. 'I went to tell them that I could not hold Tahira to her promise to marry me. I had to release her from that vow, to tell her family she is free to marry another person of her choice. I am a broken man,' he said.

I called Maqbool to check a couple of facts and I am very glad I did. I hardly recognised the voice of the downhearted young man I had spoken to a few days before. 'We are to marry after all,' he blurted out. 'When the border reopens, and I am sure that will be soon, we will see each other again. I thought I had lost Tahira, but she wants to marry me still.'

20
Taxi Driver

Kylie Morris

Months after the end of the war in Afghanistan, hundreds of men, from forty different countries, were still being held prisoner by the Americans at their base in Guantanamo Bay, Cuba. One was a Kabul taxi driver who set out for an ordinary day's work and ended up 9,000 miles away in Cuba. After finally being classified as being of low intelligence value, he was allowed to return home. (14 June 2003)

Some stories are easy to forget. On days when the news is moving fast, they flash by you in a flurry of questions, writing and filing. But others stay with you. They come back to you, they pester you, and they require you to do the right thing by them. Last October, the father of a young man who'd been taken by the American forces to Guantanamo Bay came to the BBC's bureau in Kabul. He said his son was innocent of any connection to the Taliban or al-Qaeda. In my time as a journalist, I've grown inured to protestations of innocence. Everyone didn't do it. No one is guilty. So I wasn't ready to believe this father. But after just a few days' investigation, I began to feel a churning sense of outrage. This young man really was innocent. And why was it that the Americans hadn't put aside a day or two to find that out? And why was there no legal process to ensure he'd get out?

Abassin was a taxi driver who'd picked up a passenger and then been stopped at a checkpoint. It turned out the passenger was the cousin of a warlord who wasn't on good terms with the soldiers who ran the checkpoint. Abassin was handed over, together with his passenger, to the authorities. A few months later, his dad started getting postcards from Cuba. What's worse is that Abassin's best friend, another taxi driver, who made inquiries about him, was also handed over, and also sent to Cuba. Abassin wasn't a fundamentalist, or a fighter; he was a joker. His mates at the chaotic taxi stand on the edge of Kabul had great tales: he'd been jailed by the Taliban for listening to Hindi music. He used to smuggle tapes of movies, banned by the Taliban, under the bonnet of his taxi.

We did the story. And stayed in touch with Roshan, Abassin's father. When we talked to three Guantanamo Bay detainees who made it back to Afghanistan in December, Roshan came and waited at the studio while I went to see if Abassin was one of them. He wasn't. His dad was fatalistic, but I noticed his hands shaking as he drank the tea I'd made him.

I was on duty in Iraq when I next heard of Abassin. I rang the newsroom in London to file a story, and a duty editor said: 'Hang on, there's a message for you. Kabul says your taxi driver has been released.' She said: 'Does that make any sense to you?' I couldn't stop smiling. Suddenly Iraq wasn't so bad, journalism wasn't as stupid as I'd been thinking and there was, after all, some justice in the world. When I got back to Kabul, Abassin came to the bureau. He looked thin, and was wearing new glasses, but smiling. He brought flowers, sweets and a camera; so we all took photos of each other in the back garden. It was like a reunion with someone you'd never met. Over the next few days, he told us things that I won't forget. Guantanamo Bay is a place we deliberately aren't allowed to know very much about. It was the details of what the cell was like, the bright lights that made it difficult to sleep, the sound of crying at night, the precious thirty minutes a week he was allowed out into the sunshine, the orange overalls. The fear.

We went through the censored postcards that he'd sent his father. Sentences where words had been crossed out. He remembered the sentences in full, and explained what had been cut. On one card, he'd written 'America has no justice,' and the censor had blocked out the word 'No'. It's ironic that Abassin, who was never religious, learnt to read the Koran in Guantanamo Bay from the guy in the next cell. The Koran was the only book he was allowed.

We took him back to his taxi stand and stood back while he was hugged by dozens of his friends, so pleased to have him back. A few of them joked: 'I recognise you, aren't you al-Qaeda?' During our days together in Kabul, Abassin's mood changed; he was sombre one minute, laughing the next. We couldn't do much at once, he got too tired. His friends told us he suddenly seemed older, and far less likely to come up with a funny line. He was distracted; he seemed so affected by his best friend Wazir remaining in Guantanamo Bay that he was unable to savour his freedom.

In Afghanistan, most twenty-one-year-olds have seen a lot of horror. Aside from the poverty and the invasions, they've had wars, religious strictures and inter-clan violence. So it's not unusual to be bruised, angry and resentful. But the amazing privilege of meeting this taxi driver, this ordinary man, was that despite the injustice he's faced, he bears no grudges. He says he just wants to get on with things. I hope now he can.

21
Out for a Chinese

Fuchsia Dunlop

British people may consider eating out in a Chinese restaurant fairly predictable. Almost all of the restaurants offer Cantonese cooking and a standard repertoire of dishes. But going out to eat in China itself is never boring. (5 July 2003)

Dining out is something of a national obsession in this Most Flavoured Nation, and the restaurant scene is staggeringly diverse. Two decades of economic reform have set the catering industry alight after years of stagnation in the Maoist era. Talented chefs have fled the old state-owned restaurants to find more rewarding, and more lucrative, work in the private sector. And you never know what's going to be on the menu.

In the Sichuanese capital, Chengdu, restaurateurs work in an atmosphere of frenzied competition. New food trends explode and spread like wildfire, and acclaimed new dishes are quickly plagiarised across the city. The pressure to be creative is intense: a chef in one fashionable restaurant confided wearily that he had to spice up his menu with at least ten new dishes every month in order to stay ahead of his rivals.

Successful restaurants exist on a scale which would be unthinkable in the West. One cheap and cheerful eaterie in the western part of the city has 700 seats. Another popular establishment has an upper floor which resembles a village, complete with streams of running water spanned by little bridges and a host of private dining rooms styled like traditional cottages. Downstairs, a vast open dining room has space for more than 400 guests. Yes, you can forget the idea of a quiet candlelit dinner; the Chinese like their restaurants to be as warm and noisy as a marketplace.

In the past, China's surly service culture was a legend among international travellers. But the dingy old state-run restaurants, with their indifferent food and grumpy waitresses, are a dying breed. Some have closed down, others are being sold off to shareholders who, it is hoped, will kick them back into life. And the level of luxury and service offered by the smart private restaurants is extraordinary. Dining out, of course, is an essential part of doing business in China. Extravagant delicacies such as shark's fin and abalone are traditionally used to impress associates and butter up influential officials. And many Chinese people would rather entertain lavishly in a restaurant than struggle in the kitchen at home.

In the cities, restaurants serving China's new rich vie to outdo one another in the novelty and complexity of their cooking, and the rarity of their ingredients. At one recent banquet I attended we were served with a whole fleet of small boats made from cucumbers, their dark skin carved into an intricate pattern, their hollowed flesh bearing dainty cargoes of stir-fried fish and pine kernels. And there was also braised yak's foot, and a delicious stir-fry made from just the fleshy parts of chicken's feet.

Some restaurants devote themselves to the cult of the exotic, like the one I visited, whose owner had a freezer stuffed full of all kinds of insects which he serves up to jaded city officials on a country jaunt. 'This one is really good if you mash it up into a kind of puree,' he told me, squeezing a fat white grub between his fingers. 'But I tend to use the grasshoppers whole.'

In fact, there are restaurants to cater for every taste or predilection. Some specialise in regional cuisines, others in a particular ingredient cooked in myriad ways, or a single dish such as Sichuan hotpot. Some aim to re-create the flavours and the ambience of the great official houses of the past, when wealthy men kept private cooks and entertained extravagantly at home. And then there are the medicinal restaurants for people who want to pig out in a restorative kind of way. The menus change with the seasons and offer delicious concoctions designed to treat all manner of physical conditions. There's nothing medicinal about the atmosphere, however, and when I visited one not long ago I ate so many dishes designed to bring harmony to my body that I thought I would simply explode.

And if all the luxury of the finest restaurants feels like too much, you can always drive out of town to a place which affects the simple rusticity of the Sichuan countryside. There you can play mah-jong and nibble sunflower seeds in a bamboo shed, while you are plied with vast platters of spicy rabbit and other hearty peasant fare. And if the mood takes you, you can sometimes even pick your own vegetables or catch a fish for dinner in the pond.

So as I peer through the glass of a British Chinese restaurant, scanning the menu in the hope of finding more unusual dishes among the familiar sweet and sours, I sigh for China. And I wonder how it is that, after all these years of Chinese catering abroad, so little seems to have filtered through of this most thrilling of culinary cultures.

22

Awaiting Revolution

Damian Grammaticas

*Parliamentary elections had been marred by fraud, protestors were out on
the streets and the talk in the Georgian capital, Tbilisi, was of revolution.*
(22 November 2003)

A week ago, 20,000 Georgians were clamouring at the gates of Tbilisi's presidential office. The country was teetering on the edge of revolution. A day later, by the time I'd jumped on the plane from Moscow and arrived, they'd all gone home. I should have known; Georgia is the laid back sort of place where everything stops for the weekend, even revolution.

At the airport the immigration officer who took my visa application and the fee of eighty dollars smiled. 'How about I keep ten dollars for myself,' he grinned, and then pocketed twenty. Georgia's economy has collapsed and it's the sort of place where everyone has to survive how they can. At customs you pass a sign that says: 'Your duty-free allowance is a bottle of wine, ten packets of cigarettes and two car tyres.' Why on earth two car tyres? Well, Georgia is the sort of place where the only thing that functions is the black market, and smuggling is rife.

Georgia's political crisis began three weeks ago, when the country's parliamentary elections were marred by massive vote rigging and thousands of furious opposition supporters took to the streets. Georgia's old warhorse of a president, Eduard Shevardnadze, who has a haunted look about him at the best of times, has been under enormous pressure to rescind the election results or resign.

As the opposition gathered its forces for a new assault, I wandered through Tbilisi's old town, looking for the reasons why Georgians are in revolutionary mood. It didn't take long to find them. Tbilisi has a beautiful setting, along a river beneath high hills on top of which sit the ramparts of an ancient castle. Clinging to the slopes are Georgian Orthodox churches with conical roofs. But the cobbled streets are literally disintegrating. Stunning old homes, almost Parisian-looking villas, are crumbling away; wooden balconies and shutters are rotting and crumbling. In one courtyard I climbed a rickety wooden staircase. I found Lamara Tetruashvili in her kitchen, a small woman with a kindly face, wrapped up in layers of clothes to keep warm.

She showed me her pension book. The government gives her the equivalent of just three pounds a month. But the entries for August, September and October showed she had received nothing. Often the state simply can't pay. 'Look what I have to eat,' Lamara said, holding out two rotten apples and some stale, rubbery breadcrusts. 'Dogs wouldn't eat this.' A black and white portrait hung on the wall. It was her husband, a pianist, who is now dead. He was a handsome man with fine features and a pencil-thin moustache. Lamara has had to sell his piano. Down the wall snaked huge cracks. 'There was an earthquake last year, but no one came to fix the wall,' Lamara explained. 'I'm afraid it will go soon.' Walking across her floor, which sloped at an alarming angle, made me feel seasick.

Then her neighbour appeared. 'Come and see my toilet,' gestured the middle-aged woman. What could I say? To decline an offer like that would have been rude. I found a porcelain lavatory perched precariously, almost ready to collapse into the courtyard four floors below. 'It's a bit of a worry,' the woman said with a smile. I saw blocks of flats where you have to pay every time you use the lift. Electricity is in such short supply you put a coin in the meter before pressing the button for your floor. And the taxi driver I used was a doctor, a specialist in ear and throat infections. You can't make a living in medicine, he said.

Behind Georgia's deep discontent lie stories like these. The fabric of a country falling apart. As a Soviet republic Georgia was rich. But without Soviet raw materials and Soviet markets Georgia's factories and farms have shut. Deep-seated corruption has made things worse. The blatant rigging of this month's parliamentary elections was the final straw. So President Eduard Shevardnadze, a hero in the West for his role in bringing the Cold War to a peaceful end when he was the Soviet foreign minister, has little support left at home. He's now a lonely, unpopular figure. The middle classes, too, like Temuri Chilachava have lost patience. With his beard and chequerboard jumper, he could be a university professor anywhere. Over the past fortnight he's been missing lectures to attend rallies demanding Mr Shevardnadze resign, and he's been trying to turn his students into political activists. 'I want a change for my children's sake,' he says.

His wife and daughter sit on the sofa, chuckling at one of Georgia's most popular television programmes. It's an animated cartoon that pokes fun at a bumbling white-haired figure, recognisable as Mr Shevardnadze. He blunders from crisis to crisis. When I met the cartoon's maker, Georgi Chanturia, an energetic man in his thirties, he told me: 'Shevardnadze has been around for as long as I can remember. It's time for him to go.' As I write this, Georgians from around the country seem to share that view. They're heading to Tbilisi to join the anti-Shevardnadze protests. Squads of riot police stand ready at key points around the city. Most of the police are middle-aged, with battered old riot shields. They shift nervously from foot to foot and look ready to run away at the first sign of any trouble. But then again, this is Georgia, and it's the weekend. So the revolution might have to wait until Monday.

23

Murder at the Palace

Daniel Lak

Daniel was the BBC's man in Kathmandu during some of the most devastating events in recent Nepali history. (21 February 2004)

Nepal was a bit of a mystery to me when I came to Kathmandu as a BBC correspondent in August of 2000. For nearly a decade before that, I'd been covering south Asia's two tumultuous giants, India and Pakistan. In that time, there'd been wars, countless elections, natural disasters, nuclear weapons tests and cricket, plenty of cricket. I had barely a moment to stop and appreciate either country. By contrast, Nepal seemed just the place. It was democratic yet had a centuries-old monarchy. It was multi-ethnic but everyone seemed to get along pretty well; its people were poor yet proud of their unique culture. A nice, quiet place to do thoughtful, reflective journalism, and to explore the Himalayas.

Or so it seemed from a distance. Close up, from my hilltop home in Kathmandu, the view was somewhat different. One of the first indications of that was a bruising encounter with Nepali national pride. The BBC had asked me to provide a few topics for a radio and internet debate on Nepal's future, so I prepared a selection of questions about how Nepal should deal with India. Someone, somewhere in the power structure in Kathmandu, seemed to think I was suggesting the larger country swallow the smaller one. Before I knew it, I was pilloried in the press as an Indian spy and even burnt in effigy outside parliament by a mob; a very polite mob, mind you, but a mob none the less. Nepal, I soon found out, takes the India question very seriously, and very sensitively.

Then there are the Maoist rebels. Long after Beijing renounced everything about Chairman Mao but his brand name, a group of Nepalese peasants and intellectuals are fighting to turn their country into something from the pages of the Chairman's 'little red book', an agrarian people's republic. And, the rebels say, they won't stop with Nepal. Maoism, a smiling, articulate young man told me in a distant village a week's walk from the capital, would spread outward, taking in India, China, and even, yes ... America. When I asked him about the millions of deaths in the Cultural Revolution, the Khmer Rouge atrocities in Cambodia and the Shining Path of Peru, he fixed me with a keen stare and announced to general applause from his armed colleagues that mistakes do happen and those made elsewhere would not be repeated in Nepal.

As I leave, the latest statistics for eight years of war between the rebels and the security forces are tragic and frightening. Nearly 9,000 dead, a democratic political system in ruins, tens of thousands of internally displaced or exiled people, an economy dependent on tourism and foreign aid unravelling, and a brutal pattern of human rights abuses by both sides. It's hard to find anyone outside of the cloistered Kathmandu valley who hasn't been touched by violence. No sign of a people's paradise anywhere.

By far the most powerful memory I take with me is of a night in early June 2001. A ringing phone well after midnight brought news of a stunning and incredible series of killings at the Royal Palace, including that of the beloved King Birendra, his wife the Queen and seven others. And the murderer? None other than the heir to the throne, Crown Prince Dipendra, who later killed himself. I remember putting down the phone and going up on to the roof of my house to find out if Kathmandu sounded different now that its royal family had been massacred. It didn't. Not right away. At dawn the next day, an eerie silence descended over normally busy streets. Nepalis with access to the BBC and Indian television news stood in groups quietly discussing what they'd been hearing. Their own media told them nothing, but it suspended all programming and was playing solemn funeral music. A sense of disbelief grew; call it denial, the first reaction to severe trauma. Then, as now, few could accept what I knew to be the case, that Prince Dipendra carried out the killings in a fit of rage. The deaths led at the time to anger, riots and attacks on the funeral procession. Eventually, say many here, it also led to serious doubts about the future of the monarchy in Nepal. And those haven't disappeared with time.

King Gyanendra came to the throne under the most tragic of circumstances. Within a year and a half, he'd responded to Nepal's perpetual political confusion by dismissing an elected government and assuming power himself. The people might have accepted that had it proved an effective way of dealing with the country's problems. But the feeling is that things have actually got worse; the war, the economy, national morale. There are now almost daily demonstrations calling for a republic, something unthinkable just a few years ago, whatever the utopian dreams of the Maoists may be.

Nepal has had a rough ride during my time in Kathmandu. Friends joke that I helped provoke that, as a journalist in need of stories. They forget what I told them when I arrived nearly four years earlier, that I wanted a quiet time in the most splendid country in Asia.

24
Books For All

Joanna Robertson

The world of books may be changing radically, with the marketplace now dominated by large chain stores, but in India there's a tiny establishment called Strand Book Stall which has been open for sixty years and where bookshop life goes on much as it has always done. (24 July 2004)

In the broiling blare of Sir PM Road, hidden behind an odorous cab stand, squeezed into the shade of a scarlet-flowering gulmohar tree, and sandwiched between a brand-new mobile phone service and a crumbling paper wholesaler's, is a small shop. Step over the flea-plagued pregnant bitch slumbering across the dusty doorstep and push open the narrow door. Inside, books! From floor to ceiling, a room bursting with books. Pick your way through the teetering ziggurats of overflowing paperbacks and climb the steep little staircase to a second bulging room above, the whole woven together by the perpetual upstairs-downstairs jangling ring of several antiquated telephones.

'Yes, hello. Strand Book Stall. *In Defence of Globalisation*? Yes, yes, we have it,' a voice says. Strand Book Stall. The most wonderful little bookshop in the city of Bombay, also known these days as Mumbai. To many, quite simply, the most wonderful little bookshop in the whole of India. I stumbled upon it, literally. Tripping over the step, treading on the dog (she yelped), almost falling through the door.

I was feeling rather peculiar from the midday sun. The crowded shelves of jumbled-up fiction, philosophy, history and self-help swam before my dust-sore eyes. Oh, for a lace handkerchief and a bottle of sal volatile! I felt on the brink of a Victorian swoon. Instead, a very kind man appeared, pulled up a chair, popped me into it, placed an ice-cold bottle of Coca-Cola in my trembling hand and opened a volume of Oscar Wilde upon my knee.

Before I knew it I was slurping happily to the sobering rhythm of *The Ballad of Reading Gaol*.

The very kind man turned out to be Mr Shavi, thirty-eight years' service, now shop manager. His favourite book is *The Count of Monte Cristo* by Alexandre Dumas. 'There's a lot of what you find in life between those pages,' Mr Shavi confidentially observed. 'But you should talk to Mr Shanbhag, he'd know more about it than me.'

Mr Narayan Shanbhag, now eighty years old, is the founder and owner of the Strand Book Stall. Over a glass of cognac with a little fresh orange juice, his preferred lunchtime drink during the monsoon, Mr Shanbhag is remembering.

'It was 1942. I had saved seven rupees, a great sum of money to me, and I took my rupees to a shop that claimed to be the largest bookshop east of Suez. But they wrinkled their noses and turned me away. I looked far too poor to be interested in books. I must be a thief! I vowed then and there to become a bookseller and to sell only books at a price Indians could afford.'

Narayan Shanbhag did just that. He established a humble, sweaty stall in a cinema foyer, the cheapest space available in an overcrowded city, at the edge of Bombay's clamorous harbour. His first sale was Volume One of Winston Churchill's *War Memoirs* at a twenty per cent discount to a businessman. He has since sold thousands of copies of that book. Indeed, Mr Shanbhag has become a millionaire, making his fortune and nurturing generations of new readers by selling good books at very low prices. 'A big turnover on very slim profits,' he says.

'My bookshop is a university,' Mr Shanbhag declares, raising his cognac and orange to his lips. 'Its customers over the years read like a *Who's Who* of India.' He is not exaggerating. The current president of India was a regular customer for more than twenty-five years. Even when it was just a stall, the Strand Book Stall was frequented by politicians, intellectuals, scientists, writers, police commissioners, businessmen and plenty of 'ordinary people'. One early customer was the first prime minister of India, Jawaharlal Nehru.

'I'll never forget the day Nehru first came, because he stopped in the street outside to first smoke a cheap Indian cigarette. Then he crushed the glowing butt under his foot, and walked right in.'

On his twice-yearly trips to London to buy books, Narayan Shanbhag became friends with many of the literary and publishing figures of the fifties, sixties and seventies such as W. H. Auden, Stephen Spender, Bertrand Russell, Allen Lane and Aldous Huxley. In India, he became close to the writer Nirad Chaudhuri, with whom he shared a common world and a common interest. 'Chaudhuri used to describe it as "the struggle of civilisation with a hostile environment",' Mr Shanbhag remembers, 'and he had a point!'

'Books are for everyone,' he explains. 'Knowledge has legs. It was made to walk. My ideal customer is a typist or clerk whose thirst for knowledge is as great as mine, but who cannot possibly afford 2,000 rupees for a book.'

Back outside the shop, across the filthy potholed street rancid with monsoon rains, stands a modern bank. An employee there recalls that when he was a student he was too poor to afford books, so Mr Shanbhag would lend him volumes from the shop, provided he kept them very clean. With that help, he passed his exams and joined the bank as a clerk, a clerk with a thirst for knowledge and a small monthly salary. He is now the bank manager and each day, in his lunch hour, he still crosses the street to the Strand Book Stall.

25

Economic Explosion

Rupert Wingfield-Hayes

The explosion of the Chinese economy was causing concern in countries around the globe. Already it was the world's third biggest. With annual growth of ten per cent, it was expected to overtake that of Japan. Other countries fear they'll no longer be able to compete; they won't be able to manufacture goods as cheaply as they do in China. It's a revolution based on a limitless supply of manpower.

(31 July 2004)

In Beijing this summer the latest fashion statement is a Hummer H2. For the uninitiated, a Hummer is an enormous gas-guzzling American 4X4. It's about the size of a small house. Just the thing for running around a congested city of fourteen million people! 'That has to be the stupidest car on the planet!' I commented to a Chinese friend on seeing yet another one blocking up a Beijing street. 'I can't understand why anyone would want to buy one of those things.'

She laughed at me. 'I thought you understood Chinese people,' she said. 'They love cars like that. If you're rich in China, you want to show it off.' And in Beijing there are plenty of new rich who like to show it off. I'm not talking about rich compared to other Chinese. I'm talking rich compared to anywhere. You can see it in the neighbourhood where I live on the outskirts of Beijing. Two years ago it was surrounded by cornfields. Now it's surrounded by huge new building sites for luxury housing complexes. Places with names like Grand Hills, Riviera or, my personal favourite, Yosemite Park.

Here China's new rich can buy a fully packaged American lifestyle, five bedrooms, a real log fire and, of course, an extra-large garage for the 4x4. All yours for a bargain sum of a million dollars, and there is no shortage of takers. So where's all the money coming from? Well, much of it is far from clean. In my new area there are no doubt a fair number of corrupt officials, police officers and even the odd gangster. But an increasing number are from a class that ten years ago hardly existed in China: private entrepreneurs. To see them in action you have to leave Beijing behind and head south, 1,500 miles south to the little city of Wenzhou on the coast of Zhejiang.

Wenzhou is crowded in between a wall of mountains and the wide expanse of the East China Sea. Its physical isolation has forced its people to look outwards across the sea. It's a city of traders and, interestingly, of churches. Christianity and capitalism have both found fertile souls among the people of Wenzhou. But as you drive from the airport into the city it's not the churches you notice, it's the factories. I'd been picked up by the driver of one of those factory owners. Snug inside the boss's V12 Mercedes-Benz, we sliced through the traffic at alarming speed, the driver's hand constantly on the horn. We sped past factory after factory, their oversized gates proudly displaying names like Golden Dragon Footwear or Bright China Leather. One even had a huge billboard showing Pierce Brosnan, better known as 007, purportedly wearing one of their suits. Here capitalism is raw and unregulated. The air is acrid. The rivers run black. It's not pretty, but it is thriving.

Finally the large black car slipped through the gates of the East Wind cigarette lighter factory. On its steps stood a short man with a crew cut. He was the spitting image of China's late Communist party chief Deng Xiaoping, the man who coined the phrase 'to get rich is glorious.'

Mr Feng has taken the words of his more famous doppelganger to heart. Starting with a small loan fifteen years ago, he now produces 100 million cigarette lighters a year. If you have a cigarette lighter in your pocket or your handbag, the chances are it comes from Wenzhou, and there's a fair chance it comes from Mr Feng's factory. His formula for success is simple: learn how to make something, then make it cheaper than anyone else.

The first part was easy: he bought samples of the best lighters from Japan, took them apart and copied them. But it's cheap that Mr Feng really excels at. He took a sleek red lighter from his pocket and gave it to me. 'In Japan this costs about twenty-five dollars,' he told me. 'I can make it for one dollar!'

Mr Feng's secret is his work force. In a large hangar I found 600 of them sitting behind rows of desks, assembling lighters. Most were young women. 'They're better at the fiddly work,' Mr Feng told me. But men or women, they all have one thing in common: they are all migrants from China's countryside. And they'll all work for virtually nothing. Mr Feng pays his workers

about ninety dollars a month. China today is like eighteenth-century Manchester, only much, much bigger.

There are now thousands of Mr Fengs all over southern China, setting up
factories and churning out goods. And there are 900 million poor farmers in
China's countryside, all just waiting to up sticks and move to a factory. The
implications for the rest of the world are troubling. 'Just think of it this way,'
one Chinese economist told me recently. 'If all the industrial jobs in Europe
and America moved to China tomorrow, we could fill them all and still have
plenty of people left over!'

26
Moving On

Jim Muir

*Our correspondent moved on after five years in Iran. The country was shifting
into another period of political change and uncertainty. General elections had
unseated the reformists and brought conservatives back to control parliament.*
(17 August 2004)

When I actually moved to Tehran towards the end of 1999, I hadn't got much
beyond the stereotyped images of grim mullahs and fanatical Hezbollah
members screaming 'death to America'. I didn't really know what to expect
and what I'd be able to do. But I was always mentally prepared for two
contingencies: I thought that sooner or later, for one reason or another, we
would have some sort of crisis with the authorities that might end in my
expulsion, or worse. And I also thought that sooner or later we would have
a major earthquake. Iran is riddled with fault lines; a big one was overdue.

Well, at least I was right about the earthquake, though things didn't
happen quite as I'd imagined. I was actually out of the country for a break
last Christmas when the ancient mud-brick city of Bam, in the far south-
east of Iran, was devastated in the early hours of Boxing Day morning. But
I managed to get there very quickly and flew into Bam just as my driver,
Nada, arrived in the Nissan Patrol with our equipment after a long drive
down from Tehran. My team and I were on our own for the first thirty-
six hours and the Patrol became our home and office, before becoming the
centre of a little BBC tented township as reinforcements poured in from all
points of the compass to help document the double tragedy of 30,000 deaths
and the destruction of a unique piece of Iran's heritage.

But I was wrong about having a crisis and getting thrown out. I don't
think we pulled any punches in our coverage of Iranian politics, though
some angry exiles, who believe the clerical regime just needs a good kick to

bring it down, would undoubtedly disagree. And we did features, which often made me wonder how close to the wind we were sailing, on such issues as the serial murder of dissident intellectuals, which turned out to be the work of intelligence ministry officials, and the growing and related problems of drug addiction, runaway girls, crime and prostitution in Iranian society.

All this and a lot more passed without repercussion. The only time I was aware of being in trouble was over a story in which I'd ventured to suggest there might be some links between Iran and the extremist Islamic group Ansar al-Islam, who were ensconced right on the Iranian border, just inside the Kurdish area of northern Iraq. This clearly annoyed the revolutionary guards who were in charge of the border. But instead of having me kicked out, they invited me for a discussion over tea and fruit at a villa in north Tehran, and then forgave me.

But Iran is a hard place in which to work; the bureaucracy of a divided authority often makes you feel you're trying to run through mud up to the waist. The technology rarely seems to work for long. And if everything else is fine, there's always the monster traffic jams to hold you back. But all that was outweighed by the friendship and warmth I met from the people who are as varied and interesting as the large and diverse country they've inherited. No one exemplified those qualities more than my guide and companion from the outset, my Iranian cameraman Kaveh Golestan. Kaveh was a prize-winning photographer before he turned to filming, and his tireless energy and enthusiasm, his ever-excited love for his own country and his passion for images illuminate his work for television. He was my constant sidekick on many trips and adventures round the country and beyond.

In the spring of last year we were in northern Iraq together as Saddam's regime was being blasted to bits by the Coalition. By a fateful combination of circumstances we ended up parking in a minefield. As we were getting out of the car, my producer from London, Stuart Hughes, put his foot down on to a mine, which exploded. We all thought we were being bombarded, even Stuart himself, who'd lost the bottom of his foot and later had to have his lower leg amputated. I threw myself to the ground. Kaveh sprinted off down the hill, stepped on another mine and fell on another. He died instantly. Lives were changed and one ended in much less time than it takes to speak these lines. My journey back to Tehran with Kaveh's remains was the saddest of my life. The tragedy and trauma of his death were softened only by the kindness and love his family – his mother, his sister, his wife, his son – showed me.

Through all the parties and farewells that have marked my departure from Tehran, there has been the sadness of leaving a country I came to love and where I made many good friends. And behind that there has been a greater sadness. When Iranians miss someone, they say 'Your place is empty.' Kaveh, your place is very, very empty.

27
Parallel Universe

James Robbins

A visit to Pyongyang, accompanying a Foreign Office minister, took place amid reports that a major explosion had taken place somewhere in North Korea.
(18 September 2004)

I did not want to stare, but I did want to know if anybody was actually buying anything. We were in Department Store Number One, Pyongyang. There was a lot of activity at the counter; bottles were being pushed across it, a woman had her handbag open, as if to pay. But the drama being played out for us visitors seemed frozen, or at least the action never quite reached its climax, as far as I could tell. No money appeared from the woman's hand, hovering over her bag. The man next to her fiddled with the bottles, rearranged them on the counter, but never actually packed them, or picked them up.

I was aware they were looking at me looking at them. Their smiles, too, were fixed, almost desperate, willing me to look away, to lose interest. I am fairly sure there was no sale, that the shop did not have to give up any of its precious stock. If the goods here were props in an elaborate piece of political theatre, to persuade us that stories of critical shortage in North Korea were not true, then we were proving to be far too attentive an audience. This was the cue for one of our minders to distract me and move me on with a polite and gentle push.

Sale or no sale, and I really cannot be quite sure, a diplomat who was with us told me several interesting things: first, there really was more on the shelves than there had been a year ago; more basic plastic bowls and a few more tins of fish under the glass counters. Second, the lights were on for us, in particular for Britain's Foreign Office minister, Bill Rammell. Normally, I was told, this shop, a rarity in itself, would be in semi-darkness. There is simply so little power in North Korea, it is very strictly rationed.

The day before it was a goat farm with no goats. The only billy to be seen was painted above the doorway as we went into a farm building. The goats, we were told, had been taken indoors elsewhere on the farm, to keep them out of the torrential rain. There was no doubting the rain. Excellent deep drainage channels, lined with large stones, were racing with muddy water a metre deep, water cascading down the slopes of the farm.

But apart from the weather, it was always hard to take anything else at face value. I had stumbled into a parallel universe. It had taken twelve hours of flying to get to North Korea from London, and yet I felt I had got no further than East Germany in the 1970s. Everywhere, the unrelenting grey-black of poured concrete, four- and five-storey blocks of flats. The blocks were chipped, battered and peeling. They were shapeless buildings that looked more like prison blocks than family homes. Running between them, rusting trams and trolley-buses, but no cars, not even vans. Wide city roads which must once have been crowded were all but empty. Every so often, a great cut-out hammer and sickle was attached to a wall, or a slogan praising the forward march of revolution.

The whole country, or all that we were able to see, at any rate, looked as if it had broken down, with no prospect of repair. You could see when the glory days had ended, when the Berlin Wall came down and the Soviet Union collapsed. No more guaranteed markets then for North Korea's shoddy goods, and no more big investment from sympathetic Communist neighbours either.

It is extraordinary that this utterly rigid regime has survived so long, until you consider the total repression that stifles all opposition. Reports of huge labour camps dotted across the country for political prisoners filter out from defectors. When Britain's minister challenged his North Korean counterparts, they laughed off terrible torture allegations, but they did concede that forced labour is an integral part of what they call 'rehabilitation'. Extracting that much was a bit of a breakthrough, but North Korea has a not-so-secret weapon to deter any outsider even toying with the idea of regime change.

So, to complete our surreal few days, a nuclear scare. We may never know what caused a huge cloud over mountains in the far north. Neighbouring countries are so paranoid, understandably, that it was soon labelled a mushroom cloud. Nothing in North Korea is as it seems. I had gone there expecting to come out much better informed. Reporters like to believe that. I may know a little more now, having been there, but then again …

28

Memories of the Caucasus

Chloe Arnold

*Chloe spent five years based in the Caucasus; chronicling the revolution in
Georgia, monitoring the continuing tensions between Armenia and Azerbaijan
and seeing how the oil boom has transformed life in Baku, the Azeri capital on the
Caspian Sea, where she's been living. (23 September 2004)*

It's the little things I'll miss the most; the delicious taste of tomatoes from the
Green Bazaar in Baku, the thick wedges of crumbly white cheese you get in
roadside cafés, accompanied by clumps of fresh coriander, the silky texture of
beluga caviar eaten straight from the jar, the woman who sells lemons from
a battered straw basket at the end of our street. Her forehead is etched with
creases; she saw her husband and both her sons killed during the war with
neighbouring Armenia. But she smiles whenever she sees me and always
slips an extra lemon into the bag. 'May Allah protect you,' she says.

The cool breeze off the Caspian Sea on warm summer evenings and the
music from the rickety Ferris wheel on the seafront, the young couples strolling
along the promenade or stealing a quick kiss at the end of the rusty pier.
And Baku's Old City, its crenellated walls straight out of a fairy story, the
Shirvanshah's Palace with its dungeons and portcullises and the lopsided
fig tree that grows beside an ancient stone well.

Of course, there are things I'll be glad to see the back of. The irritating
trill of mobile phones on every street corner. And the blast of car horns.
The other day I was stuck behind a man in a black BMW whose hooter
played the theme tune from the *Godfather*. He was wearing dark glasses and
shouting into two mobiles at once. Talk about a cliché. I won't miss the *gaish-
niki* either, the notorious traffic police. Nearly all the ones I've come across
are on the make, and the excuses they use to rob you of a twenty-dollar bill
get more and more ridiculous. Last time I was flagged down, I asked the fat

official spitting sunflower seed husks all over my bonnet why he was fining me. 'Because you can't stop here,' he said.

In the last three years, I've travelled all over the south Caucasus, the tiny knot of countries squeezed between Russia and Iran, Turkey and the Caspian Sea. The area may consist of only three countries, but it's a melting pot of religions, cultures and peoples, each fiercely independent and many fighting to secure a homeland not much bigger than an English county.

In Armenia, the visit by the Pope was one I'll never forget: the crowds of people lining the streets of Yerevan to catch a glimpse of him and the candlelit mass inside the Cathedral of St Gregory the Illuminator, when one of the congregation stole my mobile phone.

In Azerbaijan, there was the interview I did with Qyzyl Quliyeva, who, at 131, would have been the oldest woman in the world. Except she didn't have the documents to prove it; they didn't give out birth certificates in the tiny town of Lerik in the 1870s. She reminisced about the time of the tsar and how, later, her father, a farmer, had killed all his sheep rather than hand them over to the collective farm after Lenin came to power. I spoke to her in a little wooden house besides acres of orchards, the trees heavy with apples, pomegranates and persimmon. There was no staircase. Qyzyl pointed to a wobbly ladder before scrambling up it and into the attic, where she sat cross-legged on the floor, her skirt covered in red and yellow poppies billowing around her.

'We'll have tea,' she told her great-great-great-grandson in Talysh, the local language. 'And make it quick. I've got the chickens to feed.'

Then there was the trip to see the Mountain Jews, descended from one of the ten Lost Tribes of Israel. Azerbaijan is a Muslim nation, but this tiny Jewish community has survived countless wars and still lives in a pocket of the Caucasus Mountains. It was New Year's Eve, and the head of the Mountain Jews invited us to dinner with his best friend, a Muslim policeman. My lasting memory is of the two them with their arms around each other, knocking back shot after shot of vodka, and wishing each other health, happiness and hundreds of grandchildren as the clock struck midnight.

Perhaps the story I'm most happy to have covered was last year's revolution in Georgia. Perched on a shaky balcony overlooking Freedom Square, I watched as thousands of Georgians stormed the parliament building and forced the president, Eduard Shevardnadze, to resign. As the former Soviet foreign minister who negotiated the end of the Cold War fled in an armoured Mercedes, a man on horseback from a far-flung village rode into the square, waving the country's new flag, the cross of St George. A cheer went up from the crowd and then fireworks burst overhead as dusk began to fall.

29
Tsunami

Jonathan Head

The Indonesian province of Banda Aceh was hit hard by the tsunami which devastated countries around the Indian Ocean. Tension between Indonesian soldiers and rebels, who'd been fighting a bitter separatist conflict, was doing nothing to help those trying to get relief supplies to remote coastal communities destroyed by the tidal waves. (1 May 2005)

I counted more than sixty bodies packed in a mass of floating debris in the river below me. And I didn't know what to think any more. Each one was so grossly bloated it bore no resemblance to the human being it had once been. Squads of Indonesian soldiers moved around in rubber dinghies, hooking the corpses with ropes and pulling them back to the bank, where they were packed into body bags. At least they had body bags now; a few days earlier they'd simply been leaving them uncovered in rows beside the road. They did their work quietly, and they were watched by a silent crowd on the bridge. And then I looked again, and I saw one of the corpses was wearing a bra. It was someone's mother, sister or wife. And another, smaller, was in a striped T-shirt and underpants; somebody's daughter.

And I couldn't look any more, nor could some of the bystanders on the bridge. Nearly everyone here has lost numbers of close relatives; really lost them: they're probably dead, but their bodies are among the piles that are being dumped into mass graves outside the town, or crushed under mounds of concrete and mud, or floating in the river. They'll never be identified, never properly buried, just mourned without ceremony by survivors too shocked to make sense of their loss.

How are we supposed to report a human tragedy of this magnitude? The words and phrases used to capture the scale of previous disasters seem hopelessly inadequate this time. And there's no one to blame, no failures to rectify that could prevent a recurrence. This was a natural phenomenon so brutally destructive it almost seems evil. Standing on the bridge and staring out at the mangled, foul-smelling mess of upturned cars and smashed fishing boats and rubble stretching for miles in what had once been a substantial neighbourhood, I found myself unable to imagine the power of something that could do all this, nor the terror of the people caught up in it. You can see all the detritus, the evidence of once-normal lives: shoes, clothes, plates, toothbrushes, photographs, torn and tossed together in a ghastly grey wasteland.

It seems so appallingly unfair. Aceh had already been dealt a lousy hand before the disaster, its people caught in a vicious war between separatist rebels and the Indonesian army. It was a conflict the world took little notice of, even though thousands were killed. Sealed off from help by martial law, Aceh is one of the poorest regions of Indonesia, ill-prepared to deal with destruction on this scale.

Local people I've spoken to have asked what they could have done to offend God. These are, for the most part, devout Muslims. But nothing in their religion explains the suffering they've had to endure.

The world is here now; no one wants to miss the chance to take part in the most dramatic natural disaster of modern times; one day Colin Powell, the next Kofi Annan. The people of Aceh have never experienced such international scrutiny before. Everywhere the television crews scour the faces of the displaced in search of the personal tragedies that will bring the scale of this disaster home to their viewers. You don't have to look far; every face tells a story, some so harrowing you wonder how these people have kept their wits. Some haven't. Trauma is etched in the hollow eyes of many victims.

The Acehnese are proud of their defiant history, fighting long wars against the Dutch, the Japanese and now the government in Jakarta, for more independence. They've learnt to bear their suffering well, but I've just had a fifty-six-year-old man sobbing uncontrollably in my arms, after telling me about his two sons, both missing, almost certainly among the countless unnamed corpses. They're also bewildered by the relief effort. No one has ever cared about them before; certainly not their own government, which has sanctioned the harshest tactics by Indonesian soldiers to suppress their separatist dreams.

The temporary camps that have been established in almost every school, mosque or building are largely run by the displaced inhabitants themselves, with modest help from Indonesian volunteer groups. They seem astonished to hear that so many people in the rest of the world want to help. But just how far is our commitment to the people of Aceh going to go? We, the news media, will be gone in a couple of weeks. And if the Indonesian government re-imposes its ban on foreign journalists, we won't be back.

The UN and the aid agencies say they must be allowed a long-term presence to help get Aceh back on its feet, but they still depend heavily on the co-operation of the Indonesian military, which really runs this province. That co-operation could come at a price; of funds siphoned off, of soldiers directing the flow of aid away from areas considered sympathetic to the rebels. The army's presence here is strikingly visible. Already there are signs they're moving in to control the relief effort. That's not to say the aid workers aren't making a difference. After a shaky start, life-saving assistance is getting through to tens of thousands of victims, often through superhuman efforts.

But when I tell the Acehnese the international community is going to help them get their lives back together, they ask me when. Who's going to give them the money to rebuild their houses, their shops and fishing boats? I tell them to be patient, it will come. But knowing Aceh's wretched history of war, abuse and corruption, I can't be sure that even now they won't be disappointed.

30

A Public Hanging

Natalia Antelava

*Public executions take place infrequently in Iran and only when a crime is deemed
to have caused particular public outrage. When a man, found guilty of murdering
twenty-one young children, was put to death in the town of Pakdasht, south of the
capital Tehran, correspondents were invited to watch justice being administered.*

(19 March 2005)

Ali stood in the middle of the square, his hand raised high towards the sky.
His body was still. Only his lips twitched as they let out the most desperate cry I have ever heard. 'Kavon! Kavon,' he wailed over and again. I tried
not to follow Ali's transfixed stare. I knew what he was looking at, and I
could not bear to see it any more. There, in the blue, cloudless sky, above the
crowded square, swayed the body of Mohammed Bijeh, the man who had
murdered Ali's twelve-year-old son Kavon.

One year ago, Kavon and his two friends were playing outside Ali's family
home when Mohammed Bijeh approached them. He told the children he
would take them hunting. Instead he led them into the desert just south of
Tehran where first he killed them, then burned their bodies. Eighteen other
victims of Mohammed Bijeh died in a very similar way, a total of twenty-
one children in the course of a year. Six months ago, finally, he was caught.
During a closed trial, Bijeh confessed to all of his crimes, coolly recounting
the details of each murder. 'The vampire of the desert,' they called him. Now
his body hung over the main square of Pakdasht, the town where most of
his victims came from. Underneath it, thousands of people were applauding
and cheering. And I stood still, my throat dry, my brain trying to grasp what
my eyes were seeing.

We got to Pakdasht just after dawn. Police cars were driving through the
streets announcing the location and the time of the execution. 'At nine in the

main square,' they yelled into loudspeakers. Thousands responded to the call, by nine the square was full; women and men, young and old, gathered behind a fence built for the occasion. Young boys climbed trees and lamp posts to get a better view and dozens of people crowded the roofs of surrounding buildings. In the middle of the square stood a crane with a hook attached from which the murderer would hang. Metres away from it, relatives of the victims waited for the police to bring out Mohamed Bijeh. We, the journalists, were told to gather next to the family members.

The crowd watched mesmerised as the killer's bulky figure appeared on an improvised stage in the square. Angry cheers filled the air as the court officials chained him and carried out the first punishment, a beating, one hundred lashes. Bijeh was silent and still, but at one point his body shook visibly from the shock of the pain and he fell down. He collapsed twice during the lashing. Both times he was forced to get up. He was then brought down from the podium, his shirt soaked in blood. As he walked up to the crane, the growing roar of the crowd mixed with the chant of the final prayer that the mullahs were reading into the loudspeakers.

At that moment, the seventeen-year-old brother of one of Mohammad Bijeh's victims ran up and tried to stab him. But the boy was quickly pushed away by soldiers. A woman in a black chador, the mother of another victim, walked up to the crane and put the rope around Mohammad Bijeh's neck. As his body lurched into the air above the square, the crowd applauded and cheered. Some relatives joined in, chanting and applauding; others stood quietly, their heads raised high, their eyes, some full of tears, focusing on the dark figure that swayed above them. 'Again, kill him again,' the crowd behind us shouted.

Part of me was appalled by this shameless exhibition of death, by the sheer excitement it was causing. But it was something else that I felt most uncomfortable with. And that was my own feelings of approval. 'This is real justice,' one of the parents told me during the execution. What I saw made me sick, but as I looked at the grieving face of the man who had lost his son I found I could not disagree with what was taking place. Many will say that capital punishment is not right, under any circumstances. But as I watched the woman's trembling hands tie the knot around the neck of her child's murderer, as I heard again and again Ali's desperate cry for his lost son and as I saw Bijeh's pale face confront the community to which he had brought so much grief, the execution somehow felt awkwardly, disturbingly right.

The Early Years

1

Wind of Freedom

Erik de Mauny

At the twentieth Congress of the Soviet Communist Party, the Soviet president Nikita Khrushchev astonished the world by making a devastating assault on Stalin's reputation and on the 'cult of personality' which he had established. Erik de Mauny examined the effects of this attack on the peoples of Eastern Europe.
(1 April 1956)

Well, it's clear, I think, that what we've been seeing during the last three or four weeks is the overthrow of a god, for Stalin was in fact revered as a god in his later years. There's no other way of putting it. Supreme military genius; father of art and the sciences; leader and teacher of mankind: these were some of the praises heaped upon him. But even these are mild; mild when compared, for example, with the following rhapsodic outburst which appeared in the pages of *Pravda* as far back as 1936: 'O great Stalin, o leader of the people; you who created man; you who populated the earth; you who made the centuries young; you who made the springtime flower.' Or the following extract from an anthology published in 1946: 'Stalin – here in the Kremlin his presence touches us at every step. We walk on stones which he may have trod only quite recently. Let us fall on our knees and kiss those holy footprints.' There's been nothing quite like it since the emperor Augustus allowed himself to be worshipped as divine among the furthest provinces of the Roman Empire.

Now it's fairly obvious, I think, that such a god can't be overthrown in a day, or even a week, and in fact it's taken the present rulers of the Soviet Union nearly three years to nerve themselves for the final onslaught. For, of course, when such a great idol crashes, a great many other things happen. For example, one of the first repercussions was a report of rioting in Georgia, Stalin's native region; and the Party has admitted to sending out thousands of agitators, or propaganda experts, to explain the new line to the workers. And then, of course, there are all these activities that are not without a certain grimly comic aspect: the quiet removal of the huge portraits; the shrouding of the giant statues; the tremendous labour of once more rewriting all the textbooks and histories of the past twenty years. Indeed, the decision is bound to have its repercussions in every sphere of Soviet life: in education and economics, in art, philosophy and science. For all these things Stalin is now said to have perverted and falsified.

Well, Soviet society has had a long training in not answering back when official policy changes. But, of course, the change has also found repercussions among Communist parties outside the Soviet Union. It's here that the old wounds are being reopened, and the stench isn't pleasant. For one important sequel has been a reappraisal of the 1948 split between the Cominform and Tito. And one of the consequences of that break was a wave of treason trials throughout Eastern Europe; in fact, wherever Stalin thought he could detect the least dangerous whiff of Titoism.

Already one of the chief victims, the former Hungarian foreign minister, Laszlo Rajk, has been posthumously reinstated; for it's now been officially proclaimed, by no less a person than the Hungarian Communist Party leader, Mr Rakosi, that Rajk was condemned and executed on false evidence. And the prime instigator in laying that false evidence, according to Mr Rakosi, was none other than Beria, the former Soviet security chief, himself executed by the present Soviet leaders three years ago – Beria who, according to *Pravda*, flourished like the green bay tree under Stalin's dictatorship. And, of course, there were other treason trials: Kostov in Bulgaria, Slansky in Czechoslovakia; it's quite a formidable list. Perhaps we haven't heard the last of them yet.

For now that the process of unravelling Stalin's reign of terror has begun, it's difficult to see where it will stop, or even where it can be stopped, since the Soviet leaders will presumably want to call a halt at some point.

Meanwhile there's one interesting and even rather paradoxical fact that emerges from studying the reactions of Communist parties in Eastern and Western Europe, and that is that their leaders have not by any means all shown the same alacrity to accept the Moscow denunciations. The Eastern Communist leaders have echoed them wholeheartedly enough: at Party meetings, in their own newspapers and radio broadcasts. But in the West, and particularly in Italy and France, the Party leaders have adopted a noticeably more delicate and shrinking attitude. In fact, like the French party leader, M. Thorez, writing in last Tuesday's *Humanité*, they've tended rather defiantly to lay all the stress on Stalin's positive achievements. And there's the apparent paradox. One might say the ordinary Soviet citizen, in his tightly policed world, had little option but to acquiesce in what went on under Stalin, whereas the Western Party members at least had the advantage of distance, and might have been expected to see what was happening. And, of course, that's just the point. They did see, and they applauded. They even vied with each other in acclaiming Stalin's infinite wisdom and goodness as one carefully staged trial succeeded another. No wonder they're now thrown into some confusion. No wonder they're finding it rather difficult to put the right conviction into their appeals for popular-front governments.

Meanwhile, when something as big as this happens – and many observers think it's the biggest thing that has happened since the Revolution – it's just not possible to grasp all the motives and consequences involved. It may seem fairly obvious, for example, that the present Soviet leaders had to destroy the terrible Stalin myth before they themselves could begin to breathe freely. But it's a good deal harder to guess what the full psychological effect of their action will be on a people conditioned for more than a generation to worship the very ground on which Stalin trod. No one has suggested that the long-term aims of Communism have changed. But at least the new Soviet leaders have shown an apparent desire to ease tension abroad and create a more liberal atmosphere at home. One may say that, in the long run, they had no choice. The really vital thing is that they seem to have breathed a little wind of freedom into the huge prison of Soviet society, and who can say what this may eventually lead to.

2
The Suez Crisis

Douglas Stuart

Douglas Stuart was the BBC correspondent in Cairo when President Nasser of Egypt nationalised the Suez Canal and ordered the formation of an Egyptian Liberation Army to defend it. Britain and France were reacting angrily to what they saw as a threat to their communications with the East, and Britain was calling up reservists. (19 August 1956)

Most days I park the car in the same spot in a backstreet in the centre of Cairo and then walk to my various appointments. Over the weeks, I've got to know the people near the parking place quite well, particularly the steady customers of the small soft-drinks shop. We smile at each other, say good day and exchange platitudes about the weather; then they sink back into their chairs on the pavement and return to their newspapers and gossip. But I've noticed that the whole street seems to congregate round the door of the shop whenever Cairo Radio broadcasts the news; for popular interest in the London Conference, in fact over every aspect of the Suez crisis, is very great. But the Egyptians, although they consider themselves to be entirely in the right, are not at all bellicose. I've not encountered hostility anywhere; on the contrary, I've found a great deal of friendliness and enjoyment of even the slightest of jokes.

For example, there was the time when an Egyptian asked me: 'How are you this morning?' It was just after President Nasser had refused to attend the conference in London. I replied: 'Still confident,' and this mild witticism was greeted with shouts of laughter and I'm still being teased about it. On the other hand, the Egyptian government is doing its best to stir up popular indignation against the West. The newspapers and the radio play up what is termed the 'Anglo-French military threat to Egypt'. President Nasser has coined a new slogan to describe the efforts of the Western powers to secure international control of the Suez Canal.'This is collective colonialism,' he says.

Everywhere there are signs of strenuous preparations to meet what's called 'the danger of an imperialist invasion'. The authorities have turned schools into recruiting centres for the new National Liberation Army. This is the equivalent of our own Home Guard. The slogan of the new force is 'a rifle behind every shutter'. Women, too, are being trained in the use of firearms. Every day the newspapers carry pictures of veiled Egyptian damsels holding sub-machine guns and valiantly trying to hide their distaste. Children are not excluded from the general mobilisation. Boy Scouts are being formed into battalions and I've seen army instructors showing six-year-olds how to drill. There are no longer any playing fields or sports clubs in Egypt; the authorities have turned them all into parade grounds and military training establishments.

The Egyptian army, navy and air force are fully mobilised; all leave has been cancelled. What's more, President Nasser has signed a decree making it illegal to publish information about the armed forces without special permission from the minister of the interior. Religious leaders have announced their support of Egypt's cause. The Rector of Al Azhar, Cairo's 1,000-year-old Muslim University, has announced that for a man to defend his country is a sacred duty; he's called for a jihad or holy struggle against Egypt's enemies. To show that he meant what he said, this elderly bearded scholar doffed his robes the other day, put on uniform and accepted instruction from army officers in the use of a rifle.

The authorities have not lost sight of the need for a passive defence; they've opened blood banks, recalled doctors to duty, doubled the number of beds in state hospitals and appealed for gifts of blankets, clothing and medical stores. The principal cities of Egypt have all undergone mock air raids. In Cairo, it took me completely unawares. In my flat the lights flicked off and on twice and then the sirens began to wail; ARP-wardens ran down the streets blowing horns and shouting 'put that light out!' Within a matter of seconds the city was in darkness; only the light of the moon illuminated the white cliffs of the skyscraper apartment houses along the banks of the Nile.

This then is the paradox of the Egyptian scene. On the one hand, there's what I can only describe as the apathy of the man in the street. He follows the news carefully; he supports Colonel Nasser to the full, but so far, he's not displayed an ounce of jingoism. On the other hand, Colonel Nasser's military dictatorship, with all the skill of modern propaganda techniques, is seeking to create a martial mood among the people. The streets of Cairo are decorated with huge photographs of their leader in army uniform. An enormous silver eagle, the symbol of the revolutionary regime, blazes across the Nile at night in neon-lit splendour. A giant plywood soldier straddles one of Cairo's main shopping streets. In the air-conditioned cinemas the people watch films glorifying the Egyptian army. From time to time there's a little clapping.

Well, what's the explanation? A British friend of mine asked his servant the other day what he thought of the Suez problem. 'Colonel Nasser's right,' the man replied with conviction. 'Well, will you defend Egypt to the last drop of blood?' my friend asked. The servant's face expanded into a big grin. 'When the first bang comes,' he said, 'I'm off home to Aswan; there'll be no bombs there.' And yet I doubt whether many Egyptians feel this way. Europeans who've spent many years in the country tell me that there's a new spirit abroad, a spirit of resolution, and men of resolution do not need to be jingoistic.

3

Escape from Budapest

Ivor Jones

The Russians had invaded Hungary to suppress a revolution there. Budapest was bombed and occupied by Soviet tanks. After a week trapped by the fighting, Ivor Jones, together with a number of other correspondents, managed to get out.
(18 November 1956)

Reporters are notorious individualists but, five days after the Russian attack started, we in Budapest found ourselves almost spontaneously working together. We had to get out to tell our story. There were no normal communications, and we thought that the bigger our convoy was the better our chance would be. So, early in the morning of Friday the 9th, we began to form up outside the American Legation. It was an amazing collection of cars, more than thirty of them, some barely roadworthy, some elegant enough for a glossy advertisement, but nearly all plastered with the flag of some Western nation. We set off. We had no papers allowing us to go. Some of us hadn't even got visas allowing us to be in Hungary. But we set off. There was still some firing going on.

We crossed the Danube by what seemed the easiest bridge. There were Russian tanks at either end, but the sentries let us pass. Beyond, in the suburbs, the debris of fighting was as heavy as in the city centre. Wrecked Hungarian guns lay beside the road; walls and the sides of houses had been shot away. About ten miles out we reached a big barracks held by the Russians. We were stopped at a checkpoint outside it. There was already one tank there and some tommy-gunners. Another tank came up and I spent most of the next few hours looking down its gun barrel, which seemed to be trained directly on my car. Our spokesman sought out the barracks commander, a Russian colonel.

He was correct, almost affable. He said that, unfortunately, he had no authority to let us pass and, since we had no documents, well … We asked him to do something about it, to ring the Foreign Ministry, to do anything. He said he'd try, but nothing happened. We sat and watched Soviet troops coming and going and, with them, small groups of AVH men, Hungarian security police. The AVH were an aristocracy of sadists that kept such Stalinists as Rakosi in power. I'd met men who'd been obscenely tortured by them. Others showed me perjured documents and bogus confessions from the AVH files. Well, when the Russians arrived the remnants of the AVH came out of hiding. And there some of them were, outside these barracks. It wasn't a comforting thought for those of us whose passports weren't in order.

We stayed until mid-afternoon and then went back to Budapest, to the Foreign Ministry. We stood in the hall there, a frustrated rabble, calling for the minister, for senior officials, for anybody. The minister appeared, at least I think it was the minister. He said yes, he thought he could arrange for us to have a safe-conduct pass to the Austrian border. We settled down again to wait while permanent officials came and went. They were quite friendly. It turned out that we were to be given a document in Hungarian and Russian and signed by the deputy prime minister of Hungary, but not, unfortunately, till the next morning.

Next morning we were back at the Ministry. The documents finally arrived. But by this time we'd learnt that the Russians weren't willing to accept these pieces of paper, even though they were signed by one of their puppet ministers. He's probably well used to such humiliations. So we started all over again by going round to the Soviet headquarters, the Kommandatura. This is housed in a curious pink mansion surrounded by tanks, armoured cars and troop carriers. We stood around in the hall, an immensely tall room painted white and decorated with plaster roses. At the corners of the walls were coy statues of naked girls. And everywhere were tough-faced, square-built Russians armed with pistols and tommy-guns.

Around the edge of the room, halfway up, ran a gallery from which Soviet secret police in plain clothes looked down on us. Finally we got a sort of assurance that we'd be given passes. But not until tomorrow. Next morning we actually did get them. They were blurred and untidy and I don't know what magic formula was written on them, but they got us past the Russian checkpoints, about a dozen of them, between Budapest and the frontier. Anyway, we reached the border. As we crossed, there was some small-arms fire in the distance. We were told that it was AVH men firing at Hungarian refugees, some of the millions who were less fortunate than ourselves.

4
Detained in Congo

Richard Williams

Congo had become independent, but mutiny had broken out among the armed forces and then the wealthy mining province of Katanga declared itself independent, electing Moïse Tshombe as president. Richard Williams travelled to Katanga as United Nations troops were flown in in an attempt to keep the peace.
(10 September 1960)

We landed slap in the middle of the enemy camp. Back at Elisabethville, Mr Tshombe's military commander, Major Crèvecoeur, a Belgian officer, had assured us that the airport was in friendly hands. He was positive that troops loyal to his ally, Mr Kalonji, had recaptured it the day before and United Nations troops were there, too. So we took off in a tiny aircraft with Alan Kearn, a British pilot, to fly across the desolate Congo landscape to Bakwanga, 500 miles away.

The countryside and the few villages we passed over seemed peaceful enough, but we knew that the Africans who lived there were locked in a ferocious battle. We located Bakwanga by the great open-cast mine on the outskirts, where sixty per cent of the world's industrial diamonds are produced. That day, the mine was shut and deserted. We discovered later that the 4,000 Africans who worked there, mostly from the Baluba tribe, had all fled in fear of their lives. Ten million pounds' worth of diamonds were still locked in the strong rooms. We circled the rough airstrip once and saw black faces under steel helmets staring up at us. The blue berets of the United Nations troops were evident, too, and that seemed good enough. We came down steeply and in no time at all we were churning up the red dust of the Kasai, the most stormy province in the Congo.

As soon as we clambered off the aircraft, we knew that things were different from what we had been led to believe. A United Nations officer, a

Tunisian, approached. Behind him, glowering and staring at us, stood a large group of the so-called Force Publique, the heavily armed militia loyal to the Communist Patrice Lumumba, who opposed the secession of Katanga. They came from the notorious Thysville garrison, the first one to mutiny in the Congo. After years of special training by Belgian officers, they've been completely brutalised. We were to get much better acquainted with them later that day.

An aura of deep suspicion divided us from them, but for the moment our story that we had come from friendly territory was accepted. We drove into town with a UN commander, a brave and friendly Tunisian, whom I remember very warmly. We owe him a great deal. Among all the officers in the Congo, his task in this remote and cruel town of Bakwanga was perhaps the most difficult. He took us to the mining club, where about a hundred Belgian men, the only Europeans left, were living in a dormitory under UN protection. They were technicians from the diamond mine. There we met the devoted Australian team of the Red Cross and they recounted the horrors of the previous day, culminating in a massacre of the innocents at Bakwanga church, where seventy African men, women and children had been shot to pieces. The only survivors were six babies and a small, bright-eyed golden rhesus monkey, whom they adopted as a pet and called Ossi. The four doctors had been burying bodies all day. Their leader, Dr Fox, told me sadly: 'I came here as a medical man, not to be a grave-digger.'

Well, we decided not to hang about and drove back to the airport for a quick getaway. But by now suspicion had deepened into open hostility. The sergeant-major of Force Publique came up and barked at us that we were under arrest. We were bundled into a truck and driven, under heavy escort, to the African quarter of Bakwanga. They placed us in a small guardroom, with two armed soldiers at the open door. By this time we were hungry and thirsty, and we were very glad when the Red Cross man brought rations and a supply of soda water. The city water plant was not working.

After he'd gone, the sergeant-major returned, scowling heavily. I got the impression that he didn't like white people very much. He started shouting again, and we remained silent. 'You will be sent to Luluabourg,' he said, 'where you will be shot.' These words were to have very serious consequences for us, which we did not foresee at the time. They were heard by a large group of soldiers who had gathered outside.

As soon as the sergeant-major left, they began to crowd the small room, their tommy-guns and rifles clattering. We were sitting down and we were allowed to smoke. Without warning, one soldier snatched the cigarettes from our lips with a cry: 'Spies can't smoke!' Another poured the precious soda water over us. They took our chairs away and they removed the Red Cross rations. We asked to see the Commandant and they laughed. It seemed odd to hear laughter in that hot and crowded room.

Two more soldiers arrived, one carrying a long stick, the other with an evil black truncheon. The atmosphere was heavy with menace. By this time we were four frightened men, trying hard not to show it. We watched discipline and the thin crust of civilisation crumple in front of our eyes. The soldier with a truncheon struck a ferocious blow at pilot Kearn. We stood together in a corner, while soldiers screamed threats and imprecations. The shouting became a meaningless chant. A guard tried to protect us with outstretched arms. It didn't help very much, but we were grateful. The mob, it was nothing else by now, continued to surge. Several pairs of hands clawed at my watch. They tore my suit in a frantic search for valuables. They took all I had: documents, money, sunglasses, pen. My companions were treated likewise. Then, they dragged off our shoes and threw them away.

Fortunately the Commandant of Force Publique arrived soon afterwards and the crowd fled. He realised at once what had happened. He said quietly in French: 'You've been very lucky.' Then he told us that we'd be handed over as prisoners to the United Nations. The deep set eyes of this soldier, who was trained in the North African desert, looked at us gravely as he said: 'They can be very dangerous, you know. They kill easily.'

We were the UN Commander's guests for three days, while he and 200 Tunisian soldiers did their job fearlessly and well: the thankless task of keeping the peace in a most unhappy country.

5
Funeral Special

Gerald Priestland

Gerald Priestland was revisiting India when Pandit Nehru, who had been prime minister ever since India achieved independence, died. (13 June 1964)

'You must be mad to go on that train,' they said. 'Why spend twenty-four hours in a cattle truck when you can fly there in just over one hour?'

Well, that train was the funeral special taking the major remains of Mr Nehru for immersion in the holy Ganges at Allahabad. I'm glad I went on it, not because it wasn't uncomfortable, it was, but because it reminded me of what India's really all about. As we rumbled across the sandy flatness of the north Indian plain, bleached and corroded by the sun, people came down to the side of the line to have *darshan*, to be vouchsafed vision of the sacred relics. This was the heartland of Mr Nehru's Congress Party, and they came down from villages that one could see were still untouched by the first, second or third Five Year Plan. They stood among fields where peacocks strutted in flocks as evening gathered; they packed on to the platforms of country stations to bathe in the reputation of a man whose constant urgings to become scientific, secular and socialist they must have considered far above and beyond them. Such advice was for the learned; for them there remained the spiritual emanations from his ashes.

In the press coaches it was suffocating. Officialdom did its best. There were free issues of explosive fizzy lemonade; in every compartment there were earthenware crocks of drinking water; sweepers crawled on all fours mopping up the dust that swirled in; and at one stop great blocks of ice were dragged aboard in galvanised baths and set under the ceiling fans, so that the blast they circulated would become a little less searing.

At every stop it was like the rush hour on the London Underground. Those lounging on the seats inside stared with wonder through securely barred windows at the shoal of humanity pressed against the outside. Once the Indian reporters in my compartment told the curious peasants who peered back at us that a French correspondent was President Nasser of Egypt. The peasants replied that they were grateful for the honour His Excellency was doing them. They meant it, and I'm glad the Frenchman gave dignity to a bad joke by bowing in reply.

It was impossible to get on to the platform to make one's way to the white funeral coach, where the urn was displayed on its floodlit pedestal. But at Cawnpore, I managed to climb out on to the roof of my coach and stumble along the top of the train, jumping the gaps till I reached it. It was one of the most enthralling sensations of my life, one that invaded every physical sense. I squatted there, wedged between the roof of the station and the roof of the coach. Below, the crowd surged to and fro like a heavy sea against a cliff, uttering a continuous wordless roar. They were men, all of them men, not a woman in sight. I was battered by the sound, stifled by the heat that rose up with a strange mixed aroma of sweat, spices and flowers, the flowers they'd brought to toss before the urn. I was rocked by the beating of thousands upon the side of the heavy coach. It was like observing the very bloodstream of India, hot and throbbing, every head below a human corpuscle.

Then on through the night, with every now and again a chant of '*Chacha Nehru amar hai*', 'Uncle Nehru is Immortal', swelling and tapering off from the trackside. The final scenes at the confluence of the Ganges, the Jumna and the invisible Sarasvati River, the holiest of Hindu ends for this agnostic Westernised leader, hammered it all home; the unalterable Indianness of India. As one Indian pointed out to me, it was inevitable that Mr Nehru, despite his wishes, should have had a religious funeral. The New Delhi electric crematorium still isn't operational after eight years' work on it, and the priests are the only people who know how to set about a cremation.

And so Hinduism took its wandering son back to its bosom, with the Indian army amphibians handling the transport, and the Indian air force scoring one direct hit and two near-misses with showers of petals. On shore, a million people joined in the public holiday. There was hardly a wet eye to be seen, and the weird triangular banners of the holy men fluttered over their encampment on the sandbanks like a goblin army ready to invade the nation.

6
End of the Prague Spring

Robert Elphick

The Czech president Alexander Dubcek had introduced something like democracy to Czechoslovakia by carrying through reforms which gave liberty to the press and broadcasters and freedom of speech and movement to the people. Moscow responded by sending in the Red Army; the Czech leaders were arrested and taken to Moscow before being returned to Czechoslovakia. Robert Elphick was in Prague as the Russians tried to strengthen their hold over the country.
(3 September 1968)

The most poignant scene in Prague these days is played out daily round the big equestrian monument of the Saint King of Bohemia, our Good King Wenceslas. Since the beginning of the invasion it's been the focus for protests, hung with black flags and the Czechoslovak national tricolour. But now it's been scrubbed clean of all the posters and slogans telling the Russians to go home, and it's become something like a national shrine; a shrine, moreover, which isn't kept up by the government but by the efforts of the ordinary people.

Fresh flowers appear daily at the foot of the statue, and the national flag and the black flag of mourning get carried in informal relays by young people, old people, long-haired beatniks in jeans and spruce young soldiers. They've been keeping it up for days now, sorrowing for the people who were killed in the early days of the invasion, and also for Czechoslovakia's lost independence. By contrast, the most macabre of my experiences has been, perhaps, to watch a full-scale Soviet concert party entertaining the troops with concertinas, balalaika music and those exuberant Russian dances. It was something like a celebration at a wake.

It's now a fortnight, though, since the armadas of tanks poured across the country to strangle Czechoslovakia's attempt to mix Communism with democracy, and it's quite clear that the Russians grossly miscalculated the temper of the people here in believing that they had only to act decisively to destroy Mr Dubcek's position. They obviously placed high hopes on the veteran president, General Svoboda, as possibly providing a respectable head to a puppet regime. But the old president was having none of that, and it's reliably reported he threatened not only to resign but to commit suicide unless Mr Dubcek and the other leaders were freed and restored to their positions.

Not that this, a gain though it is against the possibility of widespread bloodshed, is making much difference to the general Soviet tactics of putting Czechoslovakia back into a rigid straitjacket. No more dreams of independence within the Communist movement; no more thoughts of holidays abroad or contacts with Western Europe, of freedom or democracy at home, or even better pay, except by leave of the masters of the Kremlin.

What's been published of the dictated Moscow settlement is already onerous enough, and nobody believes that there are not any secret clauses. It's clear, for instance, that there's no fixed date for withdrawal. It's believed they've also insisted on stopping all tourism and closing the frontier with Western Germany altogether. They've also warned the cabinet that any signs of unrest will be taken as proof of the government's incapacity to rule, and that any attempts to resist the invading forces will be ruthlessly suppressed.

Although the Russians are now withdrawing troops from some of the more conspicuous places in Prague and elsewhere, nothing can conceal the fact that their agents are taking over, as rapidly as possible, all the key posts in public life. The calculation is evidently that, having failed to push Mr Dubcek and his colleagues out of office, they'll make them do their work for them, in the expectation that as they take the unpopular measures they're told to do, they'll lose all credibility with the public. The Russians have already forced the government to bring the censors back. They've also forced changes in the Ministry of the Interior, literally over the dead body of one of the deputy ministers, who's reported to have committed suicide rather than hand his files over to the KGB.

The best that Mr Dubcek and his colleagues can do now is perhaps to mitigate the consequences of Russian domination, and wait for better times. Initially, at least, they'll be helped by the massive feeling of national solidarity that the arrival of the foreign troops has engendered, and also by the natural patience of a people to whom foreign invasion is only too familiar.

7

Nightmare in Vietnam

Anthony Lawrence

The first American soldiers had arrived in South Vietnam in 1954 and in 1970 they were still fighting there. Anthony Lawrence was the BBC's Far East correspondent. (23 May 1970)

From time to time, reports come out of South Vietnam suggesting that the morale of the American troops there is sinking. And discussion of this will grow as the American army takes in more young men from the age-groups that have been demonstrating on university campuses, smoking pot and rejecting today's American society.

Soldiers' morale is difficult to analyse, especially here in Vietnam. Wars are different now. The old vocabulary – words like bravery, discipline, morale – doesn't meet the problem. In the Vietnam war you mostly don't need brave men; you need efficient ones able to handle highly sophisticated instruments of transport and death. And the standard length of service in Vietnam is one year. For most of the 400,000 Americans still out here, the best morale builder of all is that you can actually count the days to going home.

But there are tremendous contrasts. Many of the soldiers have an easy time, with their nightly cinemas, good food and modern plumbing. Many are better off than they would be in the States. But when you leave the big bases and maintenance areas and get out into the wilds, then it's different. There you meet the real soldiers: the men of the infantry and the air cavalry units. There are about 80,000 men, less than a fifth of the total US army in Vietnam, who really meet the enemy close up: killing and getting killed. They're young, mostly drafted men, graduates, college dropouts, a large proportion of Negroes. Their nickname is 'grunts', from the way the soldier grunts as he shoulders his heavy pack. They spend most of their time out in the wild forest near the frontiers, where the enemy is always infiltrating.

They may be out for as long as a whole month at a time. And when they return it's not to a camp with cinema shows and hot showers but to a so-called fire-base with gun-pits and holes in the ground to sleep in. And their chance of getting killed or wounded is very high.

That's the sector where morale is under pressure. It's such a chancy business, this patrolling. You can go for months and meet nothing, and then three times in one week you meet some awful ambush or firefight. The man next to you goes down yelling with a leg blown off; the platoon commander is bleeding to death against a tree. It's over in fifteen minutes, but it's a nightmare; and it may come again tomorrow night. When you get back from all that, the re-enlistment sergeant is waiting for a little chat. He can get you out of all that, he says. If you're ready to sign on for a longer spell in the army, he'll get you a cushier job.

In this infantryman's life, the great thing is to come home safe, to keep your arse covered, as the soldiers call it. There's a vast gap between, on the one side, the junior officers, NCOs and men, and on the other, the higher ranks, the career officers, the so-called 'lifers'. It's the 'lifers' who believe in conventional discipline. But the men who stay out in the forests, beating the bush, as they call it, they're all, including lieutenants, on Christian-name terms, and there's no formality except that everyone does what he has to do.

'I never thought about morale,' said one young lieutenant. 'The life certainly changes you a lot. Luxury, to me, is staying in a forest clearing for one whole afternoon without having to move on. A drink from a cold stream's a gift from heaven. A bed to sleep on – unimaginable.'

What about pot-smoking? Platoon commanders confirmed to me that a lot goes on. But there'd be big trouble if some idiot smoked just before going on patrol. It brings on enormous thirst and for a while dulls perception, which is fatal.

Most of the young men I spoke to thought the army was badly run and the war a great mess. But that's not bad morale; they wouldn't run away. It's the case of old soldiers doing what can't be got out of, doing their duty. And again, in the old tradition, their main contempt is for the overweight sergeants back at the base, the generals' talk of 'kill ratios'. Their only respect is for each other and for the enemy who kills and dies like they do, along the forest trails. And they know, too, that when they get back to the States, there's no one to talk to about what they've been through; no one who wants to listen.

8
Post-war Washington

Charles Wheeler

America's war in Vietnam had ended after more than eighteen years and, from Washington, Charles Wheeler was describing the impact of the peace.
(30 January 1973)

On Thanksgiving Day in November 1954, seventeen American officers were handed sealed travel orders by the Eisenhower administration. Their destination was Saigon. The seventeen were the first American advisers to be attached to the army of South Vietnam. That was eighteen years ago. The war in Korea had ended only a year before and nearly 3,600 American prisoners were only now settling down to life with their families. Eventually that tiny contingent of seventeen men became an expeditionary force of more than half a million. But to reach that peak took fourteen years. No sooner had America reached it than the commander-in-chief was attacked by anguished doubts about the extent of the national commitment and began earnestly to sue for peace.

It took his successor four more years to secure that peace and even now the commitment hasn't been laid to rest entirely. America's involvement in Vietnam began so gradually that Americans have to go to the reference books to find out when the longest war in their history started. It has ended almost as gradually and quite as untidily. For some, the young men who expected to be conscripted and were reprieved, it ended last summer. For others, the families of the prisoners and the missing, it will end in sixty days, when the last of the captives are back from the camps and when the missing who can't be found are pronounced dead. There has been no celebration here of the end of the war, only relief; relief tempered by several other emotions, mostly uncomfortable ones. The Christmas bombing left deep scars in this country, too, and not all Dr Kissinger's listeners on Wednesday were comforted by his claim that that final surge of American military power hastened the peace. So did the atom bomb in 1945. Also, Americans are not blind to the fact that if the war is over for them, it is unlikely to be over for the people who've felt its impact most.

Americans have pored over the peace settlement with mixed feelings, admiring the ingenuity of its authors, but uneasily aware as well that to accept the simplistic assurance of the White House that this is in every respect a peace with honour requires a good measure of wishful thinking, if not self-deception. Most of them, I think, would rather it were called the best settlement we could get. After all, the election campaign is over, and there has been too much officially inspired self-delusion in recent years. But people who are finding the word honour embarrassing aren't conjuring with words like surrender and sell-out, as a few did last October. If there hasn't been an outburst of joy here, neither has there been any bitterness. Americans who suspect that their government might have been able to end the fighting sooner see no merit in a vicious public argument. Not only has there been more recrimination already than a healthy society can stand, but it's obvious that many of the lessons of Vietnam were well and truly learnt long ago. In other words, the process of readjustment to peace is well under way. It began somewhere about the middle of President Nixon's first term, say two years ago.

The war did divide American society and in some respects the damage is probably permanent. But the process of healing is already far advanced. To a lesser extent the same is true of America's economy. The war and President Johnson's policy of guns and butter caused in turn inflation, reduced profits and unemployment. It wrecked America's payments balance and weakened the dollar, creating a crisis in which America's relations with some of her allies were subjected to painful strains. But the war has never absorbed this country's energy totally, as two world wars did Britain's. And the experts would probably say that words like post-war recovery don't apply. Unless, that is, you take the broader view and assert that the real tragedy of those wartime years has been the dismemberment of America's infant welfare state. The war stopped social reform in its tracks and today, with the budget deficit huge and growing, there is no prospect that a windfall of money released by the war can suddenly be applied to the needs of the poor in the cities. According to the experts, the so-called peace dividend is effectively a myth. The country spent it long ago. So life goes on here much as before. If there are changes ahead, they're scarcely perceptible. Here in Washington, for example, there are stirrings in the Congress. Senators and others, who've been divided by Vietnam for many years, are beginning to find themselves in agreement on the need to provide checks on an executive branch that is able to take the country largely by stealth into an undeclared war, and keep it locked in conflict for years after everybody has agreed that the whole enterprise was a ghastly mistake. Now whether anything will come of this realisation that the war has revealed a grave weakness in America's system of government, nobody can say. Presidential accountability can't be created by the passage of a new law. Public opinion must first perceive its absence. This hasn't happened yet. Though the debate about power promises to occupy Washington for many months, there is no sign that the country is so far deeply concerned.

9

Travel Soviet-style

Philip Short

Philip Short, stationed in Moscow, had been given permission by the Soviet authorities to travel to the southern republics, but only by air or by train. He sent this account of his trip. (1 October 1974)

Usually if you can go somewhere by train in the Soviet Union you're also allowed to fly there, and most people do, especially over long distances. But travelling by train does have its advantages, too, as I found when I went from Baku in Azerbaijan to Makhachkala, the Daghestanian capital, a couple of hundred miles north up the Caspian Sea coast. For one thing it's punctual. The ticket clerk tells you that train number six always leaves ten minutes late and that's exactly what it does. And it's also one of the best ways of meeting Russians, for in the south, at least, a train journey is not so much a means of reaching your destination as a social occasion, a great exercise in communal living. In the sleeping compartments, men and women are lumped indiscriminately together; unshaven figures in string vests wander up and down the corridors; music programmes from Radio Moscow blare out over the loudspeaker system and you find yourself being invited in to share someone's vodka, or to meet a village schoolmaster who says he wants to be able to tell his friends that he's had a drink with an Englishman.

Each carriage has its own *dezhurnaya*, a robust lady who brings round endless glasses of Russian tea, and who is equally capable of bouncing a drunk or of arbitrating in a dispute over who has which bunk. And at the stations along the way, peasant children sell apples and tomatoes from tin buckets.

The problems really start when you arrive wherever it is you're going to, for then you have to take on the system of Soviet hotels. The lift, for instance, with its small handwritten signs, 'No service after 11 p.m.'; and when you complain that the once-daily train doesn't arrive till midnight, back comes the reply: 'Are we responsible for railway timetables?' Or your room, which turns out to be already occupied by someone else who has to move out. 'But I've booked it,' you say. And the answer to that: 'You didn't expect us to leave it empty, did you? What if you hadn't turned up?' And this, you're told, isn't sharp practice but just raising productivity for the Five Year Plan. And that's only the start. There's the bath you paid extra for to discover that there's only hot water on Fridays, and of course this isn't Friday; or the television set for which you also pay extra, whether you want it or not, because the town plan for television rental is badly under-fulfilled.

And what about the noise like a cross between a jet engine and an air-raid siren that wakes you up in the morning, the cleaning lady's vacuum cleaner? Perhaps that all sounds just too far-fetched and vituperative; and if so I must disclaim responsibility. For it's all from a report on provincial hotels by two Soviet journalists, which appeared in the central government newspaper *Izvestia*. My own experience, in fact, was rather better than that, but there was always some little quirk which made me realise that *Izvestia*'s description wasn't far-fetched at all. And there are plenty of things which *Izvestia* didn't mention. The practice, for instance, of charging foreigners ten times the Russian rates, so that a night's stay is twenty pounds instead of two; and if you query it, you're told with total conviction that it's the international norm and that exactly the same thing happens to Soviet tourists in Britain. They may even try to charge an extra twenty pounds as a booking fee.

And there are other differences in the way foreigners are treated, too. At Yerevan, in Armenia, I watched a receptionist who'd gone out of her way to be helpful to me turning away a Russian woman, who was almost in tears because she had nowhere to stay, with a completely callous rudeness and indifference. Perhaps that was an isolated case, but certainly the system of foreigners being privileged operates all the time when you travel by air.

Flights in the Soviet Union may be astonishingly cheap; as little as six pounds for the equivalent of London to Paris. But all too often they're subject to overwhelming delays, and airports in the provinces can look like transit stations for wartime evacuees – old peasants with great shapeless bundles of belongings, whole families encamped on suitcases, a woman breast-feeding a baby. They may have been there four hours or twenty hours or two days, quietly resigned. Sometimes you're lucky and there's no delay at all, but at Yerevan I waited eighteen hours to fly to Baku, and at Baku ten hours to fly back to Yerevan. You queue at the enquiries desk and at five minutes to twelve they're still telling you: 'Yes, your plane will leave at twelve o'clock,' and then it's postponed till four, and when four o'clock comes round it's the same story again. The reason, I was told each time, was the weather, but when there were enough foreign tourists waiting, they arranged a special plane, which, for some reason, the weather didn't affect. Perhaps part of the explanation lies with the kind of incident I saw as I was waiting at Baku. Just as a group of passengers were at long last about to board their flight, a petrol lorry drove into the aircraft's tail. The passengers returned inside; lorry and plane were solemnly towed away and a little old lady with a broom appeared to sweep up the broken glass.

10

The Correspondent's Trade

Ian McDougall

Ian McDougall returned to Britain after twenty-seven years of service as a foreign correspondent during which he sent more than 10,000 news stories from over forty countries in four continents. (31 August 1976)

The reason why a broadcasting correspondent has an easier time now than he did in the forties is simple: communications have improved. Communications are the only things that change in news. The news itself, despite what some may claim about there being more of it today, or less of it, remains remarkably similar from one decade to the next. And, in fact, the only really novel events that have happened in my time are space travel, political hijackings, mass tourism and the plastic explosion in household equipment, what one advertising man once described to me as 'the breakthrough in plastic toys for budgerigars'.

When I first started in the forties, as number two in the Paris office, we had to send nearly all our stories at fixed times over a microphone hook-up, a music circuit, as it's called in the trade, and only occasionally did we use the phone, because at that time, for various tedious reasons, the use of the phone for broadcasting in voice was forbidden. Tom Cadett, the chief Paris correspondent at that time, and myself used to scamper up and down a flight of stairs to a converted attic bedroom in a hotel and seclude ourselves behind a thick curtain, as if in a confessional, screaming ourselves hoarse till contact was established with London and praying that we'd emerge without dying from suffocation. It was, incidentally, the only broadcasting studio in the whole world equipped with a bidet; in that, as in so much else, the BBC led the field.

It wasn't until the early fifties that I recall being equipped with a portable recording machine. The first of these was unbelievably heavy and big enough to pack a fair-sized puppy in. The tape had to be wound back by hand, which is the perfect recipe for instant calamity. A two-year-old child would have been an easier travelling companion, and I once said so in a cable from Burma, which was the only message I sent from Burma that got any notice taken of it at all. Then we were issued, as a kind of overreaction, with a sweet little machine about the size of a schoolchild's pencil box and about as robust as a piece of Dresden china. This also broke incessantly, but at least it was so small that one could forget about it, which was more than could be said for its predecessor.

As time went by, the telephone was rehabilitated as a legitimate means of sending dispatches by voice, and the extension of the automatic system for international calls greatly reduced the need to maintain bad-tempered arguments with exchange operators in various languages. On the frontier between Malaya and Thailand, I once got through to London in a few seconds from a jungle telephone which was having its cord chewed by a sacred goat as I used it. And in the remotest part of the Carpathian Mountains of Romania, I was taken by a heavily armed escort to a railway signal box half a mile away in the middle of the night – we'd been sleeping in a train while accompanying the then Soviet leader, Khrushchev – in order to receive a call from the BBC. I thought this was good staff work on the part of the Romanian post office. I thanked my escort who, however, stolidly informed me that they had only been protecting me from the perils of mountain bears which infested the region. I then understood for the first time why they had made me change from my light-coloured pyjamas into something dark – a disconcerting instruction at four in the morning in a Communist country!

Broadly speaking, you can get almost anybody to a telephone these days, which is perhaps why some editors and producers think that there should be nothing very difficult about getting Ford, Carter, Giscard d'Estaing, Schmidt, Amin or whoever into a programme at very short notice. On one single day in Bonn I was asked to get Chancellor Brandt, then just installed in office, into three different BBC slots more or less at the same time. The trouble is that foreign politicians tend to give priority, just as do British ones, to their own audiences.

However, while improved phone systems, not to mention cable and telex and satellite, have made human contacts much faster, they've also reduced the frequency of the old-fashioned scoop, by which I mean a story which no one else has got and which, and this is the crucial point, is worth having. There's no merit at all in being first with a load of boring old rubbish. My idea of a reasonable and feasible scoop today would be for a reporter to land on Mars, or authenticate the Loch Ness monster, or prove that Mao Tse-Tung is already dead. But scoops cost money and editors tend to be closer and closer-fisted. When, some time ago, Henry Morton Stanley of the *New York Herald* questioned his editor about expenses for an interesting assignment he'd just been given, he received this magnificent reply: 'Draw a thousand pounds now and when you've gone through that draw another thousand, and when that is spent draw another thousand: and when you have finished that draw another thousand, and so on. But find Livingstone.' In fact, Stanley spent about £9,000 on the job, which would, of course, be equivalent to a far greater sum today, though still cheap at the price.

But my point is that today the editor wouldn't have put it like that. His message, probably in garbled telex, would have read, 'Find Livingstone, but remember cost-cutting has absolute priority.' Stanley's great scoop, incidentally, was fully believed in by his editor, though at the time others had doubts. A scoop today is suspected by all.

I am none the less proud that the profession of foreign correspondent survives. Democracy needs it, even though some people claim to be vague about what foreign correspondents do, and whether indeed they do anything at all. There is a lunatic fringe which thinks they drink champagne out of their mistresses' shoes and live at the local Ritz. There is another fringe, not entirely lunatic but almost so, which believes they're on Christian-name terms with everyone in their territory from the president downwards and are occasionally called in to advise on foreign policy.

My own experience throughout twenty-seven years has been that the job is extremely arduous, both mentally and physically: that drudgery is of its essence, as in most other jobs, and that the advantages of not having to keep nine-to-five hours are more than offset by the disadvantages of being on call at every hour of the day and night, a requirement which correspondents share with, almost uniquely, medical general practitioners.

When all is said and done, however, it also seems to me a profession which teaches you to cope with literally any situation without flapping and without yielding to the pressures of interested parties. Over a very long time, and on a day-to-day basis, this is harder than it sounds. It defines, too, the frontiers of your powers of endurance and rubs in the valuable lesson that the way things appear on the spot are nearly always different from the way they are visualised by the reader or listener in an armchair. Now this has nothing to do with inaccurate reporting. It has to do with the human imagination, which seems unable to cope with anything smaller than twice life-size. I don't remember being seriously frightened on a story I was actually covering, but I was often terrified when I read other people's reports of it afterwards.

11

Flight from Jonestown

Paul Reynolds

*More than 900 members of an American religious cult led by the Reverend Jim
Jones were found dead deep in the jungle in Guyana. Paul Reynolds reported on
how the body of a visiting US Congressman, Leo Ryan, had earlier been discovered
nearby. (29 November 1978)*

He lay back on the bed in the heat of the afternoon, his head propped up on
a pillow: a short, stocky man in his forties, lean and bronzed. His name was
Gerry Parkes, and in his soft, slow drawl he told me the story of how he had
led his family into virtual slavery, and how he had tried to lead it out again.
Gerry Parkes, his wife Patricia and their five children, the eldest a married
man, the youngest a twelve-year-old girl, were fundamentalist Christians
who lived in California. Many years ago Gerry and Patricia used to go and
listen to sermons given by a young preacher called the Revd Jimmy Jones
in Ohio. Jones was a dynamic young man, Parkes said, and he himself, a
methodical, reserved man, was attracted by the Jones personality.

'Everything Jones touched seemed to turn to gold,' Parkes said. 'He
looked after drug addicts, criminals, the poor and the black.'

The Parkeses moved to California and kept up their close links with
Jones, who by now had set up a commune in San Francisco he was calling
'The People's Temple'. Parkes broke off and stared ahead silently for a few
moments. His twelve-year-old daughter was asleep on the bed next to his.
'Didn't you know there was terrible repression in the People's Temple?' I
asked him. 'We rationalised that,' he said. 'We thought the punishment was
necessary to keep some of those people out of prison.'

It took the Parkes family two years to make up their mind to go to
Guyana. Gerry Parkes broke off again before resuming: 'It was the most
terrible mistake I ever made,' he said. He explained that Jones had told them

Guyana was ideal for a new type of community. The land was rich. The temperature never rose above eighty. The settlement would perhaps grow into a new city one day. Jones showed them films of the site and eventually the Parkes family sold up their house, gave the money to the Temple and set off for South America.

The family was greeted at the camp gate by an armed guard. 'I knew I'd made a mistake as soon as we arrived,' Gerry Parkes went on. From then on they lived the lives of slaves. The day began at six with a meagre breakfast. Everyone had to be at work by seven; some toiled all day in the fields, and at six in the evening there would be another meal, usually rice and gravy, sometimes vegetables as well. At around seven-thirty the people would have to gather around the camp pavilion where Jones harangued them and built up the atmosphere of paranoia which was to culminate in the mass self-destruction.

'He told us our enemies would destroy us,' Parkes said.'We had to be ready to commit revolutionary suicide. When the enemy attacked, we would foil him by destroying ourselves.'

The Parkes family arrived in Jonestown in April this year. They were not allowed to leave, so they began to work out an escape plan almost immediately. They did not dare to tell anyone else. There was no one they could trust; many of the settlers believed in Jones, others enforced his will with guns. Some even regarded the camp as a revolutionary base to help spread and foment rebellion throughout South America.

By then the visit of Congressman Ryan was imminent, and when he arrived Gerry Parkes decided this was the moment to leave. Jones tried to persuade him to stay. He offered to give back their passports, get good medical help for his mother, give them better food if only they would stay. But Parkes had had enough. He gathered the family together and along with Congressman Ryan they set out for the nearby airstrip and freedom. A few others joined them. Jones and his followers saw them as traitors, though.

'People we had got to know stared at us with hatred,' said Parkes. 'We knew we were in danger.' And they soon found out just what that danger was. As they sat in the small aircraft one of the supposed deserters with them pulled out a gun and started shooting. Other gunmen appeared from the camp, and among the five dead were the Congressman and Gerry's wife, Patricia. The death of Patricia Parkes was the price the family paid for their escape. Nor was it the only price. As Gerry was finishing his story his eldest son, Dale, came into the room. He listened to the end, then quietly went over to a wooden trunk in the corner, the trunk in which all their belongings had been shipped to Jonestown some months before.

He pulled out a photograph. It was that of a smiling two-year-old boy, half black, half white. 'That was my adopted son,' Dale said. 'We had to leave him behind.' Dale put the photo back in the trunk. 'The police have told me he is dead,' he said. 'It was the children they killed first.' Dale Parkes went to lie down on another bed. A doctor from the American Embassy came in to see how they were. The girl woke up, her face was drawn and tired. From below there drifted up the noise of a steel band. I left the room and closed the door.

12
Desert Disaster

Clive Small

*Clive Small was the BBC's Washington correspondent when an American
military mission to rescue the fifty-three hostages being held by the Iranians in
the US Embassy in Tehran ended in disaster. Eight Americans died when their
helicopter collided with a tanker aircraft in the Iranian desert and the mission was
aborted. (30 June 1980)*

_____

I had been up late at night, putting over a dispatch to London about the
growing concern in Washington that Mr Carter might be moving too quickly
towards some form of military action against Iran. Ironically, the action
everyone was talking about was a non-violent naval blockade some time in
the future. At midnight I went to bed. Not much more than an hour later the
phone rang next to my bed. A voice on the other end said: 'The White House
here, Rex Grenham speaking. Is that Clive?'

I sat upright quickly. Rex Grenham is deputy to Jodie Powell, the president's spokesman. 'I've got a statement,' said Mr Grenham. 'I'll read it and
at the end I won't take any questions. Are you ready?' I scrabbled for my pen
and notebook. 'Go ahead,' I said, shaking the sleep out of my head.

'The president has ordered the cancellation of an operation in Iran.' And
so on. As that astonishing story unfolded, I felt a fleeting second or two of
doubt. One of the strange features of Washington in the early hours is a
number of what are officially described as 'nuisance calls'. Several times my
wife and I have been woken by the phone ringing and an official-sounding
voice trying to put over a hoax of some kind. Was this another? But no.

By the time I had taken down the first few sentences of the statement I
knew this was only too tragically genuine. Rex Grenham was giving me the
first few details of an historic disaster. He spoke calmly at little more than
dictation speed. 'Rex,' I said, 'have you given this to the news agencies?'

'Jodie's doing that at the moment,' he said. 'Thanks,' I said, and he hung up.

I rattled the phone cradle frantically to clear the line and got my call through to the foreign news traffic manager on the late shift in London. I hurried through a quick sentence telling of the mission that had failed in the desert in Iran. Within minutes I was reporting the White House statement live into the *Today* programme. After putting over a news dispatch and being interviewed by the *24 Hours* programme on the BBC External Services, I dressed hurriedly, swung my car out of the garage and headed in to the BBC office in the centre of Washington.

I drove fast through the scattered banks of mist in the empty streets. It was just after three in the morning. Suddenly my mind flashed back to a hotel room in Nairobi. It was about three in the morning then and it was Sunday 4 July 1976. The phone next to my bed rang and it was a voice telling me of the raid on Entebbe. The traffic light changed and I put my foot down, and the car shot off again.

Now I was thinking about something else. Why had the White House phoned the BBC so quickly with the first news of the raid on Iran? Ever since the hostage crisis began President Carter's officials have become more aware of the BBC's ability to get news in and out of Iran through its Persian-language service. In this case, was the White House trying to get a message through to people in Tehran by way of the BBC? If so, what people? Was it the militants in the Embassy, letting them know through news broadcasts that the American operation had failed in case they heard rumours of an assault under way and panicked and shot hostages? Or could it be something else? A raid like that would have to have had supporting groups inside Iran. Perhaps the White House was hoping that BBC broadcasts would tell those groups that the raid was off and they should keep their heads down.

Well, perhaps all that it proves is the way a journalist's imagination can speculate privately at three in the morning. Still, the BBC was given the news surprisingly quickly. As I drove past those darkened houses, it looked as if no one in Washington was aware of what had happened a few hours before on that stretch of Iranian desert. The British Embassy, like the other foreign representatives here, had not been told.

But now, as I listened to the car radio, the talk shows and the phone-in programmes were well aware of the failure of the rescue mission. And nearly all of the listeners who were calling in were worried. What would happen to the hostages now? And would the disaster in the desert mean that the crisis would spread and threaten peace? The announcer interrupted.

'The president will speak to the nation at seven this morning,' he said. I parked the car and crossed the deserted street to the office. It was still dark. And it felt darker.

13

Special Information

Jim Biddulph

Jim Biddulph was another of the BBC correspondents who saw service in numerous foreign capitals and, as a result, felt privileged to have acquired some specialist knowledge. (30 November 1980)

One thing about a job like mine, you do come by all sorts of special information. I don't mean the sort of 'special information' that sends civil servants twitching towards official secrets acts, and I don't mean extraneous *Guinness Book of Records*-type information, such as the fact that the police band in Bangkok has nine bagpipers, although even that became rather special a few days ago. The sound of nine Siamese pipers wailing under your hotel-room window, while you're trying to catch up on your jetlag, is really pretty special.

What I mean is the kind of information that you file away in your mind, in case it might come in useful in future, which I don't suppose the nine bagpipers ever will. For example, did you know that in the only hotel in the island republic of Nauru you have to order lunch at breakfast time? Otherwise the chances are you won't get any. It's worth remembering, but of course only if you plan going to Nauru, which very few people do because it's composed almost entirely of accumulated bird droppings which are being dug away to fertilise the fields of Queensland. If you do want lunch, you had better hurry up.

While you're down that way, well, give or take a couple of thousand miles, don't try smuggling any Camembert cheese into Australia. I was specifically warned against this by the man they have at Sydney Airport to stop people shipping in old palm trees and other foreign matter. And don't try smuggling a durian fruit out of Thailand. It isn't, mind you, the most smuggleable thing, being about the size of a rugby football, covered in jagged spikes and with the stench of a dead skunk. It's the smell that makes it unwelcome at the airport and some would say anywhere else, come to that. Which reminds me, if you're inclined to morning sickness of whatever origin, don't use a Korean lift at breakfast time. Koreans start the day with large helpings of a kind of mulch called *kimchi*, which is a well-rotted mixture of cabbage, garlic and chillis in roughly equal proportions. If everyone in the elevator breathes out at once, as they tend to do, the lift goes up without the button even being pressed. That's the kind of thing I mean by 'special information'.

And then there's the category simply involving getting to wherever it is in the first place; moving equipment in, and the end product, a television report, out. Airport luggage trolleys become an obsession. For years there were no trolleys in the whole of India and Pakistan; only hundreds of porters, each of whom would grab one piece of baggage and head for the door. Well, they do have some trolleys at New Delhi airport now, and Islamabad has managed to buy a few, presumably using all those thousands of rupees they've collected in airport tax. But, inseparably welded to each trolley, is one of the original airport porters. The system remains the same, except that now it's on wheels. Still, it's better than the brand-new airport at Peking, which had no trolleys of any description when last seen last month.

Sending air cargo has a mystique of its own. Choose an inconvenient time to try and ship your package in Thailand, for instance, and you have to pay ten or fifteen pounds for what's called 'knock-door' fee, which is a sort of informal charge for customs assistance. In Rawalpindi, you have to employ a public scribe for sixty rupees to fill in the customs form in English. Not because it's particularly complicated, but because the scribes have managed to corner the market in customs forms.

Some 'special information' is the kind you'd really rather not have, that makes the heart sink before the journey has even properly begun. I know, because I have timed it on three occasions, that it takes the immigration men at South Korea's Seoul airport one minute fifty seconds to check each passenger's passport. Now, that is really not very long, unless two jumbos arrive at the same time, disembarking maybe 700 passengers. Multiply one minute fifty seconds by the number of people ahead of you in the queue and you almost decide to fly right out again. Except that would mean queuing at the other counter and nobody's going to give you an exit stamp without an entry stamp already being there. It's one of the many things about crossing frontiers by air. There's none of the excitement or sense of occasion you get on a road crossing, although, very often, I seem to end up looking at the frontier instead of crossing it.

I do seem to have spent an awful lot of time lately pacing along borders. Like the barbed wire and muddy stream separating Hong Kong from China. Or the dusty road with its leftover French colonial milestone between China and Vietnam, or the mountains between Pakistan and Afghanistan, or the concrete dividing lines between North and South Korea, among the barren hutments of the demilitarised zone.

Or, and very frequently this past year or so, the often invisible border, the strings and scrubland between Thailand and Kampuchea. I left that one till last, because although all borders depend on passes and other paperwork to some extent, the Thai/Kampuchea border has a repertoire of rubber stamps quite numbing in its variety. You begin with a letter from your own organisation, which is presented to the British Embassy in Bangkok. They, if you're lucky, will provide a covering letter to say you are what you say you are. Those two letters or photocopies you take to the Interior Ministry, who, in due course, provide a covering letter confirming that the Embassy say that you are what you say you are. The collection then goes to the Foreign Ministry, who write another letter, saying, in effect, that they say that the Interior Ministry say, that the embassy say, that you say that you are what you say you are. And so on, to the headquarters of the Supreme Command. No more letters. They issue two cardboard passes, one pink and one green, for different sectors. And that's all there is to it. Well, almost, because those passes will not get you past a single one of the many, many roadblocks. You take your pink or green cardboard to one or another of the several sector commanders who will swap it for a specifically dated piece of paper for a specifically designated village. The initial part of all that performance only applies the first time. Subsequent visits begin at Supreme Headquarters, and in any case you can of course short-circuit the whole system by just whizzing off on your own, which is how one of my film reports ended up as yards and yards of celluloid curling in the hot sun in the dust of a roadblock south of Aranyaprathet.

I must admit I don't like military roadblocks, even with proper passes. They always seem to be manned by absent-minded enthusiasts who fiddle with the triggers of their guns as though they're trying to remember exactly what happens if they pull them. Unofficial roadblocks can be equally disconcerting. The one in Thailand erected on a main road by monks seeking contributions to their temple wasn't too bad. But I was stopped abruptly on the road from Peshawar a couple of weeks ago by a crowd of Afghan shepherds. They clustered round the car, plucking at the doors and uttering hoarse cries. One man was disembowelling a sheep, on the very crown of the road. One of his companions managed to get the passenger door open and levered himself in beside the driver. He growled and motioned urgently forward. The driver obliged. As the speed built up, the man shouted over his shoulder that a bus somewhere ahead had hit one of the Afghan sheep and roared on without stopping. And a sheep, he added, was worth 200 rupees. Well, eventually up ahead, we saw a bus and our passenger insisted that was the one. So we overtook it.

My driver wanted to look for a policeman, though goodness knows where he thought he was going to find one. But, in any case, our passenger insisted he would handle it himself. The bus pulled up behind us. Our Afghan unwound himself from the car and strode over to the bus, with his moustaches bristling, his huge headdress making him look ten feet tall. He seemed to clank as he walked. He reached up to drag the driver from the cab, but abruptly from behind the driver a fist shot straight out and hit the Afghan straight on the nose. His headdress fell off, his eyes streamed tears, his moustaches drooped. The bus passengers screamed in triumph. Our warrior was suddenly revealed as a rather undernourished seventeen-year-old who snatched up his headdress and dashed away into the forest beside the road. The bus drove off in triumph. We never did know if it was the one that killed the sheep.

Refugees and roadblocks seem to go together. And there are just as many roadblocks at sea as there are on land, if you know what I mean. But there's a great deal more to be said for being arrested by boat than by a foot patrol. It's almost always a politer experience. When Malaysia was being inundated by Vietnamese boat people, the authorities were determined to keep refugees and journalists apart, especially when there was a whole boatload of refugees anchored a couple of miles off the coast. It became a sort of game with the marine police, and, with a little preparation, not too unpleasant. For days the routine scarcely varied. Day after day, we tried to board the ship using a variety of hopefully innocent-looking small boats. And day after day, the marine police would swoop down at the last moment, arrest everyone in sight and send them under armed escort chugging up the estuary to the nearest police station. It was almost like a picnic; providing you set out with packed lunches, cooler-boxes of soft drinks, an envelope of money to pay the boatman's fine and a taxi ready waiting at the police station. 'Special information' again.

Altogether, for a non-nautical person, I seem to spend a great deal of time on boats, official and otherwise. In the South Pacific there are still plenty of places that are accessible in no other way. And sometimes an arrival by boat can be a grand occasion. The only time I've ever sailed into Sydney harbour was on the deck of the royal yacht *Britannia*, and you can't be much grander than that. Although sailing into Shanghai a couple of months ago with the Royal Navy ran it close. With the navy, 'special information' tends to be interesting, rather than useful. You may know very well that only a fool gets involved in apparently innocent party games in a petty officers' mess afloat. But, come the moment, and there isn't very much you can do about it. For days after, I had an egg-size bump on my head, for confused reasons involving a blindfold and a soup ladle. I pass the information on for what it's worth, but that can't be very much.

Even with the very smallest boats, 'special information' tends to have restricted use. I have spent many, many long nights cramped in small rubber dinghies with troops and police in the waters between China and Hong Kong, waiting to catch illegal immigrants. The only answer as the hours drag by seems to be transcendental meditation.

Most of my 'special information' tends to be immediate and severely practical; for instance, I know exactly where in Pakistan I can buy a brass safari washstand, which is bound to come in useful one day. But some of it, well, I don't really know. Just under a year ago, soon after the Soviet invasion of Afghanistan, one of the newly appointed ministers in Kabul complained to me that the ousted regime had run off with 20,000 gold objects. He was particularly embarrassed about this because the gold had only been unearthed a few months ago by a Soviet-led expedition. The new masters were obviously beginning to ask questions.

I was recounting this story a few days later to an acquaintance, an elderly lady, and she said: 'Good Lord, I know exactly where all that stuff is! Nobody stole it; they just changed museum curators six times in a year so I suppose they've lost track of it.' She proceeded to describe the place and even the room and the special locks guarding the treasure. It was only a few yards from where the complaining minister had been sitting. That is certainly 'special information', but probably useless. For I know the Afghans have rediscovered their gold. And I haven't seen that minister's name mentioned recently. It's impossible to get a visa to Afghanistan to check it out myself. So, as I say, as information it probably is useless. On the other hand, if the gold has not been found, perhaps something could be arranged. 'Man with special information seeks visa for self and camera crew.' Absurd? Well, yes of course, but you never know …

14
A Sense of History

Angus McDermid

Angus McDermid worked for the BBC for twenty-three years before retiring in 1980. When asked to choose the most memorable period of his career, he recalled his years as West Africa correspondent, as a roving reporter in a turbulent post-colonial period. (13 December 1980)

'Candidates,' the advertisement for the post read, 'should have a sense of history.' And that was perhaps not so much for purposes of background but for the knack of recognising the historic moment when it happens. But being there is often a matter of luck. Who among the delegates at the Commonwealth Conference in Nigeria in 1966 could have realised that a revolution was being planned under their very noses; that their host was to be brutally murdered and that the conspirators were only waiting for them all to go home? But the ominous signs were there and the journalists who stayed on for an extra few days did have their revolution. 'Stick around a bit' isn't a bad motto and there is no substitute for seeing for yourself. All else has to be assessed critically on a sort of sliding scale of credibility: 'Why am I being told this? Could this really have happened?', and so on, eliminating at least the obviously bogus from the travellers' tales and always remembering that in Africa, as elsewhere, a correspondent is accountable, sooner or later, for what he writes and says.

The roving correspondent has one great advantage: comparatively few people in Africa, whether African or European, have a really first-hand knowledge of the continent as a whole. The Africa correspondents, however, might visit a score of countries in as many days. They were a hardy, resilient lot, perpetually filling in forms in triplicate for visas, dodging stray bullets or burning the midnight oil in some deserted telex office simplifying the complex, explaining the irrational, self-sufficient, used to frustrations and rebuffs and always good companions. Some had their problems; there was the stateless cameraman whose record of arrests was well above average, so much so that getting him out of jail became a little repetitious. Perhaps, he eventually admitted, they are suspicious because my uncle was editor of *Pravda*. And there was a South African who boasted of having offered mercenaries to both sides in the Biafran War, which didn't exactly endear him to his colleagues.

No correspondent likes to get too close to events. He must, in the philosophical sense, always be the onlooker and he must always be free to rush off and file his story, too. Yet the correspondent in Africa, especially one who broadcasts to the world, must on occasion feel, a little uncomfortably, that he clearly and identifiably must have influenced the course of events, and not only through his dispatches

After the first coup in Nigeria I was invited to the Great Volta Dam in Ghana. My escort, a young officer, wanted to know exactly how the Nigerian army had succeeded. I emphasised the secrecy which I felt to have been the essence of their success, and within a few months President Nkrumah of Ghana, away in China, leaving an exhausted treasury and a starving army at home, was overthrown and a radiant army officer told me that in a country swarming with secret police and informers the greatest achievement had been to keep the army putsch a secret.

The dire events in Nigeria flowed from a simple administrative process; the first census after independence demonstrated that the northerners could always outvote the rest of the population. And this was one of the political factors that led the country into civil war. Regular correspondents recognised the ominous polarisation and considered how best to cover the war when it came. My first move was to make for the back door to eastern Nigeria through the Cameroon Republic. Shortly after I arrived, the local Biafran radio announced, to my dismay, that I'd been declared *persona non grata* by the federal government back in Lagos, a serious matter for me. To check on this meant a long journey back to Douala, the Cameroon capital, where I learnt, as I suspected, that the radio news item was bogus.

Some zealous Biafran propagandist thought that I would be persuaded to stay in Biafra and the secessionist status would thus be enhanced by having a BBC man based on their side. Once back in Lagos I was reassured by the federal spokesman: of course we wouldn't dream of prohibiting an old friend like you. But if you ever set foot in Biafra again you will never be allowed back into Nigeria.

So I stayed on the federal side, someone else went to Biafra and, realising that their plan had backfired, the Biafrans made me a target for some imaginative abuse. I was the intelligence chief at the centre of a web of spies, manifestly ludicrous, the poor man's Richard Dimbleby, a rotten reporter and for good measure a bloody liar.

Reporting in Africa requires no special skill, but it does help to be knowledgeable about telecommunications. My mother was a Post Office telegraphist, so I suppose it's a matter of instinct. I've managed to get dispatches back to London by methods that would make the telecommunications purists recoil with horror and on one occasion I persuaded the censor at the Lagos telephone exchange that Welsh was a permitted vernacular, at least for long enough to get a few words through to my wife.

Danger, well not too much. You don't think about it at the time, nor does it do to reflect on the decrepit aircraft, the unregistered helicopters, the elderly pilots. 'Gentlemen,' said one dapper little ex-squadron leader as he threw away the bottle and climbed aboard, 'you're in for a bumpy trip.' But I've had worse.

I've only been deported twice; not, alas, on major 'publish and be damned' issues of principle, and I haven't been held under arrest for more than a few hours at a time. There is an art in knowing when to leave, as on Zanzibar when the BBC were officially banned from the island for 999 years.

The good things that happened? Well, I always think of the humble skipper of the dhow which ferried me across to Zanzibar. He saw me being arrested and taken away on the quayside, and in the best maritime tradition, and at great risk to himself, went into the town and told the British authorities.

Lighter moments? Well, inevitably there are some bewildered tourists around wherever there is a moment of high political drama. I remember with affection the fifty American ornithologists who wondered why they were arrested for being on a sandbank in the middle of the Congo River, which is an international frontier. All those binoculars for watching birds? A likely story.

There were, too, the African oddities, the strange tribes which had gone their own ways; like the highly mechanised basket weavers or the curious sect on a remote Nigerian island with an advanced boat-building industry and equally advanced in communal family living. They're the stories that I never got around to writing. There were, too, the ones that everyone has written; the tipsy elephants drunk on fermenting berries, the animals in the game park near Nairobi Airport so tame that they crowd up to the railings of the next-door drive-in cinema when there's a good film on.

There were moments of despair and frustration, others of pure enjoyment. The fulfilment of boyish fantasies; driving alone for 1,000 miles in search of a story, and, rarest of all, the momentary glimpses of the real Africa, the true and barely comprehended forces at work, when you realise humbly that in Africa the western correspondent can only scratch the surface.

If there is a reward, it's that of having acquired at least a working knowledge of a vast and complex subject, of having survived a sometimes lonely life, of having relied on personal decisions and of developing a measure of self-discipline. A prime minister in southern Africa once told me that nothing in Africa was ever finished. He was thrown out by his own party the next day, but he was right in the sense that it's unwise to predict with absolute finality about any series of events there. Yet when last year the Zimbabwe Conference decided, after years of wrangling, the future shape of that country, I ventured privately to remind Mr Joshua Nkomo that I'd first interviewed him on the issue twenty years earlier. What about all those ups and downs? 'Yes,' he reflected frankly. 'It's all a game, isn't it?' Which, I suppose, means that to understand African politics, it's a good thing to have a sense of humour as well as a sense of history.

15
Famine in Ethiopia

Mike Wooldridge

The famine in Ethiopia gathered in intensity until thousands were dying every week. Mike Wooldridge was finding out that relief workers were unable to get to many of the worst-affected areas which were in remote countryside regions.
(25 October 1984)

On only one other occasion in my life have I seen anything quite like the tragedy I witnessed last weekend. This was when I saw bodies being pulled out of the rubble after the earthquake at Tabas in Iran six years ago. But even though the aftermath of the earthquake was horrific and many people in the area were denouncing the Shah's regime for not having built quake-proof houses in Tabas, you felt that it was essentially an unavoidable disaster and that the high death toll was probably inevitable. No one, I think, could say the same about the ninety to a hundred deaths occurring every day at Korem in northern Ethiopia and the unknown number of people dying of starvation in the countryside, unrecorded by Ethiopian officials and the media.

A relief worker based in Addis Ababa, who last week paid his first visit to Korem since the death toll there rose so alarmingly in September, felt that an entirely avoidable disaster was taking place. He's right, but to have prevented it happening would probably have required more foresight and political will than either the Ethiopian or foreign governments have shown so far; and perhaps above all else, an end to the wars being fought over some of the most drought-stricken terrain. There are signs now that both Ethiopia and the countries in the best position to give substantial help are taking significant steps to prevent the disaster reaching an even bigger scale, such as the Ethiopian air force ferrying grain with its Soviet-supplied Antonovs, fuelled by the United States. But at the same time, aid officials say so many people are now completely destitute, with no access to food supplies, that the situation is bound to get worse before it gets better.

It will be a miracle if Melkamu Getahun survives this famine. He's an eight-year-old boy I met in Korem. Unlike others who grab at your clothes to plead with you to get them some food or help them to get medical attention, Melkamu's father simply came and stood in front of me with his son and gestured to me to look at him. He was extremely thin, with his ribs barely covered with skin. He wore just a flimsy cotton shirt for protection against the burning daytime sun and the chill nights. He looked as if all his life had already been drained out of him.

Through an interpreter, Melkamu's father told me he had harvested no crops for three years and the family had survived by gradually selling all their belongings to buy food. When they'd virtually run out of things to sell, they left their home and walked to the relief shelters at Korem, in the hope of finding a place in a shelter and some food. But the shelters and the rows of plastic tents were full and, he said, they'd not been given any food. His wife and one of his sons had already died. The day before, he'd sold his vest to buy something for Melkamu and himself to eat.

The surprising thing was that he related all this with evident sorrow but with little sign of anger, and I found this with many of the other men I talked to. It's the new arrivals who tend to agitate most for food and clothing and shelter, even demanding that the hard-pressed local officials send off messages to their superiors for more supplies that are probably not available. Those who've been there longer tend to be more fatalistic. Relief workers say many of the men go to great lengths to feed their families before themselves and the psychological strain of doing this is showing. Men in their twenties and thirties would normally be the last to die in a famine in Africa, but they're dying first in this one.

The Ethiopian authorities face a genuine dilemma over the tens of thousands of people gathering in the roadside towns like Korem. The more food they send into such towns, the more people arrive and the more chance there is of epidemics such as measles, which has killed many children in the past few months. The solution, everyone agrees, is to get food out to the people in their villages. In some areas, the mountainous terrain makes it very difficult to do that. In Tigre, where one and a half million people are said to be short of food, that would clearly mean reaching an agreement with the rebels that they would not interfere with food sent from government-controlled areas.

The tragedy now taking place in Ethiopia has a profound effect on anyone who sees it at first hand, however fleetingly. I asked a church worker how he coped day in, day out, with seeing so many people starve to death. 'All you can do,' he said, 'is to distribute what food there is as widely as possible and help those who are dying to do so with a little dignity, even on the distinctly undignified deathbed of a piece of cardboard on the floor of an overcrowded relief shelter.'

Africa

1

A Bloody End

Elizabeth Blunt

As Liberia's rebel factions fought for dominance of the country, the president,
Samuel Doe, was captured and killed. (29 September 1990)

For months Liberians had talked of little else; if Doe would go and when Doe
would go. Everyone had a different scenario: he would finally lose his nerve
and beg the Americans to helicopter him out; he would leave Monrovia for
his home village and make a last stand among his own people; or perhaps
he would stay until he went down in the flames of his bunker, the Executive
Mansion. What no one ever thought to imagine was the way that President
Doe did meet his end, being carried off from under the noses of an international peacekeeping force in a hail of bullets.

By the beginning of September, the situation in Liberia had reached one
of its periodic states of uneasy equilibrium. Rebel leader Charles Taylor and
his men had taken most of the countryside, but not the seat of government,
where Doe was still clinging on, or the port area of Monrovia, which was
held by a rival rebel faction. Five West African countries had tried to break
the stalemate by sending in a joint force with a mandate to negotiate and
maintain a ceasefire, and to use it to bring in an interim government which
would hold the ring until elections could be held.

The peacekeeping force worked slowly, but two weeks after it landed it
had made some modest progress. Those men of the rebels in the port area,
Prince Johnson's faction, had agreed a ceasefire and West African troops had
gradually deployed in their area, despite harassment by Charles Taylor's
forces. For what was left of the civilian population of Monrovia, there was
now a little space in which they could move fairly safely.

But the city was a sad sight. Past the bullet-holed buildings and the
wrecked cars, endless lines of thin, weary people trekked to and fro all day

long, searching for food. The city was under siege; no ship had come in since July and no produce from the countryside could get into town. Liberians basically live on rice, and rice had finally run out. Now there was nothing except boiled wild greens and whatever could be stolen from the port. One day street vendors might have boiled sweets, another day it would be mayonnaise. The mayonnaise is sold by the tablespoonful; it is a common sight to see customers licking their spoons just to keep hunger at bay.

It was at this point that President Doe, who had not been seen out since July, took it into his head to visit the peacekeeping force in its port headquarters. He swept in with a large entourage, ministers, television cameramen and heavily armed guards, and he went up to see the force commander, General Quainoo. But ten minutes later another line of jeeps burst into the port, this time carrying the rebel commander Prince Johnson and his young fighters, flaunting scarlet T-shirts and curly, permed wigs, and armed with every conceivable kind of weapon. Members of the rebel group swear that they did not come to the port to kill the president. But when he arrived unexpectedly, on what they thought was their territory, the opportunity was too good to miss.

Soon there was a full-scale row going on between the two groups; voices were rising and guns were being cocked. Prince Johnson himself, flamboyant and irascible, was stamping about, shouting and raving, as officers from the peacekeeping force tried to calm him. Then he went to the window and shouted: 'Men! Open fire! Open fire!' And the gun battle began.

At least from inside the force headquarters it certainly sounded like a battle, a battle fought at close quarters with rifles, machine-guns, grenades and even anti-aircraft guns. For an hour and a half the only sound apart from the gunfire was the begging and pleading of officers from the peacekeeping force trying to stop the carnage. For, in reality, it was less a battle than a massacre, as the rebels mowed down the president's people, chased them into port buildings and machine-gunned them where they were hiding.

When they finally pulled out the president, they shot him in both legs, bundled him into a jeep and drove away. They left seventy-eight bodies behind, all from the president's entourage. They took President Doe to the rebel base camp. Whatever happened that night can only be imagined: by the following morning, the president's body was on public display, its fingers smashed, its ears and private parts missing. It was a bloody end for one of Africa's worst rulers.

In a sense that was the moment that everyone had been waiting for for months. And yet so far it has solved nothing. Now the two rival rebel groups are slugging it out for dominance, with the peacekeeping force getting more and more drawn into the fighting. The day before the shoot-out, a team of six aid workers arrived to assess how they could get food and medicine to people in Monrovia. The day they arrived, the port was being shelled. The next day, it was the scene of Doe's capture. The following two days, stray bullets were flying in the centre of town where the aid workers were staying. They left without having seen more than a couple of square miles of the city, and with the message that until the fighting stops, it is going to be very, very hard to send in any kind of help.

2

Cape of Good Hope

John Simpson

> *John Simpson was the correspondent in South Africa in the seventies, when apartheid was at its height. He returned to the country for the historic general election which swept Nelson Mandela to power, and found it a changed place.*
>
> *(5 May 1994)*

The other day there was a service of thanksgiving in St George's Anglican Cathedral in Cape Town for the peaceful conclusion to the elections here. The congregation sang 'O God Our Help In Ages Past', with that slightly apologetic note in the voice that marks the influence of the English and their mild religious faith the world over. There were Indians and coloured people and Africans and whites there, and their words floated up to the groined roof of Sir Herbert Baker's incomparable piece of Edwardian Gothic. 'A thousand ages in thy sight are like an evening gone,' they sang. 'Short as the watch that ends the night.'

It did indeed seem like just a few beats of recorded time since I'd been based here and watched the cruelty and wastefulness of the system that had now been swept away by the ever-rolling stream of history. In front of me in St George's were the rich stained glass and the delicately carved granite, but I scarcely noticed them. Other images were running through my mind instead: playing with my daughters on the beach at Cape Town on Christmas Day 1977 alongside all the other white families, while a row of black children sat on a low wall at the back of the beach, watching the enjoyment they were forbidden, by law, to share. I remembered our landlord showing us round the lovely colonial bungalow we'd just decided to rent in a pleasant suburban street in Johannesburg.

'We really must get this painted nicely,' my wife had said, looking at the squalid little hutch where the servants would live. 'These people are just animals,' the landlord had retorted in his heavy Austrian accent. 'You'd be wasting your money.'

I remembered standing in the sweltering heat of a library in central Johannesburg while a thoughtful black American politician explained to the attentive crowd why the most painful sanctions were necessary against South Africa. He told us about his own child, whose legs were twisted by some childhood disease and who had to wear leg-irons which caused him a lot of pain. The politician told us with tears in his eyes how hard it had been for him to fasten the irons on his son's legs every morning, with the child begging him not to do it because it hurt so much; how he'd had to keep on saying, 'Unless I do this, you'll never grow tall and straight,' and how each time his son had nodded and helped him to do up the buckles.

And now, here in Cape Town sixteen years later, we were giving thanks for the healing of the disease; achieved not through revolution and bloodshed but peacefully, by compromise, reconciliation and understanding. I suspect that I was much more conscious of the extraordinary changes that had come over this country than most of the congregation were. They, after all, had had four years to get used to the abandonment of apartheid and the move towards a pluralist society.

To me the change still loomed overwhelming. What they were celebrating was something rather different: the series of uncharacteristic changes of heart which had brought us through the elections so peacefully. The series began with F. W. de Klerk, whom I'd known as a stony-faced minister of education. If you wanted a bigoted defence of apartheid, or someone to explain why Nelson Mandela had to stay in jail for the rest of his life, then F. W. de Klerk was your man. And he was the one who had let Nelson Mandela go.

Then, much later, came the other changes of heart: General Constand Viljoen broke away from the white irreconcilables and formed his Freedom Front party, which enabled even the far right to take part in the elections. And, even more importantly, Chief Mangosuthu Buthelezi decided to give up his alarming campaign against the holding of the election, as a result of which hundreds of people had been killed and wounded, and to enter the lists with the other political parties.

If you add to this the collapse of the white extremists, Eugene Terreblanche and the rest, and the failure of the brief terrorist campaign, then you can see that South Africa has a great deal to give thanks for at the moment. Of course, things aren't always going to go smoothly; the fierce accusations of ballot-rigging and the postponement of the formal announcement of Mandela's presidency show that. Countries don't live happily ever after, any more than people do. But the manner of a revolution dictates the pattern of the political system that follows it. A peaceful transfer of power is a pretty good assurance that, however great the ensuing problems are, they won't be resolved violently.

On the evening of the day the thanksgiving service was held in Cape Town, I drove with my television crew to the beach to watch the sunset. As soon as we got there I recognized it: it was the beach on which I'd spent Christmas Day in 1977. They'd knocked down the low wall where the disconsolate black children had once sat, and in the last light of the setting sun a young coloured couple were drawing hearts in the sand and laughing when the waves washed them out. A little dog danced on the wet shore as the dark rich reds of the sky faded and the waters of the Atlantic went from amethyst to black. I've been fortunate to see many of the extraordinary changes that have come over our world, from the collapse of the Berlin Wall onwards. But I haven't seen anything better or more encouraging than what's been happening here.

3
Cattle Country

Jane Standley

British farms were in the grip of BSE or 'mad cow disease' when our correspondent went to meet the Dinka and Nuer tribes in southern Sudan. There, they worship their cows. The animals provide food and fuel, and are even used as currency. (18 April 1996)

In the harsh yellow-grey scrub of Tonj county to the west of Upper Nile province, the talk was all about 'mad cow disease'. Does it make your cows in Britain really crazy, do they run around in circles or do they try to escape from their herders? What has happened to your cattle camps? The intense questions about the dreaded BSE quickly exceeded the depth of my understanding of the blight on British cattle. Napoleon, a southern Sudanese Dinka, held his hands to the top of his head and waved them like horns as he made mooing noises. Napoleon would never be able to comprehend why I didn't know all there was to know about mad cow disease. His ancient Dinka tribe knows EVERYTHING there is to know about southern Sudanese cows. Cows are at the heart of traditional Dinka ritual and life; there are nearly one million in Tonj county alone and there are millions more, and precious little else, in the vast open terrain of southern Sudan. And there are hundreds of cow words in the Dinka language; towns, water holes, children are all named after cows.

A young man names his cattle after the barter goods he used to acquire them, chicken, maize, soap. Without a herd he cannot marry. When he does, his wife is given a 'darling name' after his cows. The language of lovers in southern Sudan is that of the cow.

The camp fire crackled as we gathered around the radio to listen to the news about Britain's mad cow crisis on the BBC World Service. Napoleon and his colleagues, George, Darlington and Manasses, all work with aid agencies to try to protect the treasured cattle of southern Sudan from devastating diseases. Not BSE, but rinderpest and bovine pneumonia. They couldn't quite understand why a BBC reporter had come to see Sudanese cows while those of her home country were so threatened. A gulf of cultural misunderstanding existed when it came to cows.

We were camped out in the open under the clearest and darkest of African skies after five hours of bouncing along the dusty tracks of Tonj county to reach the vast cattle camps of the dry season. Every year the herders move their cows and their families to the wetlands, known as the *toich*, where something approaching grass continues to grow. The herders are born with the map of the migration running through their blood. But I couldn't see much wetness myself; it was as hot as standing in front of the dry blast from a kiln, and the pink tongues of the cattle curled around tiny blades of grass. But, for centuries, it's been enough to keep the Dinka alive.

It's a bumpy journey from Marial to Langkap, neither a metropolis large enough to appear on any map of southern Sudan. Not that there are really maps, or roads, or electricity or even more than a handful of one-storey brick buildings across hundreds of thousands of miles of vastness. Most people live in mud huts with conically pleated rush roofs, called *tukuls*. Southern Sudan is pretty much as it was one thousand years ago , but every jolt of the journey was worth it; it is a truly magical place. Naked children smeared in ash to protect them from diseases borne by insects ran along after our sturdy four-wheel drive vehicle. At stops to repair punctures, shy women wearing only a scrap of material around their waists came to take a look. Many had never seen a foreigner; one woman asked why my skin had peeled off and I was so ugly and white. Ebony-black old men leant on their spears, gleaming younger men patted traditional Mohican-like hairstyles and jangled strings of elaborate beads.

I had gasped aloud at the first glimpse of the cattle camps. The sight was unbelievable. Wisps of smoke from hundreds of cow-dung fires curled up into the sky, shot through with rays from the peach-coloured sunset. Brown, black and white speckled backs topped with curling horns spread on for ever. Tassles swung from the hugest horns of the favourite bulls. Herders and cattle alike were bedding down after a day's grazing on the *toich*. Deafening mooing was the bass line in the cattle-camp symphony. Women called their family's herds in, securing their ropes as they came forward to individual pegs. To heathen like me, the jumble of cows appeared indistinguishable. But their tenor-voiced herders moved through, calling each cow by name and singing lullabies to calm them for the night.

Cows and owners need to be calm now. After centuries of surviving drought and pestilence, southern Sudan's cattle culture is looking another threat in the face, that of war. The civil war pitching southern Christian rebels against the Islamic government in the north is now in its thirteenth year, and cows have become the favourite spoils. Pro-government militia have been raiding cattle camps in Tonj county and the pattern of dry-season migration has been disrupted. It's the traditional hungry season in the south, made worse by the looting of already depleted grain stores and the rustling of cattle at gun point. The Dinka people rely on the milk of their cows at this time of year, even bleeding them for nourishment when they're really starved. But many cows have been taken and access to all the wetlands has been curtailed by fighting. Napoleon tells me many of his fellow Dinka don't know if they'll make it through this hungry season. He's despairing as he talks of how Dinka rituals and traditions are cracking at the edges because of the war. Napoleon is only a nickname, a joke, he says. But people are now calling their children after the fighting, instead of after cows. Little ones are called 'Grenade' or 'AK47' or 'Bomb'.

Napoleon sighs, but cheers himself with the fact that the Dinka cows are at least safe from BSE. The questions resume: 'Are British cows physically as well as mentally sick?' Ducking my shameful lack of bovine knowledge, I busily open tins to begin cooking on the camp fire. The words 'It's going to be a beef stew' are out of my mouth before I even realise. 'Is that mad beef from Britain?' Napoleon cries, grabbing the can. 'No, the can's from Britain, but the beef's from Argentina.' Come to think of it, Napoleon, you should go there, one day. The Argentines love cattle, they have millions of them, but I'm not sure if the cows all have names.

4

End of a President

Allan Little

The final days of the regime of President Mobutu of Zaire were characterised by
rumour and fear as rebel forces approached the capital, Kinshasa. (24 May 1997)

Wednesday 14 May. Rebellion enters the city, first in disembodied form. It comes in the shape of hearsay and rumour and rising apprehension. It comes out of the dense, damp immensity of the rainforest in silent, menacing legion and along the teaming tributaries of the great river by steamer and ferry boat and dugout canoe. The rebel advances out there travelling the same silent hidden paths and it's all the more menacing for being unseen and unheard. A stalking night hunter closing in on its prey by stealth.

We know the rebels are coming to take the city and we know that when they descend it will be decisive and immediate, but we don't know how far away they are, or how imminent their strike. We wait in the highly charged city, gripped by rumour and feverish counter-rumour, and we try to separate fact from fancy, legitimate balanced concern from mounting paranoia. Everyone feels this; Mobutu's soldiers are behaving with more and more brutal abandon. I have seen this ready impulse to violence everywhere in this country; that single heartstopping moment when a red-eyed angry soldier holds you at gunpoint and you wait for his bitterness and fury to spill over into physical cruelty.

Or when the mood of a crowd switches from benign disregard to mass collective rage. Today George has been arrested at the airport with his crew. Our interpreter, Clyde, who has been working with us for weeks and has become a valued friend, steering us through the uncertainties and anxieties of this place, has been beaten up by six or more members of the supposedly elite, supposedly disciplined, special presidential guard. They were perfectly friendly at one moment, but then suddenly turned on him. He has been badly hurt. George and the others could do nothing. The Zairean army in defeat is capable of almost anything.

Thursday 15 May. At 12.30 we hear from two sources simultaneously that the army has been routed and is in retreat. The airport road is crazy now, swarming with pumped-up Zairean troops heading into town. Shops and offices are closing early. The people want to get home as quickly as they can. They are afraid of the rebel advance, it is true, but they are much more afraid of what their own troops will do when the end draws near. The army hasn't been paid properly in months. It is the soldiers' habit to ransack the city, to embark on a frenzy of looting and pillaging in which anyone who gets in the way risks being mown down in a volley of machine-gun fire. It happened in Goma, in Kisangani, in Lubumbashi. Today, I wrote in my diary, there will be an attack and a pillage; it could be tonight. When the news of the retreat reaches here, it will set the city on edge; it is the end for the Zairean army; the last defensive position has gone, collapsed. The airport is next, then the city. I am carrying my passport everywhere I go now. I find myself nervously checking from time to time that it is still in my pocket. I do not want to be separated from it. I am reacquiring, unconsciously, old habits from Bosnia. I sleep with a torch beneath my pillow; I leave my room key in the same place every night so that I know instantly where to find it if I need to leave in a hurry. If it starts tonight, we must stay here in the Memling Hotel in the centre of town.

British Embassy advice is that foreign nationals must assemble at the InterContinental Hotel and wait for evacuation by the Marines across the river. But it is too far to the InterContinental; we would never make it. I'm convinced that we are now nearing the end of the Mobutu regime. The only way we can avoid a bloodbath here is a military coup. The generals must tell the president that they are not able to defend the city and that some kind of surrender must be negotiated.

The radical opposition are going into hiding, convinced that there is a hit list of people to be murdered before the end comes. My colleague, Richard Downes, is reading Emily Dickinson and quotes aloud, 'because I could not stop for death, he kindly stopped for me; the carriage held but just ourselves and immortality.'

There is a new rumour abroad, and it is bizarre and chilling, that the end will not come until a certain cremation has been carried out. No one knows what this means, but rumour is the currency here and it is out of control. Television news tonight at 8 o'clock reported the onset of the dry season as its lead story and warned parents to protect their children from dry-season illnesses. 'We are sorry,' says the newsreader, 'that we are unable to bring you our usual photomontage of the president's activities today. This is due to technical reasons.' What kind of fantasy world is the regime living in? Up there in his hilltop palace at Camp Chachi, Mobutu is in a kind of presidential never-never land in which presidents never grow old and armies never suffer defeat.

Friday the 16th. Mobutu has finally left for Gbadolite, his home village in the jungle in the north of Zaire, he and his entourage sneaking out of the city unannounced at the crack of dawn. It's over, he won't be back. Our sources tell us in confidence that the generals did indeed go to him last night and they told him that they could not defend the city and that the only obstacle to a peaceful transition to rebel control was his continued presence here.

But now the hiatus. The Mobutu regime is entering the last phase of its last catastrophe and we are about to go through the most uncertain and perilous twenty-four hours. The dictator's departure has left a dangerous power vacuum. But there is a glimmer of hope. General Mahele, the army chief of staff, summons the BBC to his office today. His staff brief us. The general's view is that he cannot contemplate sacrificing an entire city for the future of one man. Those days are gone. It is the general's way of signalling that he is prepared to do a deal with the rebels. Rumour is rife that since the rebels got to within mobile-phone range of the city there have been clandestine channels of communication between them and General Mahele's people. It is an act of extraordinary courage.

News from the airport as night falls: defensive positions there have collapsed; the army, both the rank and file and the presidential guard, have abandoned their positions and are heading into the city. Still the fantasy world survives. The absurd information minister briefs us again. The president remains head of state; the government remains in control.

Saturday 17 May. George wakes me with a phone call at three in the morning and his news chills me to the marrow. General Mahele has been assassinated by hardline Mobutu loyalists. The regime has turned in on itself, fragmenting in its dying hours. I am instantly awake and shivering. I feel the familiar, unwelcome knot in my stomach and that cold, pulse-quickening chill spread, from my feet through my legs, stomach and chest. My throat tightens. General Mahele was our hope of a peaceful handover. He was the man who risked his life to open a channel of communication with the rebels and who, it seems, has paid the final price. The streets are ringing with small-arms fire, single resounding shots echoing through the empty city and the deep duga-duga-dug of heavy machine-gun fire rolling across the rooftops through the still heavy night air.

We assemble in our television edit room. A well-placed contact has called to say that renegade presidential guardsmen are on their way to our downtown hotel to take foreign hostages. Clyde, our interpreter, still traumatised from his beating, tells us his friends in the military have warned him to stay away from the BBC today. The BBC were the last people to speak to the assassinated General Mahele. It was the BBC who broadcast and made known to the world General Mahele's intention to bring rebel troops into the city by peaceful means.

A newspaper colleague calls from elsewhere in the hotel. 'Stay away from the hotel lobby now,' he says. 'Something is going on down there.' It is now impossible to separate rumour from fact. We have become part of the city and are susceptible to its mood swings. The mounting paranoia has engulfed us and we choose a room that is furthest from the stairwell and lift and we wait. Another call, another colleague, another rumour. The European ambassadors have agreed an evacuation; Belgian paratroopers are to secure the area around the hotel. It will take twenty minutes for them to cross the river. In the silence someone says: 'Never in my life did I imagine I could be overjoyed to hear the sentence "The Belgians are coming."' And we all laugh and the whole absurd edifice of rumour and paranoia falls away. The rebels are in the eastern suburbs; the presidential guard is fleeing, too preoccupied even to loot or pillage.

One rumour stands up: the Delphic reference earlier in the week to cremation. In his last hours in the city President Mobutu had the remains of an old friend disinterred from their grave at Camp Chachi and cremated so that be could take them into exile with him. They were the remains of the late president of Rwanda Juvenal Habyarimana, who was assassinated on 6 April 1994. His death immediately triggered the genocide in which up to a million Tutsis and moderate Hutus were murdered. The genocidal regime lost the war and fled to eastern Zaire and the protection of Mobutu Sese Seko. It has come full circle. The shockwaves from that assassination have at last toppled another great African tyranny.

Sunday the 18th. The long march from the east is over and the war is won. Today I walked with the rebels to the corrupt centre of the Mobutu empire; a single-file column of exhausted men, earnest and disciplined, snaked its way up the hill to Camp Chachi. They had come from Kalemie, far away on the shores of Lake Tanganyika, and they had progressed through the heart of this huge country at the pace at which a man can march. They scarcely fired a shot. The dereliction to which Mobutu's regime has reduced the country has finally worked to its benefit. The army was rotten to the core and could not put up a fight. Kinshasa was spared the bloodbath it feared. This was not a war at all. It was a people's uprising.

From the impenetrable vastness of the rainforest and along the tributaries of the river, hope has marched into the city on bare feet and weary legs and now there is retribution. In a suburban street, seven members of the old secret intelligence service have been set upon by the mob and killed. Their bodies piled together have been doused with petrol and are burning. I and the public know what all schoolchildren learn: those to whom evil is done do evil in return. While the reek of burning flesh fills the air, the crowds sing songs of freedom and liberation through the smoke.

5

Mrs Robinson Visits

Mark Doyle

A brutal civil war in Sierra Leone created more refugees than any other African war. And not only were millions left displaced, thousands had also been mutilated by the rebels. (3 July 1999)

One of the great problems of reporting from Sierra Leone is that the full picture has not been seen by the outside world. Great swathes of the country are occupied by unpredictable rebel forces and are too dangerous for journalists to enter. In Sierra Leone, it is as if the early period in the Kosovo crisis, before the world became aware of it and NATO intervened, had gone on not for weeks but for several years. When the United Nations Human Rights Commissioner, Mary Robinson, visited recently, she said there had been more loss of life in Sierra Leone than in Kosovo. More suffering, more mutilations and more basic violations of human rights. And it does not take much effort to see the results of what is happening in the Sierra Leone countryside.

Just a few hundred metres from where Mrs Robinson's helicopter landed, there is a camp for people displaced by the war. It specialises in helping those who have been mutilated by the Sierra Leonean rebels. For many years now, the rebels have used terror as a deliberate tactic. They chop off people's limbs and then send the mutilated people, bleeding and traumatised, into the government-held areas, as a warning to others not to support the government. Conservative estimates say this has happened to around 10,000 people.

One of them is Moctar Diallo, a confident, straight-talking schoolboy, who had his hand chopped off by the rebels. His story is a credible and depressingly common one. Moctar told me that once he knew he was not going to escape mutilation by the rebels, he asked them to chop off his left hand because he was right-handed. But the rebels refused this request, and just to make absolutely sure that no surgeon would help Moctar to sew his limb back on, the rebels put the severed right hand on a tree stump and chopped that in two as well.

Moctar Diallo is highly educated by Sierra Leonean standards, and as soon as he knew I was a journalist he suggested that I would like to meet the youngest known victim of the rebel atrocities: two-year-old Maimouna Mansarray. She lost her arm inside a mosque when the rebels attacked civilians cowering there. She was strapped to her grandmother's back and as the grandmother ran away she was shot. The bullet killed Maimouna's grandmother and left the little girl with just one arm. Maimouna smiles a lot, and seems not to realise that she is different from other people. This is not surprising. The man who was looking after her when I visited only has one arm as well. And another man, somehow doing his washing at the time I was there, had no arms at all.

The Sierra Leone war has created more refugees than any other conflict in Africa, about 500,000 people. But this is just the total of those who have fled to neighbouring countries and been registered by the United Nations. Far more people are internally displaced by the fighting. UN aid workers believe these may number more than two million.

One of these people is Sheikh Foday, a teacher by trade, whom I met in another squalid camp for displaced people inside Freetown. Sheikh Foday did not want to talk about his own problems, which to my eyes were dramatic enough, but about the problems of Sierra Leone's children. 'Imagine having hundreds of thousands of children displaced for several years,' he said.

'Suppose further,' the displaced teacher said, as we stood in his muddy camp, 'that those children were deeply traumatised by the horrors that they had seen. And then imagine that the vast majority of their teachers, those that are left, are traumatised as well, and ask yourself what future Sierra Leone has,' he said.

By any standards, Mrs Robinson's comparison of Sierra Leone with Kosovo was shocking. Here was the former president of Ireland, a highly respected European figure, saying that the human rights situation in Sierra Leone was worse than that in the Yugoslav province. It may be that a debate about which situation is worse is fruitless, like somehow comparing Hades with Hell. But the UN Human Rights Commissioner's comments do raise several questions.

If the situation in Sierra Leone is so bad, how come there are 50,000 NATO troops in Kosovo and just a few dozen unarmed UN observers in Sierra

Leone? If the needs are so huge in Sierra Leone, how come independent aid agencies there, such as Oxfam, say that their funds are being cut to help finance projects in Kosovo? And if it is objectively true, as no less a person than the UN Human Rights Commissioner says, how come journalists who report these things are sometimes accused of exaggerating?

I don't mind being accused of exaggerating. Back in 1994, before the extent of the genocide in Rwanda was widely accepted, lots of people said we journalists were overdramatising the situation. We were not. And now, perhaps it's not an exaggeration to suggest, just tentatively, that the international reaction to Sierra Leone might have been very different if all of those people with their limbs chopped off had been white.

6
Child Sorcerers

Jeremy Vine

Everyone was being blamed for the years of fighting which had devastated the Democratic Republic of Congo. Some families who were down on their luck were saying it was the fault of their own children, whom they accused of sorcery.
(16 October 1999)

The track that runs to the home of the Mahonda family is blocked by big rocks, so we stopped our jeep and walked. At the top of a slope we found their place, not the shack we were expecting, because this area is miserably poor, but a nicely situated house with solid walls and decent furniture. In front of it, an intense-faced Pandi Mahonda was trying to fix the motor which powers his maize grinder. Nothing remotely supernatural in this, you might think, as he ploughs his screwdriver blade into rusted troughs in the side of the motor. But actually it is taking on profound significance for the Mahonda family, who've added together a series of recent events that have befallen them, and have decided they've fallen victim to witchcraft.

The events are listed by Kalumbu Ngisa, Pandi's partner. Money went missing, she says. The icebox in the kitchen shattered. She was ill, and doctors couldn't help, and then she crashed her car. So what with all that and the grinder motor, she explains, the suspicion of sorcery fell on her two sons, aged eight and ten. It seemed to her and her friends that they were witches. I look at them, sitting either side of her. Nothing sinister in these plump faces, but there is fear in their eyes now for sure. Ikomba and Luwuabisa are the names of these two little boys.

It's becoming a craze in Kinshasa now. Because of crushing poverty, families feel bad luck is haunting them, and they lay the blame on their own children. Fourteen thousand have been thrown out of their homes in this one city, according to local child welfare organisations. In some ways they're the lucky ones; because if a family suddenly decides a son or daughter is guilty of witchcraft, that child can be in immediate peril.

That was the case with Angella, a fresh-faced ten-year-old, who told me that when her mother was hit by bad luck and decided she was a witch, family members tried to put her in a sack and dump her into a river. Then they wired her up and gave her electric shocks. But what happened afterwards to Angella is still more disturbing. Cast out, she ended up in a sect run by the self-styled Prophet Onokoko. There are dozens of sects like his. The Prophet is a broad-backed smiling charismatic Congolese man with gold-rimmed glasses, who walks fast and likes to dress in black. At his sect he 'delivers' children; meaning they go through a process where they're asked to 'vomit up the devil', as he puts it. He produces hazy Polaroid photographs from his inside breast pocket. They show various objects vomited by children. It makes disconcerting viewing to say the least.

There's a shell in the shape of a horn. That, he says, came from little Angella. After she vomited it she was at peace because the horn was a devil. Another photo shows a young smiling boy with a hugely bloated stomach. There is a flash of white over his shin, where the picture wasn't exposed properly but the Prophet says: 'That white mark is a devil in his leg. He had to be given several deliverances.'

We raise the case of the boy at the Kinshasa offices of Save the Children, where Mahimbo Mjoe has been monitoring cases of what are called *'enfants dits sorciers'*, children said to be sorcerers. He says Save the Children discovered that boy had died, because the procedures used to prepare children for exorcism damaged his insides so badly. In the sects, he says, children often have soap inserted into their anuses. The objects they vomit have been put into them unnaturally, Mr Mjoe tells us. 'Witnesses have seen it happen,' he says. 'As far as we're concerned,' he goes on bluntly, 'what's happening in Prophet Onokoko's organisation is child abuse pure and simple.'

We didn't film a session held to deliver young people, because we didn't want to encourage their maltreatment. But we saw a nineteen-year-old in a state of complete hysteria as her devil was supposedly 'delivered' and around fifty children watched, all knowing they would have to go through something just as intense before their families would take them back.

In a small room the Prophet meets the Mahondas. The two boys look very scared as a group of adults sing and pray around them, gradually getting more and more worked up. The Prophet is moved by a spirit to shout 'OUI', yes in French, which means the boys are witches. He shakes their hands and grins. The singing stops. 'Yes,' he says, 'it is confirmed.'

The boys will have to stay in the sect until their demons have been driven out.

There is a sub-plot here; the Italian government is giving this place thousands of dollars a month: building a dormitory in a place where charities say children are being abused. The Italian ambassador, Pietro Ballero, simply told us he didn't think it was his business to interfere with local customs. But the practices are causing grave concern among locals here, too. The police have arrested some sect leaders, but Prophet Onokoko continues his work with a cloak of respectability given to him, bizarrely, by the Italian government. It's depressing stuff. A war waged by adults has caused hardship which is blamed on children. In this sect alone 230 young souls wait for deliverance, but not the kind this Prophet is offering.

7

Farm Invaders

Ben Brown

Hundreds of white-owned farms were being taken over by squatters led by veterans of Zimbabwe's liberation struggle in the 1970s. (15 April 2000)

'You'll be okay,' the white farmer promised us. 'If the militants do come to get me,' he said, 'they'll arrive at the front gate. You can slip out through the back one.' It sounded like a perfect plan. Sadly, though, it had a fatal flaw, because when a few minutes later I watched them invade Mike Mason's farm in the northern district of Tengue I realised with a growing sense of nausea that they were blocking off both gates simultaneously; it was a two-pronged attack cutting off our escape route. We were well and truly trapped.

Before, reporters have always covered these land grabs from the outside, but we were on the inside and for the next few hours we would be stranded here, under siege, effectively held hostage by about 200 extremists. They were armed with their usual array of clubs and machetes, knives and iron bars, and they were seething with what they see as historic injustice. I wouldn't have been so worried except that I knew mobs like these hate the press in general, especially the British press, with no greater demon in their eyes than the BBC. One of the leaders of the so-called 'war veterans', Rex Jesus, is particularly hostile to us and he was rumoured to be on his way. I'd been warned that whatever his name, this Jesus does not turn the other cheek.

But while I and my BBC colleagues were hiding and quivering with fear in the farmhouse, Mike Mason himself was calmly striding up to argue with the mob at his gates. They told him to sign a piece of paper handing over his land to them. He told them to go to hell, or words to that effect. The argument grew more heated. It ended with them breaking through his front gate and Mr Mason rapidly retreating inside his house with us right by his side.

Frantically we locked every door, every window, pulling curtains so they couldn't see us. With great foresight Mike Mason had evacuated his wife and three young children just a few hours earlier. Now the militants were inside the compound and baying for our blood. They kept banging on the doors, telling Mr Mason he should let them come in and search his home. They suspected he was a member of the MDC, the party opposed to President Mugabe. Coolly Mr Mason used his radio to call in help from fellow white farmers nearby and from the local police, but there weren't nearly enough of either to disperse the increasingly menacing mob.

By now we'd sealed ourselves into a small corridor. The leaders of the militants were at the window shouting in at Mr Mason, again demanding that he sign away his life's work to them. He told them he'd only do so if ordered by the government. They said they were the government. I was so alarmed at the prospect of the crowd bursting in and beating us up or worse that I wanted to say to Mr Mason: 'Come on, just sign the piece of paper, just give them what they want.' Anything to get them away from here. Anything to save our skins. But these farmers are made of sterner stuff than that and I was rather ashamed of myself.

After about three hours of growing terror, Mr Mason decided to help us make a break for it. But the mob were in a state of total frenzy now and at the back gates they started attacking him, beating him across the head, the chest, the arms. Some of them surrounded our car as we attempted to drive out. They were rocking it, trying to turn it over with us inside. We hastily abandoned the vehicle, sprinting back to the relative safety of the house, the furious crowd at our heels.

Later a police superintendent finally managed to persuade the farm invaders they should let us make an undignified exit and we did so with huge relief, though to get out we had to pretend we were visiting tourists; we carried a suitcase stuffed with some old clothes from Mr Mason's bedroom and we left behind our television equipment.

These are dangerous days in Zimbabwe, as President Mugabe lets his country slide into ever greater economic and social chaos. And dangerous not only for the whites here; some of Mr Mason's black farm labourers were also badly beaten up by the mob. Increasingly farm workers want to fight back against the invaders who threaten their livelihoods. It's not just black against white, it's black against black as well, and Zimbabwe approaches the twentieth anniversary of her independence next week with a sense of terrible foreboding.

8
Passport for Sale

Cathy Jenkins

Living in Somalia could be a difficult business. Acquiring a Somali passport was much easier. (27 January 2001)

Somalis like to say that Bakkara Market in Mogadishu is the biggest in Africa. I don't know whether this is true, but it is certainly a maze of narrow alleyways and once inside you lose all sense of direction. Somalis also boast that there is nothing you could possibly want that you can't buy in Bakkara Market. The open-fronted kiosks are piled high with goods imported from all over the world, duty free of course. But real business is often done in the small rooms behind the counters.

I'd come to the market to see Mr Abdul Kadir Ali Mohammed. He owns a photographic studio and the reason I particularly wanted to see him was that, as well as doing passport photographs, I'd heard that he would also issue me with the passport itself – that is, a Somali passport. Since in war-torn Somalia there is no immigration department, if Somalis want to travel anywhere they have to arrange their travel documents themselves.

It is a task which Abdul Kadir and others like him have cheerfully taken on, not least because it's a very profitable business. In his studio I have the choice of buying a diplomatic passport or a normal one. I opt for the latter, since the prospect of becoming an instant Somali is intriguing enough, and at thirty dollars I think it's a fair price for the opportunity.

The process of my becoming a Somali citizen lasts about fifteen minutes. That includes the time taken by Abdul Kadir's assistant, Said Afrah Guled, to snap a new photograph. The resulting image is very like the photograph I have in my usual passport, which clearly states that I'm a British citizen. This doesn't bother Abdul Kadir. Nor does the fact that neither my father's name, Waldo Stephen Howell Jenkins, nor that of my mother, Dorothy Margaret

Jenkins, suggests in any way that I might hail from an ancient Somali family. My parents are in fact Welsh. But never mind.

All these details, plus my date of birth, my profession and my place of residence – Mogadishu, of course – are carefully recorded on page three of my passport. My photograph is affixed to page two, and I'm invited to sign my name just below. This done, Abdul Kadir stamps the page twice, scribbles a signature which is not his own but that of a former deputy director of immigration whose name appears on the stamp, and hands it to me. I have, it appears, just become a Somali and I'm roundly congratulated by everyone in the shop.

Despite allowing their country to fall into a state which the rest of the world calls anarchy, Somalis are extremely proud of, well, being Somali, and they empathise completely with my wanting to be one, too. My passport is green with the words 'Somali Democratic Republic', written across the top. The Somali flag, blue with a white star, is in the middle.

Leaving Somalia, I'm a bit sad that I don't manage to get an exit stamp on my visa page. I fly out of Mogadishu on a small plane which has just delivered a consignment of khat, the mildly narcotic leaf which is widely chewed by Somalis and which is flown in every day from Kenya. There are no officials checking my documents as I climb aboard. But I do get the only seat on the plane which has a seatbelt. Perhaps the pilot thought I was the sort of Somali who would naturally hold a diplomatic passport.

9

A Proposal

Ishbel Matheson

A flight into Sudan, where civil war had continued unchecked for nearly twenty years, led to a meeting with one of Africa's last warrior tribes. (22 June 2002)

Our plane dropped out of the sky, and skidded bumpily to a halt. We could feel the heat already, prickling our skin. 'We'll be on the ground for just ten minutes,' said the man from the Norwegian aid agency. 'We need to refuel.' We climbed out of the plane, on to the hot dust. Through the yellow savannah grass and delicate acacia trees, tall warriors, brightly dressed women and a ragtag of merry children came towards us. We carried mineral water. They carried AK47 rifles. We hadn't landed in just any part of Sudan. This was Topoza country.

We had heard all about the Topoza on our flight across the green mountains which mark the boundary between Kenya, Uganda and Sudan. Our guide was a loquacious former Catholic priest with many years experience in the south. There are several warlike tribes around here, but the Topoza, in his view, were the most bloodthirsty. 'The Topoza, they don't take prisoners,' hissed the priest. 'They would kill you and enjoy it.' Fortunately for us, the Topoza were in the mood for visitors. A small crowd clustered around. They stared. We stared back.

Many of the women were bare-breasted, their shining dark torsos and faces adorned with symmetrical scars. They wore intricate bead collars and bracelets of red, green and yellow. Their hair curled in dainty dreadlocks. They were extraordinarily beautiful. I, on the other hand, was treated more like an exotic creature in a zoo. Hands reached out, daringly, to touch my white skin. The freckles were rubbed to see if they would disappear. Then, my soft fair hair was gently stroked.

They gestured towards a bald American colleague, asking: 'Where is his hair?' He rubbed his chest. They giggled. 'And on my legs,' he said. He pulled up his trousers to show a very hairy white leg. They screamed with laughter. One of the women looked at me. She pointed to her breast and then at my chest. Another pulled down her wrap, to show her breast. The message was clear: let's see yours.

Listeners, I did not reveal my biggest assets to the Topoza warrior women. I did, however, by way of compensation, offer them a flash of my belly button. The reaction, I am pleased to report, was pretty close to ecstatic. All of this took longer than ten minutes. An hour later there was still no sign of the fuel. The pilot was arguing loudly with someone on the other end of a satellite phone. We settled in for a long wait.

A herd of cows wandered past, their bells ringing gently. The Topoza, like other pastoralist tribes, judge wealth in terms of cattle. 'How many cows do you think I would be worth?' I asked an old Topoza man, who'd been standing for some time on one leg, leaning on his stick. He leaned back on his stick, sucked his teeth and cast a swift, practised eye over the merchandise. After some consideration, he held up two fingers. 'Two!' I said incredulously. 'You must be joking.' Apparently, the old man thought I would be no good for heavy work.

I found some shade beside the plane with a Kenyan colleague. 'Do you know,' he said, looking at the naked children running past, 'I can't believe that people still live like this in Africa.' And theirs is, indeed, a vanishing way of life. The warriors of East Africa, the Masai, the Karamajong, the Turkana, are being forced to abandon their nomadic ways, to lay down their arms and send their children to school. Governments here seem to see these tribes, and their wild, unfettered ways, as an affront to modernisation.

The Topoza, perhaps paradoxically, have a better chance of surviving. They are after all in Sudan, a country that's been at war for nearly two decades. Peace would bring schools, longer lives and do-gooders from across the world. You don't get the impression that the Topoza are much interested in all of that. The pieces of modern technology from our world, the satellite phones, laptop computers, cameras and sound recorders, scarcely attracted a second glance.

I lay under an acacia tree, watching the large butterflies flap past, smelling the fragrant, clean air. The old man squatted beside me. He held up three fingers. He was upping his offer. It happened to be my birthday; I'm not getting any younger and am of an age when a woman really should be thinking of getting married. The fuel truck was lumbering through the bush

towards us. This was decision time. I looked at the blue sky, with its little
puffs of white cloud, picked up my bottle of mineral water and headed back
to the plane.

10
Celebration in Mozambique

Barnaby Phillips

Celebrations were held across this southern African country to mark the tenth anniversary of the peace accord which brought a long-running civil war to an end. Barnaby Phillips, who lived there in the early nineties, went back to see how the country had changed. (3 October 2002)

I was looking for my old flat, and I was sure I was in the right place. Eight years have passed since I left Mozambique, but my memories are vivid. It was my first foreign assignment, and I fell in love with the country. I had been back a day and had had no problems navigating my way around the capital Maputo, so I was in the right place, and yet everything looked so different.

Directly opposite the flat, where I remembered a ruined building full of homeless children, stood a gleaming skyscraper, at least twenty storeys high. On either side were new shops; new restaurants and hotels stretched down the street. Maputo has changed – dramatically. The sense of confidence is tangible, the signs of new investment everywhere.

I remember a charming but run-down city, its streets still littered with the rusting hulks of old cars which the Portuguese settlers left behind when they abandoned Mozambique back in 1975. Now the city is the hub of one of the fastest-growing economies in Africa. I remember the road from Maputo to South Africa being a single-lane track, pitted with potholes. You drove along it at your peril; there was the constant risk of bandit attack. These days, it is a well-maintained double-lane highway, and it takes the hordes of South African tourists and investors just a few hours to drive down from Johannesburg.

I have spent most of the past decade reporting from Africa. More often than not I was in countries which were obviously going backwards, where life was better twenty or thirty years ago than it is today. Sierra Leone,

Angola, even Nigeria, come into that category. But as Mozambicans mark ten years of peace, they have reason to celebrate. Theirs is still one of the poorest countries in the world, but it is at least heading in the right direction.

The road north of Maputo was also a revelation. Back in 1993, the countryside on either side of that road was deserted; no people, no livestock. At regular intervals we used to come across the spooky remains of ambushed vehicles; in some of them you could still see skeletons of those who had died a horrible death. Now that same countryside is alive with activity. People are farming; they have goats and chickens. The sad little towns we used to pass through are now bustling, with shops and cafés and garages. Economists say that too much of Mozambique's recent growth has been concentrated in Maputo, but I could see that much has changed for the better even in the countryside.

For the Mozambican leaders who signed the peace accord, this is a time of reflection. The president, Joaquim Chissano, told me that Mozambicans carry no hatred or rancour from the war. This seems incredible. The sixteen-year conflict was exceptionally brutal; civilians were killed indiscriminately, hospitals and schools deliberately targeted. But the president has a point. It is remarkable that, ever since the ceasefire was signed, Mozambique has never looked likely to return to war. In truth the fighting was to a large extent fuelled by outside forces; once the Cold War ended and South Africa abandoned apartheid, those forces melted away, and I don't think they will come back.

I remember very well the rebel leader Alfonso Dhlakama. His Renamo guerrillas had a bloodthirsty reputation. The first time I met him was deep in the bush, and he was in military fatigues. He has long since exchanged the uniform for smart suits. These days he looks a little older; his hair is going grey. In the garden of his comfortable Maputo home, he told me that Mozambique had changed for the better. But he said it's because he fought for democracy; it was he who convinced the ruling Frelimo party to abandon Marxism. I am not sure that everyone would agree with Mr Dhlakama's analysis, but perhaps it's more important that he seems content to play the role of civilian politician and leader of the opposition.

Mozambique's progress is still fragile, and it has come at a price. Economic and political liberalisation have made for new opportunities to make money; they have also led to rampant abuses. 'Everybody is at it,' a leading lawyer told me. 'There's corruption all over, in the judiciary, in the police, in the government.'

In the 1970s and 1980s Mozambique was a country led by idealists, people who believed they were building a fairer, better society. Now too many prominent Mozambicans seem too interested in making money – fast. And woe betide those who stand in their way. Maputo is still in shock from the murder two years ago of journalist Carlos Cardoso. Cardoso had got too close to a major banking scandal and he was gunned down in the streets. No one has stood trial for the murder and last month one of the suspected assassins somehow escaped from a maximum-security prison. It is clear that powerful people have ugly secrets to hide.

'Perhaps,' one old journalist friend told me, 'the war destroyed much more than we ever imagined.' He said he always thought that it would only take a year or two to repair the damage. 'But now, ten years on, I see how much still remains to be done; not just to repair buildings, but to repair a whole society,' he said. Well, he's right, of course. But in a continent dominated by bad news, let's salute Mozambicans, who have made a pretty good start, and who are now daring to dream of a better future.

11
Seven Funeral Choirs

Alastair Leithead

Of all the African countries affected by HIV/AIDS, South Africa was among the hardest hit. Thousands of orphans were being left to fend for themselves. Yet correspondents covering the story were finding it difficult to secure the attention of their editors and listeners back in the UK. (20 May 2004)

I just do not know whose story to tell you first. Maybe it should be that of Nonhlanhla, the young mother so stricken by AIDS that she struggles to carry water the fifty metres or so from the nearest tap to cook for her children, one a baby of eighteen months who, like his mother, is infected and will soon die.

Perhaps it should be that of Mimi, who is HIV-positive, but is doing well on her drugs that postpone the deadly outcome of the virus. She can afford the pills because she sings in a choir where all fifteen members are infected and their tours and CD sales make enough money to buy the drugs.

Or it could be that of the doctors who cannot afford to give the medication, or the volunteers who visit the sick in their homes, doing little more than giving comfort, or the grandparents who have watched their children die and now tend to parentless grandchildren.

These stories can be told ten thousand times over in a country where 600 people die every day of AIDS-related illnesses. Imagine, 600 people every day! If a plane crashed and killed 600 people in South Africa, there would be a huge international response. If that happened every day for a week, the world would make sure it never happened again. But it is just not news, because it happens every day.

Covering the AIDS epidemic as a journalist, sometimes you have to let such suffering wash over you. It is the only way. You struggle to find the words, new words, to describe the extent of this disaster.

The story I will tell you is one that caught me by surprise and brought it all into sharp focus. It is Gugu's story. She is a small, youthful-looking woman in her fifties with beautiful round eyes, a wonderful smile and a habit of fiddling with her necklace when she talks to you, like a shy schoolgirl. She lives in her small mud shack with her children. She approached us, smiling and keen to talk about politics, which I was covering ahead of the South African election, the third since the end of apartheid. She was bright, intelligent and opinionated. And in her interview she described her life, what little had changed in ten years and how she was still living in poverty.

Suddenly and unexpectedly, she began to sob in the most terrible and pitiful way. 'Come on, Gugu,' I said to her. 'What's wrong?' Then she spoke, fast and through tears, of her awful secret. That she was HIV-positive, she had just been tested, she was getting sick, her joints were hurting, she was weak, and what, she wondered, would happen to the children? The house would be taken away, they would have no one to look after them, they would not go to school. I just did not know what to say. I felt all her pain hit me in a moment. The impact is harder when the words are so unexpected.

Under the hot sun on a Saturday afternoon a couple of weeks later, my mind drifted back to Gugu. As I stood on the hillside in the cemetery, seven funeral choirs merged into a discordant cacophony; the buses brought mourners to and from the graveyard; every third one of them was probably HIV-positive. More graves lay open, waiting for a dozen church services to finish; a queue of hearses awaited their turn, as some of those 600 people were laid to rest. Soon Gugu will join them: the friendly, smiling face, the big eyes, the beads lying still, the orphaned children.

If Gugu's story isn't worth telling, then what is?

12

Massacre in Darfur

Hilary Andersson

The United Nations was describing the situation in the Sudanese region of Darfur as the world's worst humanitarian crisis. More than a million people had fled their homes after months of fighting. But this wasn't just a story about refugees; it was one of ethnic cleansing and mass murder. (13 November 2004)

Far above the desolate and windswept floors of Darfur's deserts lie the mountains of Jebel Mara. It's a mythical, remote part of the earth. As you approach it from the searing Sahara, the temperature drops, the grass grows long and high. It is a paradise, but of course it lies within a hell. Why is it that where the worst horrors happen nature always seems to be indulgent?

It took two months to find a way of getting inside Jebel Mara. It involved slipping out of government territory secretly, travelling cross-country, contacting rebel commanders on satellite phones and picking our way through lands still simmering with violence; lands that have been almost completely emptied of one ethnic group, Sudan's black Africans.

We drove the route and we reached the mountains. Our contact, a rebel spokesman, had travelled two days by donkey from the other direction to meet us. And then there we were, in one of the most remote corners of the earth. The point of our journey was to find out what had happened in these mountains. Because the real story of Darfur has never been told.

The refugee camps are just a symptom of the problem. There is no drought in Darfur; there have been incredible rains: Darfur has flowed with a wealth of water this year. Water that's flushed sewage through camps, instead of nourishing the people.

Darfur's nightmare is man-made, orchestrated, systematic, even perfected. Darfur is in the middle of a gigantic wave of ethnic killings. That is what has forced the refugees into the camps. That is what is still forcing new refugees to the camps in huge numbers. There were a million in the camps once, now it's nearer two million. The world may think the problem is getting better because Sudan's government finally let aid through, but it's not; it's getting worse.

For months, when the world first woke up, too late, to Darfur's crisis, I was told stories by refugees of fields of bodies lying beyond the camps' perimeters. But we could never get to them. It was too dangerous. It is possible that genocide has been occurring in Darfur for two years, and that it is occurring right now as I speak. We, the world, have been ignoring it.

Up in the Jebel Mara mountains we reached the town of Kidinyir, a town that was utterly silent, except for birdsong. The destruction was so complete and weirdly spectacular that it looked surreal. In the school the books had been torn into shreds. The children's desks were all at angles. We found the women who had survived the attacks on the town living in small groups in the mountains. We catalogued their stories.

The attack was like most others in Darfur. Government planes bombed from the air while their Arab militia, known as the Jenjaweed, waited outside, surrounding the town. As the civilians tried to escape the Jenjaweed moved in, shooting anyone they could. The killers went into the school, into the classroom of a bright twenty-three-year-old teacher called Hikma. Children began to jump out of the windows. The militia men shot at them at close range.

We counted the mothers of eighty children who had been killed in a series of attacks on Kidinyir. It seems unbelievable because Kidinyir is a small town, but here it was; names, stories. Awful details.

The Jenjaweed grabbed Hikma and shouted racial abuse; they called her a slave, they called her stupid because she was from a black African tribe. Then two men began to rape her; they took it in turns, one raping whilst the other held a gun at her. It lasted two hours.

Fatima was down the road. Her entire village was on fire. The Jenjaweed burst into her courtyard. Her hut was in flames. They grabbed her three-year-old boy and threw him into the fire. He burnt to death. Some of these stories would be hard to believe except I have heard them so often and in such horrific detail. Every person we interviewed from Kidinyir collapsed in tears while they were speaking.

There is another town, Sallaya, where a few months ago they burnt more than thirty people alive, first tying them up. We spoke to a man who watched it all through a crack in his wall. He could feel the heat of the fire in his village bearing down on him, and thought he would burn to death himself.

So what does the world do? At the moment we are doing nothing at all that is helping to stop the violence. Part of that is because, almost two years after the killings began, most nations, Britain included, can't decide whether or not to use the word genocide – perhaps because the word implies a moral imperative to act, and intervention is not in fashion? Genocide is a powerful and dangerous word which should never be used lightly. It has a strict legal definition, which is not about the scale of the killings, but the intention behind them. Genocide is the deliberate attempt to destroy an ethnic group in whole or in part. This may be happening in Darfur. Surely if genocide, the ultimate crime against humanity, matters, we should at least have the courage to define where it is happening and quickly; and then either act, or admit we live in a world that tolerates it.

In Stanley's Footsteps

Tim Butcher

They said it couldn't be done. That it was impossible today to do what Henry Morton Stanley, the Welsh-born explorer, had done almost 130 years ago when he became the first white man to chart Africa's mightiest river, the Congo. A trip in his footsteps would not just be foolhardy, it could be suicidal. (23 December 2004)

Early research showed the sceptics could be right. The overland bit of the trip from Lake Tanganyika to the river's headwaters cuts through territory where cannibalism is still practised and the network of roads, riverboats and railways set up by Belgian colonialists has crumbled to nothing in the war, rebellion and chaos since they left in 1960.

And if rebels and logistics don't get you, there is always disease. Leprosy has returned, malaria is everywhere, and what about Ebola, the ghastly haemorrhagic fever named after the Congo tributary where it was discovered?

But I refused to believe a part of the world could simply slip off the map. For four years I badgered aid groups, missionaries, politicians, diplomats, peacekeepers and even pygmies. And after a lull in the Congo's latest civil war I journeyed to the western shore of Lake Tanganyika where Stanley made landfall in September 1876 aboard the *Lady Alice*, a collapsible rowing boat built on the Thames, named after his fiancée and carried by bearers halfway across Africa from Zanzibar.

'I can show you where Stanley is buried here in the village,' slurred Idi Kavunja, chief of the lakeside village of Mtowa. He was hopelessly drunk and talking nonsense; Stanley is buried in England. But then he became aggressive and abusive: 'Give me money' were the last words I made out. It was a sad start.

The local town of Kalemie was no less disappointing. Albertville under the Belgians, it was once a transport hub connecting trains loaded with rice, cotton and produce from the huge Congolese hinterland with boats to Tanganyika and beyond. My mother passed through here in 1959, the last year of Belgian rule, at a time when it was fully integrated in Africa's transport network. Now it is cut off, abandoned and cholera-ridden.

'I remember you could hear the whistles of the liners as they left the port and sometimes you could even hear the band playing on the top deck in first class,' Geneviève Nagant said. She arrived here from Belgium in 1951 as a young colonial social worker and never left. On her wall she had paintings, tribal stick figures on a black background, just like ones my mum purchased all those years ago. But in the garden she had something different, a crater from a rocket blast. Albertville has been fought over repeatedly, by Che Guevara, the left-wing revolutionary, Mike Hoare, the mercenary, and countless others.

'Why do you stay?' I asked the unmarried mademoiselle. 'Because when you plant a seed you must tend it before it will blossom' was her elegant response.

The 600-mile overland hike to the upper Congo was a journey back in time. Buses used to cross this region daily along a Belgian road network maintained by *'cantonniers'*, or local labourers. All that has gone, washed away by seasonal rains and consumed by the advancing Equatorial forest.

United Nations peacekeepers and aid groups don't venture into these parts, the stronghold of black magic-using Mai-Mai rebels and murderous Interahamwe fugitives from Rwanda.

So I was scared when I left the lake on a small motorbike, picking my way along tracks just thirty centimetres wide. I passed a village where a skull and other human bones lay on the ground, the result of some forgotten, bloody skirmish. I biked through burnt-down, abandoned villages and caught the occasional glimpse of people in rags who ran away, petrified of outsiders.

And the secret weapon to get me through these terrors? A pygmy called George Mbuyu, a tiny man who stared down red-eyed Mai-Mai wearing hideous necklaces of animal teeth, body parts and fetishes. 'Don't worry, I know these people. They will not hurt you,' he said reassuringly. He might have only come up to my chest, but in the badlands of north Katanga he was a giant.

But the most moving sight? The Ho Chi Minh trail of Congolese survival: cadaverous men we saw by the hundred in the middle of nowhere, pushing pedal-less bicycles laden with jars of palm oil for hundreds and hundreds of miles, hoping to make the equivalent of a few pounds by trading them for another commodity like salt. Pencil-thin, these men were on six-week round trips, drinking when they passed a stream, eating what they could scavenge in the bush and sleeping on the trail when the sun went down. There are no shops here, no houses to rest in, no respite from the brooding, endless forest.

'There is nothing in my home town, Kongolo; this is my only chance to feed my family,' Muke Nguy said before heaving his tottering bike down the trail. 'What's that?' I asked, pointing at a loop of vine on his shoulder. 'My bicycle repair kit,' he said. The sap makes a gummy resin, ideal for mending flat tyres. I shook my head in sorry disbelief. Think how great Africa could be if the skills and talents of its people were released from survival and self-preservation.

In 600 miles I saw not one other working motorised vehicle. I met village elders who told me VW Beetles used to pass regularly in the sixties, but now their own teenage children had never seen a car. This is a part of the world in regression. The hands of the Congolese clock are not just standing still, they are spinning backwards.

At night I fell asleep in thatched mud huts re-reading Stanley's diary. He too wrote of burnt-down villages and human skulls littering the ground. Has nothing changed?

When I first glimpsed the river, it was huge. Two thousand miles upstream from the Atlantic Ocean, it was already wider than the Thames in London. But what should be one of the great transport arteries of Africa, shuttling goods and people along a fluvial superhighway, was clotted.

It took weeks to negotiate my way downriver past towns like Kibombo, an eerie-looking place where I spent a night. People here cannot remember when the electricity last worked, and I saw a ghostly scene of guttering palm-oil candles throwing shadows on the looming hulks of abandoned colonial-era buildings.

The riverside town of Kindu is now home to a large United Nations head-quarters, fitted out with air-conditioning, satellite uplinks for the internet and a canteen where I had my first fizzy drink for a month. Behind the razor wire these peacekeepers lived in blissful isolation. Most of them did not even know that not many years ago thirteen Italian peacekeepers had been dragged through these same streets, disembowelled by a mob and eaten.

It was shortly after leaving Kindu that I had my only truly serene moment in the Congo. There is not a single working Congolese motorboat on this stretch of the river; the rusting remains of a fleet of paddle steamers, tugs and barges can be seen rotting at various spots on the bank, and the only river traffic is made up of pirogues, canoes made from hollowed-out tree trunks.

One evening I took a pirogue and four paddlers and we headed into the midstream of the Congo just a short distance south of the Equator. The sun had set abruptly but, as the night rushed in and the sky, forest and river merged into one impenetrable whole, an amazing thing happened: an angry red moon rose full in the east. As the water lapped against the pirogue and the four paddlers sang a gentle Swahili harmony, I watched as the slow-climbing moon shed light over one of the world's most benighted regions.

A few days later and I finally reached Kisangani, the City on the Bend in the River. Once an industrial and intellectual centre where multinationals like Unilever maintained large factories, it is now broken. It used to be called Stanleyville, in honour of the explorer who first passed here in a flurry of poisoned arrows and spears from Wagenia tribesmen rightly suspicious of outsiders.

All traces of Stanley have been removed. Where his statue once stood there is now just an empty plinth and a spring where hookers from the local Hotel Des Chutes wash their smalls.

A few whites cling on: a French-born trader who married well into the clan of Mobutu Sese Seko, the post-independence dictator who single-handedly bankrupted the country then known as Zaire; a Greek trucker who somehow maintains the town's tatty Hellenic Club with its daily menu of tzatziki and moussaka.

And there was eighty-three-year-old Father Leon, a tiny, beer-drinking, chain-smoking priest who came from Belgium to the Congo in 1947. He remembers clearly 24 November 1964, the day Belgian paratroopers dropped into Stanleyville to rescue him from Mai-Mai rebels. But the paratroopers only landed on the right bank of the river. On the left, ten priests and fifteen nuns were tortured and murdered.

'I still have a picture of Heinrich Verberne, who was killed that day. He was standing in for me when he was captured by the rebels, so perhaps it should have been me,' Father Leon said quietly. 'Why are you still here after all these years, after all these horrors? I must go where there is need and in the Congo the need is great.'

It took weeks to find a boat downstream towards Kinshasa and the Atlantic Ocean, where Stanley's epic journey ended on 9 August 1877. The national transport company has long since stopped operating and I was forced to board a Congolese boat chartered by the UN. For days it crawled along the river's sweeping arch across central Africa.

Penniless villagers would paddle out in pirogues and bravely try to latch on to our boat to sell the crew smoked monkey, fresh fish, edible grubs or cassava bread. It was a hazardous exercise and often they were overwhelmed, sunk by our wash, shouting forlornly for us to stop. It was a scene Stanley himself would have recognised, and after my journey was over it stayed with me as the perfect metaphor for the region: brave, talented people are simply being left behind, wallowing in the mighty Congo river as the rest of the world steams by.

The Middle East

1

Farces of Freedom

Tim Llewellyn

The release of another British hostage, the former Battle of Britain pilot Jackie Mann, was greeted with obvious delight and relief in the West. Other captives were to follow, including the Archbishop of Canterbury's special envoy, Terry Waite. But amid the euphoria, seasoned Middle East observers saw the whole affair as a maudlin and cynical exercise. (28 September 1991)

The ritual begins when word reaches Damascus from Beirut by devious means that the hostage is free, and that the kidnappers have handed him over to Syrian military intelligence. After they have looked him over at the former Beau Rivage Hotel on Beirut's waterfront, the dark tower that now houses the Syrian spooks, the men who really run Lebanon, the freed man is then subjected to a wild, two-hour ride over the mountains of Lebanon to Damascus.

There he is delivered to the Syrian Foreign Ministry, a building that combines the grandeur of a post-war Midlands town hall with the comfort of a 1950s railway station waiting room. He is then in the hands of the Syrian officials and the Western ambassador concerned. After a quick check to make sure that the ex-hostage is presentable (and sane), he is led in to face the public, that is to say the cameras. This is his first contact with what might pass for the real world after his years of isolation, abuse, deprivation, torture, hopelessness, depression and despair.

Escorted by the diplomats and officials, he is stood or seated between them, in front of the press, like a prisoner at the bar, blinking into the glare of the buzz-click-buzz of the camera shutters, while the homilies are read out. The Syrian minister thanks Syria for all it has done, whatever that might be, and makes hopeful noises; the Western diplomat does likewise, except that this week the British ambassador added to the fun by thanking the world's two great kidnapping and abduction nations, Iran and Israel, for all their help as well; presumably this was on the grounds that they are now giving it all up, for the time being anyway.

The prisoner at the bar, I mean the free man, is then allowed his few carefully prepared words under close supervision. Usually these are bland, happy and grateful; but at least this week the much-reduced figure of old Jackie Mann, although his voice had been bullied out of him by his captors, managed to convey to us that he was, rightfully and understandably, angry beyond articulation at the aimless evil to which he had been subjected.

But what no one seems to ask is, why is this all really necessary? For a start, other than running Lebanon now, what is Syria's role in all this? It is hard to believe that a country with as pervasive an inside knowledge of Lebanon, the Iranians, armed factions, criminals, drug smugglers and all the various villains who have been loose in Lebanon these past sixteen years did not know precisely where the hostages were. Let us be charitable and say the Syrians knew, but did nothing for fear of harming the captives in a gunfight. Did they pass on private assurances to the Western governments concerned? Were the relatives then privately advised that X was okay, or that Y needed this or that medicine?

There's no evidence to suggest any of this happened. And even if word did leak out, would the relatives or the press have been told? It seems that the Americans are already outraged that Jackie Mann has been allowed to tell the truth about his 865 days of purgatory. Perhaps Syria and Iran have put pressure on the kidnappers now that both countries want to be friends with the West again; and Syria, in its new and commanding role in Lebanon, is in a better position to exert such pressure. Certainly Syria could obstruct any release process if it so chose, which is worth bearing in mind. Is it a coincidence that no British hostage was freed until after Britain and Syria had renewed diplomatic relations earlier this year?

More obviously, Syria wants the kudos arising from a hostage release, however spurious, and it wants political control over the event. When my old friend Charles Glass, the American writer and journalist, escaped his Lebanese kidnappers in August 1987, after being held for two months, he was brought to Damascus in the time-honoured manner; he had no choice. As Charles says: 'When you're coming out of an experience like that, and you're in safe hands, you'll do anything, say anything, you're so grateful and so manipulatable.'

When Charles arrived in Damascus, an American diplomat told him he hadn't escaped at all; the Syrians had worked in their mysterious way and the kidnappers had allowed him to escape. So when his turn came to be prisoner at the bar he should thank the Syrians, and he did. What a coincidence, I thought at the time, that this was just when Syria and the United States were making strategic friends again after years of mutual distaste.

Hostages are a cottage industry for the Syrians, with everyone on the take: the hotels who house the hundreds of journalists and technicians and charge them double for their phone calls, calculating the room and phone bills at a completely artificial rate to the dollar; the thousands of dollars, both over and under the table, for allowing the media to use their satellites and facilities (a darkened air-conditioning duct in our case); the extra charges for expediting visas; the bribes at the airport for taking equipment in, taking it out, the bribes inside Syria for keeping it there. When this whole affair is over, there will be a terrible financial anticlimax in Syria, but hundreds if not thousands of much better-padded bank accounts.

Jackie Mann was released at 8.20 p.m. on Tuesday 24 September in West Beirut; he could have been safely back in the arms of the RAF within the hour, reunited with his wife a few moments later: the British base of Akrotiri on Cyprus is thirty minutes away by VC-10, or an hour by helicopter; England is just over four hours away. But it seems the last thing to be considered is the hostage's own comfort or convenience; there are many political and economic matters to be taken into account first.

2

The Shabbiest Farewell

Brian Barron

Brian Barron was the BBC's last correspondent in Aden in the mid-sixties before the British withdrew and the territory became independent as South Yemen. Three decades on, he was back seeing what had changed in the years since British rule.
(27 November 1997)

There can be few more evocative names than Steamer Point. Here for well over a hundred years the world's shipping, from rusting old tubs to the sleekest liners afloat, put in for fuel. Aden is just four miles off the busiest east–west trade route. Once it welcomed more ships than Singapore or Rotterdam. Generations of sailors, among them Joseph Conrad, have come ashore at Prince of Wales pier in the shadow of Little Ben, a colonial clock-tower that today has fallen on hard times. Beside the tower and its clock-face without hands is a ruined house, pockmarked with bullet and shell holes, a reminder of the half a dozen civil wars that have punctuated thirty violent years of independence.

The backstreets of Steamer Point are choked with hundreds of tons of uncollected rubbish; for Aden's goats, it is paradise. The souvenir shops that once prospered from steamship passengers are barred and shuttered. Only the Aziz bookshop is open. Mr Aziz, calm and collected in late middle age, sits in the doorway, clutching a large radio tuned to the BBC World Service. 'All the other shopkeepers have gone,' says Mr Aziz. 'They left because of the troubles. Because very few ships come here. They've gone back to India and Pakistan and the Gulf.'

A mile away is Mallaa Main Street, dubbed by Fleet Street headline writers in the sixties as 'Murder Mile'. Often the Arab nationalists in the independence struggle didn't differentiate between soldiers and civilians. One of my friends, a young English civil servant at the start of his career was shot in the back getting into his car. What a waste. What a pointless action. To be fair, the British forces were not paragons either.

One steamy morning in a nearby district I arrived to find Colonel Colin Mitchell, known to the media as Mad Mitch because of his gung-ho style, directing a group of squaddies who were stacking, like a butcher's delivery, the corpses of six Arabs on the pavement. They'd been shot as they tried to ambush a patrol. 'It was like shooting grouse,' said the colonel. 'A brace here and a brace there. It was over in seconds.'

A totally different version of such tragedies is displayed in Aden's Military Museum. Scattered throughout the dusty rooms are clapped-out bits of military hardware from the independence struggle and oil paintings depicting British brutality. The faded black and white photos of the stalwarts of the uprising, all in their twenties, all members of the NLF, the National Liberation Front, are the images of dead men.

Thirty years ago I watched them disembark at Khormaksar airbase just hours after the last British forces had left by helicopter. The NLF leadership had flown in to inherit their kingdom. Little was known about them except that they were Arabs from outlying provinces who'd been trained by George Habash and other Palestinian radicals in Lebanon.

Within minutes the new regime was talking about scientific socialism. Soon we realised that Britain's blunders had ushered in the Arab world's first Marxist state, named the People's Democratic Republic of South Yemen. For a while the comrades were hailed as liberators. In fact, they'd liquidated the only other Arab faction which posed a threat. In the two decades that followed they fell out and murdered each other one by one, a classic example of a revolution devouring its children.

With such a burden of recent history you might think that Aden would have had enough. A new course would be in order. In fact, they have tried, but with only mixed results. The opportunity came when the Soviet Union collapsed. Moscow had turned South Yemen into a client state. When the roubles ran out, the handful of surviving Aden revolutionaries were bankrupt and friendless. They sold their country's independence to their cousins across the border in North Yemen; the two countries were united as the Yemen Republic. It was an unequal alliance because there are six times more northerners than southerners. Three years ago the unhappy south tried to secede and civil war was the result. After besieging Aden the northerners finally won.

Today Adenis seem sullen. One Arab journalist told me: 'This is not unity, it's occupation. There is an incredible amount of resentment against northerners who've come down here and bought up prime buildings and commandeered what they want.' He finished with a warning: 'If nothing is done, there's going to be an explosion.' And explosions there have been in recent weeks: a series of bomb blasts blamed on southern dissidents. The secret police have rounded up scores of suspects.

Beneath the towering dark red walls of an extinct volcano nestles the Crater district. Bored men sit and squat in doorways. Women swaddled in black veils hurry past. Islam is ascendant, Marxism reviled. Apart from the soaring chorus of the calls to prayers five times a day, not much is going on here. Unemployment could be as high as seventy per cent of the population. For decades the Communist authorities bought the acquiescence of the people by employing them in a vast, Soviet-style bureaucracy. Private enterprise was banned. Now work is hard to find. The one glimmer of hope is a major project to redevelop Aden port with international help. It has become the forgotten destination of the seven seas.

Today, older Adenis look back on British rule with affection. The failure to provide durable institutions, the ugliness of the last two years of Pax Britannica, the indecent haste of the evacuation, all are excused or forgotten. No doubt twenty-three years of murder and tyranny, followed by seven years of tension and another civil war, are enough to gild the colonial era. But of all our imperial farewells, this still seems the shabbiest by far.

3
Bird Language

Chris Morris

Every day we hear more and more about the communications revolution and how it is changing our lives. The world, we are told, is getting smaller and we can talk to anyone anywhere at the click of a mouse. But for some people, like those living in Turkey's remote mountains near the Black Sea, even talking to the neighbours provides a hefty challenge. (13 January 2000)

———————————

I arrived at Halil Cindik's house as he was having a chat with his friend Kucuk. You know the sort of thing, just a couple of neighbours chewing the cud across the garden fence. Except in this case they were somewhat further apart, several hundred metres apart in fact, across a rather wide valley. They're used to it, of course, having grown up in this land of vibrant green mountains and steep wooded slopes near the southern shores of the Black Sea. Houses in the village of Kuskoy perch precariously above little more than thin air.

Now, the telephone only arrived in these parts a few years ago. So for generations if you did want to talk to your neighbours there was no choice. It was not so much sing for your supper as whistle down the wind. Kuskoy literally means the Bird Village and if you can't whistle, well, you're probably not from round here. I would try to give you a quick example, but sadly all I could manage was a rather unpleasant raspberry sound. I can accompany my favourite tune on the radio as well as anyone, but this is no ordinary whistle. Intensive training from my hosts on how precisely to angle my tongue and rest my forefinger on my front teeth produced only further embarrassment. In the end, I had to settle for another cup of tea and the dunce's hat in the corner.

Kuskoy's champion whistlers, on the other hand, do it loud and proud, with a decibel level anywhere between noticeable and ear-splitting. Halil and

Kucuk make it look and sound ever so easy, but ear-plugs could occasionally be an advantage. I wouldn't want to get caught in a heated argument on a long winter's night. And argue they can, because there's a whole language of whistles which about 1,000 people in and around Kuskoy use. Anything they can say in Turkish, they can whistle as well. And when your best friend is just across the valley but it takes an hour of rock scrambling to get there, it's a pretty useful talent to have.

At the moment they have twenty-nine separate whistled noises, one for each letter of the Turkish alphabet. But there could be more; just alter the angle of the tongue and away you go. Education in the fine art of whistling begins at an early age, and it's a bit like learning to talk; all the local kids pick it up in the end. Practice makes perfect, and the shrill sound of local chatter echoes down the valley more or less constantly. No one really knows exactly when it started, only why. But the writer Xenophon described people shouting across valleys in the same region more than 2,000 years ago. Long-distance whistling in Kuskoy is passed down from generation to generation, and it probably has a long history.

There are a handful of other villages around the world where the same tradition thrives in similar remote regions of Mexico, Greece and Spain. But Kuskoy believes it boasts the largest concentration of whistlers on the planet. It's determined that its language will not be allowed to wither and die as people move away from the village and modern technology intrudes into the mountains. Most people in the area are farmers of one sort or another, and they still whistle as part of their everyday business. News that a lorry might be coming to pick up the tea harvest, or that someone in the valley round the corner has some leaves to sell, whistles quickly through the community. It's much more than a gimmick.

But can this extraordinary language really survive the technological onslaught? Regular telephones were one thing, but mobiles and laptops are quite another. No telegraph poles, no fuss, and no need to venture out on to the roof to whistle across the valley in a sudden mountain storm. It is a significant threat, and the locals admit that sometimes they get a little lazy. But they are determined that what they call their 'bird language' will continue to flourish. As we all get swept along faster and faster by the giddy currents of the communications revolution, the message from Kuskoy is simple; that sometimes the old ways are still the best ones.

4

The Dinner Party

Jeremy Bowen

Jeremy Bowen was the BBC's Middle East correspondent, based in Jerusalem, for five years. As he prepared to leave, he looked back over a period in which the assassination of the Israeli prime minister Yitzhak Rabin had been a pivotal moment in the history of the region. (23 September 2000)

I heard a rustling in my garden the other morning. Was it just the breeze in the palm trees? I listened again. No, something, somebody was moving around. So I investigated. My visitor was an old lady, bent almost double, wearing a traditional Palestinian embroidered dress. She was working hard, harvesting prickly pears from the great bush of cactus down by the wall at the bottom of the garden. She did not stop when she saw me. The prickly pear, the fruit of the cactus, is a delicacy here at this time of year. Israelis call them *sabras*. They like them so much that they have adopted the name *sabra* as the nickname for native-born Israelis. Because, like the fruit, they say they are prickly on the outside and soft and sweet inside. Palestinians never really get the joke.

'I planted this cactus,' the old Palestinian lady said. 'I always come to take the fruit.' She pulled up handfuls of grass, which is long and dry and yellow like straw at this time of the summer. She rubbed the *sabras* with the dry grass and packed them in an old milk crate. Still bent double, she tied string around the milk crate when it was full and dragged it away.

This was not just a chance encounter with a neighbour. To start with, Palestinians do not live here any more. Our village is called Ein Karem. It is built around two wadis, river valleys which are wet in winter and dry in summer. There are beautiful old houses made of white and pink Jerusalem stone, fig and cypress trees, Moroccan synagogues, church bells and quiet lanes. Christians believe it is the birthplace of John the Baptist. For more than five years now, it has been my haven in what has quite often been a tense, violent and exhausting city.

Until July 1948, two months after Israel declared itself independent, Ein Karem was a Palestinian village. It still has a mosque; disused now, of course, because the Palestinians who lived here ran away, or were driven out by the advancing Israeli army.

When I signed a contract to rent a house in Ein Karem in March of 1995, I felt slightly uncomfortable about the history of the place. I used to say, look, the house is great, the village is lovely and this is not my war. It always sounded a bit hollow, to my ears at least. Once a Palestinian colleague, who was eating dinner in our house, offered, somewhat acidly, to take me to Balata refugee camp on the West Bank to see some of Ein Karem's original residents.

But now I do not feel at all defensive about living here. If the people here want peace, they must not try to unpick history. You cannot change what has happened. Instead, you have to find a way to live with it. Everybody who lives between the River Jordan and the Mediterranean, on the land that contains both Israel and what, one day, will be an independent Palestinian state, lives with the consequences of a single historical fact: Israel was created by war. In 1948, Zionists took the territory they needed to found their state by force. The only chance for peace is to come to terms with that, to realise that the land must be divided between the Arabs and the Jews. That, really, is what the peace process is all about.

More and more people here, I think the great majority on both sides, realise they are travelling down a one-way street; away from endless confrontation, and towards what?

Well, in the end I think it is going to be some sort of accommodation, maybe even peace. There will be more bloodshed along the way, but afterwards they are going to settle it around a conference table, and that is what has changed. The man who gave Israelis the decisive push that set them on their journey was the former general Yitzhak Rabin. On Saturday 4 November 1995, he was Israel's prime minister.

That night we had our first dinner party at our house in Ein Karem. Rabin was attending a peace rally in Tel Aviv. I did not think it would make a story for the evening news. Anyway, my competition, the ITN correspondent, was among our dinner guests. We were tucking into the main course when the bleepers and phones around the table erupted. Rabin had been shot. The dinner party broke up in about ten seconds. He died later that night, killed by a Jewish extremist. When we got home about three days later, the food was still on the table. The ITN fork, loaded with the next mouthful, was lying there, abandoned.

In many ways, everything that has happened between the Israelis and the Arabs ever since has come from that night. Rabin's assassination was a seismic event in Israel's history. Rabin was able to make the Israeli people feel safe in a way that nobody else could. He had had the guts to take difficult decisions and the vision to see that they were necessary. Making peace would still have been slow and difficult. But I think that had Rabin lived they would have got further, faster.

We had some tough times here after that night. Mistakes by his successor Shimon Peres helped to provoke a series of suicide attacks on buses and crowds of people that killed dozens of Israelis. Like everyone in Jerusalem, I started to feel very nervous when buses surrounded my car in a traffic jam. You could see people twitch visibly when they heard an ambulance siren. Had there been another attack? Two sirens would get people ringing home to check their families were safe. I met a friend, a colonel in the Israeli army, for lunch in Jerusalem. He told me that, even though he was carrying a gun, he would cross the street if he saw a group of young Palestinian men. 'After all,' he said, 'what if they blow themselves up?'

Israel put the West Bank and Gaza under closure for months at a time, and Palestinians suffered real hardship. At times Israeli soldiers would stop them travelling from village to village, let alone to their jobs in Israel. The Palestinian economy was devastated. More and more children in Gaza's refugee camps started suffering from malnutrition.

I thought one moment in that crisis said everything about Israel, about the insecurity that lies close to the surface in this country even though, in the Middle East, it is a superpower. One Monday afternoon in the spring of 1996 there was a suicide bomb attack in the centre of Tel Aviv. It was the fourth Israel had suffered in eight days. As I drove into Tel Aviv, still a couple of miles from the bomb, I saw men yelling and sprinting down the road. Cars raced around sounding their horns. People had started to panic. The cabinet met in emergency session and came very close to sending the army to reoccupy areas of the West Bank, which would have made matters much worse. But Israelis pulled themselves together quickly and got back on buses to go to work. This country can lurch from panic to resolve in a day.

I think Israeli insecurity comes from two main sources. First, it comes from the fact that the Israelis took their land by force and have had to fight to keep it. That will not go away until they make peace with the Arabs. More deeply, insecurity comes from Jewish history.

Most mornings when I am in Jerusalem I go running in the forest near Ein Karem. I always pass the iron gates of Yad Vashem, Israel's monument to the six million Jews who died in the Nazi holocaust. When the survivors came here, they were not treated very well by the Zionists, who had been fighting the Arabs and the British and occasionally each other. The Zionists saw themselves as strong, virile, independent; and too many of them thought that holocaust survivors were just the opposite. Some of the traumatised new immigrants were even taunted with the nickname 'Soapy' because of the Nazis' attempts to turn their victims into soap.

It is different now. The whole country comes to a halt when the sirens sound on Holocaust Day. People get out of their cars and stand to attention in the street. Buses pull over and the passengers get out of their seats. The noisiest people in the world fall silent for two minutes. When the sirens stop, Israelis drive off and resume their incessant mobile phone conversations as if they had never stopped.

Palestinians say they suffered their own holocaust in 1948, when nearly a million of them lost their homes to the advancing Israelis. To my mind, losing a home, even losing a land is not the same as genocide. But this should not be about comparing tragedies. Palestinians are still haunted by 1948; and they are still losing their land and their homes to Israel's territorial ambitions.

The first Christmas I was here we filmed a Palestinian farmer near Bethlehem. It was a perfect winter's day, which around Jerusalem means a deep blue sky and a temperature people in the UK dream of in June. The farmer's lambs leapt around a rocky landscape of pure biblical beauty. Two Christmases later I went back. The farmer was still there, but he had given up keeping sheep. A new Israeli road had been cut through his quiet valley. Earthmovers were tearing at a landscape that had not changed in 3,000 years to build houses for Jews. In classic Jerusalem fashion, Israel was putting more facts on the ground. Israelis dream of being accepted in the Middle East. Slowly, it is happening. The process would go faster if they were better neighbours. They need to learn that Arab lives are as precious as Jewish lives.

I was in Qana, in south Lebanon, the day that Israeli gunners shelled a United Nations camp, killing more than a hundred Lebanese civilians. Israel never apologised. They claimed that Hezbollah guerrillas had entered the camp and were threatening Israeli commandos who were in the area. Even if that was true, and it has never been proved, it is no excuse for killing a hundred defenceless people. That day I asked an Irish UN officer what would have happened if Hezbollah had killed a hundred Israeli civilians.

'Simple,' he said. 'Clinton would be at the funeral, we'd be in our bunkers and the Israelis would be in Beirut.'

Will I miss this place? Of course. I will miss the sunshine, the fiery sunsets that cover Jerusalem's hills with dazzling gold. I will miss the majesty of the Dome of the Rock, the shining mosque in Jerusalem's Old City. I will miss walking through Damascus Gate in the city walls and smelling the herbs sold by Palestinian women, mint, basil and zatar, which is thyme that grows wild in the hills of the West Bank. I will miss Israeli informality. When Yitzhak Rabin, as a young man, first went to armistice talks, someone had to show him how to knot a tie. This is a country where you can go to a funeral in a T-shirt. I will miss everything. But I know Jerusalem will always be here. And, with apologies to my successor as BBC Middle East correspondent, I will be back.

5

Life and Death in Jerusalem

Paul Adams

Paul Adams said he would never forget his stint working in the Middle East.
It wasn't just the range of stories he covered, the fighting between Israelis and
Palestinians and the attempts by the wider world to broker a lasting piece between
the two sides. No, Paul had another reason for believing that Jerusalem was a place
where he and his family would always belong. (14 April 2001)

A heavy blanket of English cloud hangs over Jerusalem. Drops of rain cling
to the mosquito netting. It's chilly and damp. But the seasons are chasing
each other across the sky. Twenty-four hours ago, I sat in the sun-drenched
garden in shirtsleeves, watching my two-year-old son, William, scamper-
ing on the grass, inspecting bugs, dancing in the sprinklers that water the
lawn. Summer will soon be here and the hills I see from my study window
will fade to brown under a bleached sky. The house is empty, every sound
echoing through rooms devoid of books, pictures and carpets. The material
distractions of three and a half years that have helped to create a sanctuary
from the turbulent world outside have all been shipped away.

In these last weeks, we have concentrated on making the most of life here;
one last picnic in the forest, one last barbecue on the magnificent rocky cliffs
overlooking the Dead Sea. Reminding ourselves that, for all the bitterness
that surrounds us, life here has been good.

But last night, as darkness fell, the sound of gunfire echoed once more
across the valley from the nearby Palestinian village of Beit Jala. The crack
and rattle of small arms followed by the heavy, shuddering sound of Israeli
helicopter gunships. William sometimes looks up when he hears the throbbing of rotor blades passing over the house. He points in the air and says
'opters'. Another year here and he would probably start to understand what
the 'opters' are doing. In time, he might even come to dread the sound, as

I do. For the sound of those helicopters haunts me, dragging my thoughts back to the end of last year.

On a cold, blustery night in November, I returned home with my wife Susanna. On a steep, curving road lined with olive trees, we stopped to watch events in Beit Jala. The gunships were overhead, firing into the village. Burning brightly, the rockets seemed to take an age to reach their targets. The spectacle was dramatic, but we were wrapped in our own thoughts of impending loss. The following day, we went back to the hospital where William had been born. I waited in the corridor while our second son was delivered, lived for a few moments and died. We had had a week or two to prepare ourselves; by now, we just wanted it to be over.

But as I waited, a doctor told me there had been an attack on a bus carrying Jewish children from a settlement in the Gaza Strip. Some of the children had been terribly maimed. I stared at the floor, where the jumbled patterns of tiles dissolved and resolved into faces, frozen in expressions of pain and horror. An Arab woman was wheeled by, gasping with the onset of labour. At the other end, the door to the nursery swung open; a newborn was being shown to its proud Jewish parents.

The hospital psychologist came by to see how I was doing. I didn't feel much like talking and mentioned the news from Gaza, hoping, I think, to deflect the conversation. The doctor shook her head. 'I don't understand,' she said. 'There's so much hatred. We just want to feel safe.' My mind churning with the hateful way of the world, I went to the recovery room to share a few moments with Susanna and the baby. Impossibly small, his eyes still shut and his arms folded in a protective gesture across his chest, it seemed he had heard all about the world outside and wanted nothing to do with it.

So much hatred and so much grief; the past seven months seem to have been about nothing else. But the sensitive hospital psychologist was missing the point. As the bombs explode, carrying away the lives of innocent civilians, it is simply not enough to talk of hate. Of course, it is there, welling up, visible on the burning streets of every town and refugee camp of the West Bank and Gaza Strip. But it does not spring from some innate predisposition, as many Israelis would seem to believe. Calling it anti-Semitism may be tempting, but it's wrong.

The Palestinians have ample reason to mistrust and resent their powerful overlord: the destruction of more than 400 of their villages following the establishment of the state of Israel in 1948; the exodus of hundreds of thousands of refugees, many of them driven from their homes by force of arms; the conquest of what remained of their homeland in 1967 and the subsequent decision to colonise the West Bank and Gaza Strip, a disastrous policy, illegal under international law, which lies at the very heart of today's violence.

In each case, Arab rejectionism helped to seal their doom, but the Palestinians can hardly be blamed for holding Israel, the victor, responsible for their suffering. The peace process, entered into by their own leadership and promising so much, came to be seen as the final insult.

Most Israelis do not understand that the Palestinian population feels cheated by the past seven years. They believe, wrongly, that most Palestinians now rule themselves, that the occupation no longer exists. That the uprising which erupted last September is nothing more than a brutal means of negotiation launched by a cynical Palestinian leadership.

In Gilo, the Jewish settlement which faces Beit Jala over a deep ravine, Israelis are dreaming of better days. The settlement, which sits on a hill, guarding the southern flank of Jerusalem, has been targeted repeatedly in recent months. The shots fired by Palestinian gunmen have done little damage, certainly not when compared to the gaping wounds inflicted by Israeli helicopters and tanks, but the threat of a bullet passing through a window has been traumatic enough. When the shooting began, in October, a wall of concrete blocks was quickly erected to shield Jewish homes on this new front line. The wall, and the tanks that took up positions on the hill overlooking Beit Jala, provided a vivid symbol of the new depths to which Israelis and Palestinians were plunging.

I returned to the wall recently, on a day of fog and driving rain, and found it covered by a mural. There, in gentle colours and soft lines, was, bizarrely, an idealised version of Beit Jala, the very Palestinian village the wall was put up to confront. The real Beit Jala is now a place where gunmen hide, waiting for nightfall. But the mural shows an idyllic, sunlit place, where the conflict no longer intrudes and the only Arab is an old man in traditional garb, apparently bearing a gift of fruit as he climbs the hill towards his Jewish neighbours in Gilo.

One day, perhaps not soon, the wall will be torn down and the two sides will look at each other without fear and suspicion. But for now it is, like the mural, little more than a fond hope. The past three and a half years have had their fill of fond hopes, all of them dashed.

Early last year, I travelled eagerly to Switzerland for a summit at which it was thought President Clinton would try to steer the Syrian leader, Hafez al-Assad, towards a deal with Israel. By the chilly waters of Lake Geneva it all came to nought. Two and a half months later, President Assad was dead. In July, another summit, at Camp David. Bill Clinton trying again, this time with Yasser Arafat and Ehud Barak. More high hopes and an even greater sense of disappointment when it, too, failed.

I still can't bring myself to part with a receipt from a nearby branch of Kentucky Fried Chicken. It records that I purchased something called a Combo Eight with three pieces of corn on the cob. But it also says: 'We welcome the summit and the prospects for peace.'

By the time the peacemakers made it to the Egyptian Red Sea resort of Taba, in January, it was all too late. The negotiations were real, some of the most fruitful in years, but Ehud Barak was kicked out of office a couple of weeks later and the talks counted for nothing. So many moments of hope, I confess I have allowed myself to be carried away more than once. And yet I leave Israelis and Palestinians in worse shape than I found them.

Israelis, who dream of getting on with their lives without the fear of being blown up on a bus, have retreated under a tough shell bearing the name of their new prime minister, Ariel Sharon. So far, it doesn't appear to have made them any safer. Palestinians, who yearn for statehood on equal terms, despair that Israel will ever give them the chance. More and more of them have come to believe that violence is the only way.

There is never a good time to leave, and this feels worse than most. To turn our backs on Israeli and Palestinian friends, every one of them fearful of what the coming months will bring, seems almost cowardly. 'Think of us,' they say, and we will, a great deal. But the situation here may get much worse before it improves. As the hills around our Jerusalem home fade to brown, a long, difficult summer lies ahead.

We buried William's brother up on Mount Scopus, among pine trees; Jerusalem's walls, spires and domes spread out below. In a city where the living so often invoke the dead as they lay claim to the land, where graves and bones are so important, we have inadvertently become part of something we never expected. We are leaving a piece of ourselves behind. The experience of life and death in Jerusalem has given us the feeling that we belong here. A dangerous sentiment perhaps, and a warning that it is time to leave.

6
Dinner with Arafat

Lyse Doucet

*The Palestinian leader, Yasser Arafat, was under mounting pressure to bring
to a halt attacks against Israel, its troops and its settlements. The Israeli prime
minister, Ariel Sharon, maintained that Arafat was irrelevant and he made it clear
he would work to develop an alternative Palestinian leadership. Chairman Arafat
was under virtual house arrest in his compound in Ramallah, but he was in no
mood to cave in. (14 February 2002)*

If Yasser Arafat was granted one wish, it would certainly be a Palestinian
state with Jerusalem as its capital. Once he had a touch of Jerusalem in his
life. The glorious turquoise blue of its sky was exactly the colour of his Volks-
wagen Beetle. When he told me about his car, he cast his eyes around the
dining room searching for the right shade, and there it was, in the panorama
running along the wall, a shimmering Jerusalem sky cradling the golden
Dome of the Rock.

His advisers around the table nodded in agreement; it was exactly that
colour. It is hard to imagine the symbol of the Palestinian struggle inside
that small gumdrop of a car, but maybe he didn't drive it that much. He
had seven cars then, including a Ford Thunderbird. That was when he
lived in Kuwait, a young and, it seems, successful engineer. But now Yasser
Arafat is seventy-two, under Israeli siege and on a low-fat diet. And, it has
to be said, he hasn't looked so well in years. There's a bounce in his walk
and his trembling lip, said to be a sign of Parkinson's disease, is under
control.

I took a long sideways look as I sat to his left, straining to see what tiny
pins he wore on his lapel. I could make out a Palestinian and an American
flag, the stars of the European Commission and there was a ridge across his
chest underneath his trademark fatigues. Was he wearing body armour?

Would it be rude to ask? What should you ask when you have dinner with the Palestinian leader? Conversation is a risky business.

I inspected the spread of salads, olives and cheese arranged along the table. Yasser Arafat made his way through his low-fat choices; vegetable soup followed by round slices of egg without the yolk, neatly chopped fruit and tidy squares of sesame bread, which he dipped in a black circle of poppy seed oil blended with honey. Every so often, he held out morsels for me to taste.

I asked him about the olive trees. Like Yasser Arafat, they are a symbol of Palestinian resistance. He said fifty per cent of these groves have been uprooted by the Israelis in the name of security. One of his aides piped up: 'We call them Roman trees, they have been on the land so long, 300 years.'

Yasser Arafat glared at him. 'Not 300 years,' he snarled. '2,000 years.' I felt for the man, who momentarily crumbled under his leader's piercing stare. Yasser Arafat, I realised that night, is a leader who does keep facts and figures in his head, and he's not one to suffer fools gladly. But he does like to talk about suffering; not his, but the suffering of his people.

When we retired to his office next door, I explained I would have to sit on his side of the desk to achieve the best radio recording. As the clock ticked past midnight, his command of English and his emotions gathered strength.

'What about Ariel Sharon's plans to isolate you and develop new leaders?' I asked. He burst out laughing with his wide Cheshire cat grin. 'If Mr Sharon thinks he will drive Yasser Arafat out, does he really have the measure of the man? He thrives under pressure.' The Palestinian leader reminisced about his days in Beirut in the 1980s, surrounded by Israeli tanks, warships and planes. And he recalled his days on the run, when he slipped in and out of Palestinian towns.

But that was Yasser Arafat of old. Now he is also the chairman of the Palestinian Authority, under pressure from Israel and the world to stop the violence. 'Would he arrest the thirty-three people on the list of the US Secretary of State Colin Powell?' I asked. 'Ask my security forces,' he fired back.

I asked him if he feared civil war, and he demanded to know if this was an interrogation. The temperature shot up a few degrees with every question. I could see his aides staring at me; one stood bolt upright, and then it seems I pushed the red button. I asked about the alleged Palestinian militant Raed Karni, who was said to be in prison, but it turned out he wasn't. Yasser Arafat exploded. 'This is not fair,' he shouted. 'Why have you come here with such bad questions?'

I protested that this was the question asked by every Western envoy. He leant so close I was only conscious of the iris of his eye, a milky grey-brown marble bulging from his face. His finger stabbed the little pocket of air between him and my cheek. 'Finished,' he declared. But what about Jerusalem, I insisted as calmly as I could. 'You will visit me there,' he cried. 'In my capital.'

Anger boiled over, partly I think because Yasser Arafat knew he had to get out of this corner, and partly because, like all Palestinians, he believes violence is not the issue; that the West has adopted Israel's approach and does not see it for what it is, a just resistance to Israeli occupation.

The interview was over and I had seen a glimpse of the fighter. I told him so and I think it pleased him; he planted a kiss on each of my cheeks and signed some photographs. As we drove away in one of his official cars, I heard a haunting strain coming from the vehicle's radio, the song written in 1995 to mark the assassination of Yitzhak Rabin, the only Israeli prime minister Yasser Arafat remembers as a man of peace and a friend. The Palestinian official in the car quickly shut the radio off, realising it was tuned to an Israeli channel. As it cut out, a dark silence seemed to envelop Yasser Arafat's compound.

Zina's Story

Stephen Sackur

As the Americans carried out a succession of bombing raids on Saddam Hussein's capital, Baghdad, events were being followed closely in one household in Brussels. (24 May 2003)

'They've bombed Mansour,' says the woman on the sofa, not taking her eyes off the television screen. She's looking at grainy night-time footage of Iraqis standing bemused in front of a black gash in the ground. 'Four 2,000-pound bombs ...' the reporter intones. 'The building, a restaurant. Saddam Hussein was said to have entered just forty minutes before the strike ...' The woman is frowning, staring intently at the images. Looking for clues. And as she stares she's trying, trying so hard, to remember. Back twenty-five years, back from womanhood to childhood, back to her Mansour. Heat, dust, distant laughter; memories of a big villa on a broad Baghdad avenue. Could this be it? Could the Americans have dropped their bunker-busting bombs on her street? However hard she stares, the woman can't be sure. Until she was fourteen years old Mansour was her home; now it's an idea in her head, a longing in her heart. This confusion of images and impulses is what it means to be an Iraqi exile in wartime.

The woman on the sofa is one of millions of souls driven from Iraq by the cruelty of Saddam Hussein. She is also my wife. Zina's story isn't unique, it isn't special; in fact, it is numbingly familiar. Her father was from Sinjar, a hill village in the north. He established a business in Baghdad, did well, lived well. But all the while Iraq was being slowly strangled by the fascism of the Ba'ath party. For Zina, the schoolgirl, that meant little more than mandatory marches in oppressive heat, mindless chants in praise of Saddam Hussein. But for her father it meant grave danger. As the political atmosphere worsened, Zina was sent abroad to boarding school. It was there, in cold, wet England, that she was told her father was dead, executed by Saddam's enforcers. Her mother was placed under house arrest and then kicked out of the country after a terrifying year. The family hasn't been able to set foot in Iraq since.

There have been strange twists on the road from then to now. In 1991, Zina and I were about to get married. I was sent out to cover the first Gulf War by the BBC; for a few short weeks I believed I might bring her first news of her country's liberation from tyranny; but it wasn't to be. The year afterwards we settled in Cairo. Before one reporting trip to Baghdad I naively suggested to Zina that I might visit her former home, the villa in Mansour. She looked at me as if I were mad. 'As soon as you do that, they'll be interrogating the neighbours. Stay away,' she said. She was right.

We've had three children in the course of our travels. They love to listen to their mother's tales of Baghdad, but to them Iraq shimmers untouchable on a distant horizon. Ironically the two youngest were born in the United States. American passports they could have, Iraqi passports they could not. Maybe that will change now. The tyrant's grip on this ancient land has been conclusively loosened. For the first time in three decades Iraqis have that most precious commodity, hope of something better. When the time is right Zina will make the journey home, to trace the fragments of a shattered childhood. But for now she must wait. And listen to her husband's tales from the city she left behind.

Before my first visit to Baghdad after the war my wife handed me a scrap of paper: 'Shari-al-Emiraat – Emirates Street', Zina had scrawled on it. Followed by a cryptic number: '4/2/3'. Underneath she'd added some helpful details: 'Big green gate. White house with a high wall. Near the old Ministry of Oil, behind the Mansour race track.' This was the road map to Zina's past.

I jumped into my air-conditioned car with Saad, one of the BBC's local fixers. Within minutes we'd crossed the Tigris. We were in Mansour, comfortable, middle-class Mansour, and we followed an armoured American Humvee right into Emirates Street, a soldier perched upright in the back of the vehicle, his bronzed arms cradling a machine-gun, his pose a curious mix of indolence and menace. We stopped close to a small office block which used to be the Ministry of Oil. Yes, we'd found a crucial landmark, but quickly my confidence turned to frustration; Baghdad's street numbers had been completely overhauled in the last two decades. Zina's address meant nothing to the bewildered people I approached on Emirates Street.

Forty-five minutes later, I called Zina on my satellite phone. Inevitably we managed to have a row about her directions. 'It doesn't make sense,' I said. 'The race track's on the wrong side of the road, and besides you've got to be more specific about the height of this wall of yours.' 'For God's sake, I was fourteen years old,' she shouted from Brussels. 'All I know is, when I left, that wall was higher than me.'

Down a small side street, then a right turn and finally we found it. The gate was no longer green, the wall wasn't so high, but I knew this was it. There were two slender, strikingly tall date palms close to the house. I had seen them before, in a dozen fading family photographs. We walked into the garden. It was overgrown; yellowing grass came up to my thigh. The house looked dilapidated, but it was intact. No bomb damage, no sign of looting. And there was something else; a line of washing on the roof, flapping in the hot wind.

I knocked. For a long time there was no answer; then a fumbling at the metal door, and an old man in a grubby *dishdashu* robe appeared. Saad helped to explain who I was, why I was here. The old man, whose eyes were cloudy and whose chin was covered in grey stubble, suddenly grabbed me, hugged me tight and kissed me so vigorously I thought my cheeks would bleed. His name was Abu Majid. For years he'd been guarding the house, he said, paid by the company which my father-in-law used to run. 'You, the husband of little Zina,' he murmured, now holding my hand. 'Thanks be to God, thanks be to God.'

One day soon I will come back to Baghdad with Zina and with our three children, who never knew their grandfather and who, for now, know nothing of his country. We'll go to Emirates Street, drink sweet tea with Abu Majid and begin to reclaim a past confiscated by Saddam Hussein.

8
The Bloodiest Day

Paul Wood

A devastating attack on Shiite shrines in Iraq, in which nearly 200 people were killed, took place just after a temporary constitution had been agreed by the various factions on the country's Governing Council. The document was intended to provide the basis for a handover of sovereignty by the US-led occupation authority, but there were fears that the attacks would ruin attempts to create the only democracy in a major Arab state. (6 March 2004)

Below our hotel balcony, a powerfully built young Iraqi Shiite was repeatedly head-butting an Iranian visitor to Kerbala who'd been injured in the bombing. The blade of a ceremonial sword flashed, but the Iranian managed to get into an ambulance and wrench the door shut. It was a few minutes after the street had been engulfed in an orange ball of flame and white hot metal. The crowd was howling that outsiders were to blame.

That, presumably, was what the bombers wanted, to get Shiites to lash out and eventually turn their anger on Sunni Muslims. The slaughter of the pilgrims in Kerbala and Baghdad was an attempt to suck the Americans into a civil war and wreck the transition to democracy. The open society which Britain and the US want Iraq to become had taken shape just a day earlier, if only on paper. After much delay, the Iraqi Governing Council agreed a transitional constitution.

As Council members emerged bleary-eyed from their overnight marathon of negotiation, we were in what I find the most beautiful spot in all of Iraq: between the two mosques in Kerbala. There were high walls of pale yellow brick around the holy shrines, the gates edged with tiles in pale turquoise. Shafts of sunlight were glinting off the tear-shaped golden domes; inside were Persian carpets on white marble and intricate geometrical mosaics. The sacred ground of Kerbala was packed with hundreds of thousands of pilgrims for Ashora, the anniversary of the martyrdom of Shia Islam's founder. It was a religious occasion with deep political significance. This was the first time in decades that Iraq's Shiites could mark their calendar's most holy day in freedom. There could be no more tangible sign of the changes the coalition has wrought in Iraq.

The Shiite clerics leading the prayers that day have turned out to be far more politically moderate than some had feared. They have no plan for an Iranian-style theocracy in Iraq, but the Americans have still had some nasty surprises. One was when the senior Shiite Ayatollah on the Iraqi Governing Council, and the man who might be the next president of Iraq, announced a defence pact with Syria.

Another disturbing sign was how the authorities treated foreign journalists in Kerbala. The religious police looked suspiciously into the viewfinder of our camera at every opportunity. Filming the ritual of young men cutting themselves with swords was banned. The clerics felt this was not the image they wanted to project. 'You must do what I say because I have the biggest stick,' said a member of the religious police, waving his truncheon. 'This is worse than Saddam's time,' said our translator.

Worrying, too, was how in the immediate aftermath of the bombing the crowd turned on anyone not recognised as a fellow Iraqi Shiite. Perhaps that's not surprising, given the brutality of the bombings. The pilgrims were wedged so tightly together that the sound of the multiple explosions was muffled. Body parts flew through the air; a severed hand was thrown ten metres up and landed next to our TV position on the hotel roof; people were set alight. But, despite the hospitality of Iraqi Shiites in more normal times, this is a tribal society and difficult ground in which to plant Western-style pluralism.

The good news for the coalition is that calm was quickly restored, with unity slogans chanted at the behest of the clerics: 'We are all Iraqis and no one will divide us.' So far this is not a sectarian conflict between Iraqis. The bad news for the coalition is that most pilgrims in Kerbala blamed the Americans. 'The US will pay for every drop of Shiite blood spilled here,' said one cleric.

The bombings also fuelled demands to let the Shiite militias take over more security duties. The path to elections will become more fraught with danger as different religious and party militias grow in strength. This is the Lebanon scenario for Iraq. As usual there are contradictory signals: on the one hand, a document which sets out the most liberal constitution ever for an Arab state; on the other, a dramatic worsening in the security situation which could undermine what political progress has been made. And, as with many other aspects of the Iraq occupation, America's relationship with the Shiites is turning out to be far more complex than it envisaged.

9
Before It's Too Late

Frank Gardner

Our correspondent Frank Gardner, an authority on the Arab world, wrote a dispatch for From Our Own Correspondent *describing the worsening security situation in Saudi Arabia. Al-Qaeda was active in the kingdom and there had been attacks on foreign oil workers. He said that British and other Western expatriates there were in danger and expecting further attacks. A day after filing the report, Frank was seriously wounded when he and his cameraman Simon Cumbers came under gunfire in the capital, Riyadh. Gardner survived the attack, but sustained serious injuries and was being treated in hospital. Cumbers, who was thirty-six, was killed. (5 June 2004)*

This is not the Saudi Arabia I know. In fifteen years of coming here, I have only once before seen a sandbagged gun emplacement outside my hotel, and that was when Saddam Hussein's tanks were massing on the border with Kuwait. Now the soldiers manning the checkpoints are distinctly nervous, their fingers on the trigger guards of their assault rifles, their faces darting through car windows, checking documents, looking in glove compartments, asking questions.

Superficially, much is the same here. Saudis and expatriates still go about their business in the stifling, 40-degree heat; shops close for prayers; people go home for siestas after lunch, then re-emerge into the evening traffic jams. Life goes on. Saudis I meet are embarrassed, almost apologetic, about the tight security. They shrug their shoulders and say: 'It will soon pass, God willing.'

But last weekend's extended al-Qaeda raid on a housing compound and other buildings in the Gulf town of Khobar has seriously rattled its expatriate community. It was not, as some have suggested, a direct attack on the oil industry. Those killed by al-Qaeda last Saturday included bankers and caterers. The oil facilities themselves have not yet been attacked. But this was the most violent thing to have happened in Khobar since a US Air Force accommodation block was blown up eight years ago, killing nineteen airmen.

Western expats in the oil-rich Eastern Province of the country had grown almost blasé about the terrorist threat. Al-Qaeda was something visited on other people, mostly in the strictly conservative capital, Riyadh. Now that has changed and so has the mood. In the shopping malls where expats used to linger (remember, there is no public entertainment), they now take their purchases and walk quickly to their cars. Many lock their doors; some even check under the chassis for bombs.

The Britons here tend to live in housing compounds, walled oases of comfort where they can mingle with other Western families, use the communal swimming pool, even indulge in some illegal home-brewed beer, all out of sight of the Saudi authorities. But this cosy cocoon has recently been punctured. Saudi security has failed to protect these compounds on several occasions. Twice last year, al-Qaeda fanatics were able to shoot their way past the guards at the gate, then drive truck bombs into the heart of the compounds. Investigations are still continuing into how the group that attacked Khobar last weekend was able to run amok in the compound for hours on end.

Expats I spoke to have little confidence in the defensive abilities of the unarmed security guards. Most are paid less than £300 a month and many have no training at all. Even at those compounds where the Saudi National Guard has set up sandbag defences with machine-guns, people worry whether they could withstand a full onslaught by al-Qaeda zealots who have no fear of death.

At the headquarters of Saudi Aramco, the national oil company, a long line of cars tails back at the gate, waiting to get through security. Mirrors are passed beneath vehicles, sniffer dogs stand panting in the shade. In the distance, just visible in the heat haze, is a radar installation sitting on top of a rock outcrop. It is supposed to give warning of any unidentified aircraft, so that Saudi fighters based nearby can scramble to intercept them. It all looks impressive, but one American, whose husband works for the company, told me she was waved through last week without any ID card. It worried her, as she pointed out that members of al-Qaeda cells here in Saudi Arabia have taken to disguising themselves as women. In fact, only last week, one was shot dead wearing women's clothing in the mountain town of Taif.

On Wednesday afternoon, I went to the British school in Khobar to attend the memorial service for Michael Hamilton, the Briton who was killed in last weekend's raid. The gathering looked ordinary and yet here we were commemorating something utterly alien to this normally placid community. Bankers, diplomats, teachers and oil workers stood silently while tribute was paid to a man they had so often waved to across the street, only to hear he had been slaughtered on Saturday, his body dragged round town from the bumper of a car. I saw tears in the eyes of several Saudis present.

When the service was over, his widow walked out, clutching the arm of a friend, her eyes tight shut. This is a country that thousands of Britons have made their home for years. Now, slowly, they are coming to terms with the fact that if the terrorist attacks on Westerners continue, they may have to consider leaving Saudi Arabia before it is too late.

10
Hot Mood

Hugh Sykes

What went wrong for the coalition forces which had invaded Iraq and toppled the regime of Saddam Hussein? Many of them had been welcomed as heroes when they arrived in the country in March 2003. Increasingly, though, they were becoming reviled as they presided over a security situation which was steadily deteriorating. (3 July 2004)

As I look through my photographs from Iraq last year, there are so many happy faces, so many smiles. In Baghdad, Basra, Kerbala and the small town of Hilla near Babylon, people kept on saying: 'Please, take our picture, mister!' Once it was a group of fellow diners at an outside kebab café; another time a group of women heavily shrouded in their black chadors caught my eye, pulled the cotton away from their faces so that it only covered their hair, and the flash lit up their smiles in the night. Many Iraqis I met also said, openly and loudly in large gatherings in which anyone could hear them: 'Thank you Bush, thank you Blair, we love freedom.'

At a café in Basra, two sailors sat with me as I smoked a hubble-bubble pipe and explained how much better their lives had become thanks to the invasion. One of them, Abu Dijassem, said: 'We love the British.' I nodded gratefully, thinking this was just a pleasantry for my benefit, and he said: 'No, no, we really do, look!' and he brought out his wallet. In the little plastic window where people usually keep pictures of their families there was ... David Beckham. 'Ah, you like Manchester United, then,' I said. And a little voice at my elbow corrected me with news that was only a couple of days old. 'No, no! Real Madrid.'

'Oh, hello, who are you?' I asked. 'I am Moataz. I am ten years old.' 'And you like your football?' 'Yes.' And I had a flash of inspiration. I told him: 'I live in London, near Highbury, where Arsenal play.' 'Ah,' said Moataz.

'Patrick Viera, Thierry Henri, David Seaman.' And he did a perfect goalie's save from his chair.

It seems a long time ago, another world almost, that happy evening in the Basra coffee house. And as the occupation deepened, Iraqis began to feel that their liberation was being damaged, diluted, diminished. One man said to me: 'Freedom is not freedom if we are occupied. So please, now that you have set us free, go home, and leave Iraq to the Iraqis.'

But the coalition didn't trust the people they'd set free. The Americans, especially, retreated behind rolls and rolls of razor wire, pointed their revolvers and their rifles at passionate but peaceful crowds, and barked orders in English at people for whom courtesy is one of the essential qualities of life.

In Hilla, a quiet town full of devout Shia Muslims delighted that Saddam had gone, two local petrol station attendants, Faris and Riath Hussein, joined crowds lining the main road to cheer the coalition troops as they passed through on their way to Baghdad. Two days later, Faris was driving Riath along the same road. As they approached a checkpoint, they thought they were being told to carry on. They carried on. US marines opened fire. Faris was killed and a bullet hit Riath through the front of his head, blinding him in both eyes. I counted nineteen bullet holes in their Toyota car, parked outside the home that the brothers and their families shared. I sat with Riath. Two girls came into the room. When I asked him if they were his daughters, he broke down and wept. 'I don't know,' he choked. 'I can't see them.'

In the photograph I took of Riath, with five-year-old Noor and six-year-old Rana, the confusion and fierce resentment on the girls' faces is a vivid metaphor for some of the fundamental mistakes the coalition made and their angry consequences. Many of my Iraqi friends say this is true, including one man in particular, Dr Hussein al-Shahristani, the nuclear physicist who spent twelve years in Abu Ghraib prison for defying Saddam Hussein. He refused to work on Saddam's nuclear-weapons programme. He told me this week that what had gone wrong from the very beginning was the Americans' mistrust of the Iraqi people.

'They considered every Iraqi a potential enemy,' he complained. Instead, he says, they should have realised they had a resourceful and highly educated people mostly grateful for their liberation, and eager to be left to get on with recovery and reconstruction themselves. And, he believes, the consequences of this haughty, insulting attitude were an eventual loss of patience with the coalition, the rise in violence that has now become routine and, crucially, the loss of support of the vast majority of decent, peaceful Iraqis who might have refused to tolerate much of the terrorism and insurgency if they had been treated with more respect.

And the greatest danger he sees now is the already-developing unholy alliance between al-Qaeda and the well-funded, well-organised and highly disciplined former Ba'ath party machine, the secret service of Saddam Hussein, his principal instrument of terror and control creeping back into key positions once again in councils and committees across the land.

There are two continuing failures which my Iraqi friends most deeply resent. They still feel unable to walk the streets of their capital city in the relative cool of the evenings because of crime, kidnapping and suicide bombers. And, above all, they cannot comprehend how the richest and most powerful nations in the world have been in Iraq for fifteen months now and still the electricity supply is unreliable. For the second summer in succession, they are having to endure daily temperatures of 55 degrees in the shade without a reliable power supply for their ceiling fans. Long before the serious violence erupted last year, a man in a crowd warned me, 'You must make our lives better quickly because in the hot weather we grow angry.' 'Hot weather,' he said, 'hot mood.'

11

A Sniper's View

Orla Guerin

The struggle between Palestinians and Israelis was as intractable as ever. Violence continued, albeit at a relatively low level; the conflict, while not as intense as it sometimes had been in the past, was still managing to intrude on the everyday lives of innocent civilians. (14 August 2004)

They say if you live long enough, you see everything. Rana Malhas now feels that she has. She was born in Turkey eighty-two years ago. But this gentle, welcoming old woman now lives with relatives in a stone house inside a courtyard with grapes on the vine. Her home is in Balata, a refugee camp on the edge of the city of Nablus. The area is a stronghold of Palestinian militants, who have dispatched many suicide bombers. This week, inside her own home, Rana was held for hours at gunpoint by seven heavily armed Israeli troops, and we were held with her.

We were filming with a local doctor, Ghassan Hamdan, when he was called to treat Rana. Her house had been occupied by Israeli soldiers. They were driving in and out of the camp, drawing stone-throwing youngsters out on to the streets. It looked like a game of cat and mouse. Outside the house there was no sign of any military presence. Dr Hamdan went in and we followed soon afterwards. But before we found him, Israeli troops found us, forcing us at gunpoint into a disused room on the upper storey, first the cameraman, then the producer, then me. There we saw Rana, trapped in a chair in the corner, a white headscarf on her silver hair. She was neatly dressed and alert, flanked protectively by the doctor and a Palestinian paramedic.

Soldiers seized our phones, confiscated our camera tape and, when we tried to leave, forced us back, at the barrel of a gun. Dr Hamdan stood upright, calm and polite, showing more resignation than surprise. 'Three days ago soldiers kept me like this for hours,' he said. 'It's happened to me about ten times in the past few years.' All the soldiers were young; some were cocky, sprawled around on the floor. A few busied themselves around the largest window, where a sniper rifle was fixed in position. The commander and the sniper kept their eyes trained on the road below. We could hear shouts, the familiar sounds of clashes, but the disturbances were small.

Rana leant forward to speak. Her immediate concern was for us. 'I'm so sorry this has happened to you in my house,' she said. 'And that I can't get you some coffee.' Dr Hamdan pleaded to be allowed to move her; Rana's blood pressure was high. The soldiers refused. As the minutes stretched into hours, he asked how long we would be kept there. 'You'll be here until we kill someone,' a soldier replied, in perfect English.

'We're being held illegally,' I said. The soldiers nodded in agreement, but still refused to let us go. 'You could compromise our operation,' one said, 'by revealing our location.' But there are few secrets in Balata. Local people already knew that troops had been in the house and might still be there. There were ugly moments as the doctor continued to plead for his patient. 'Rana is old,' he said, 'and needs to rest. Why does she have to stay?' 'Because her son blew himself up near my house,' one soldier taunted, and then laughed. Rana has no children.

Later a few threats were murmured in my direction. 'She'll get out of here in a body bag,' one soldier said in Hebrew, assuming, incorrectly, that we would not understand. The sniper kept scanning the crowd down below, never leaving his rifle. Other soldiers joined him at the window, suddenly tense. 'I see a gun being handed around,' one shouted. Others agreed. Then a deafening noise, as the sniper fired one round, hitting someone on the street. We later learnt that a fifteen-year-old boy had been shot as he stood near an ambulance. Palestinians deny he was carrying a gun. He was seriously injured, but is still alive.

We were kept in the room, at risk of incoming Palestinian fire. But there was none. After three and a half hours we were freed and the soldiers left the house. Downstairs, over coffee flavoured with cardamom, Rana told us how her ordeal began. 'I went upstairs after breakfast,' she said, 'at about seven-thirty, to talk to my birds, the doves. I hadn't seen them for two days and I missed them. Then the soldiers made their appearance. They didn't let me move, or go to drink water,' she went on. 'I've seen a lot of things in my life, but I was face to face with my enemy. Because of my age, I was frightened.'

After our release, we complained to the authorities. In a statement the

Israelis expressed regret and promised to investigate, but said the soldiers were in Nablus because of specific warnings about possible attacks. There was no apology for Rana, or Dr Hamdan.

12
Space from Sinai

Nick Thorpe

Israel was planning to dismantle its settlements and withdraw its troops from the Gaza Strip. The plan was welcomed by the Egyptians, particularly those living in northern Sinai in the border area between Egypt and Gaza, who were hoping that an Israeli withdrawal would lead to greater stability in the region.

(2 September 2004)

The dates are nearly ripe in El-Arish. They hang in great clusters round the trunks of the palm trees like shopping bags left by passing Bedouin. You can already buy them, still attached to their stalks, in the market in the main street; one kind yellowish, the other a darker brown. But my companions caution against buying yet. In two weeks' time, they will be sweet, they say.

This town was known in Roman times as Rhinocolorum, 'Noses cut off', after a punishment inflicted on those who were sent into exile here. Nowadays it seems a more cheerful place; at ten o'clock one evening, a little dark-haired girl poses for her father to photograph her in front of the big market tents; inside, there's a chaos of the old and new: fluorescent fringed schoolbags from China, cottons from Egypt, finely embroidered cushion covers sold by almond-eyed tribeswomen and strong-smelling saddlebags for camels, made of coarser wool.

On the edge of El-Arish, groves of palm trees guard the last houses. Then it's the open desert of northern Sinai, twenty-five miles to Rafah, on the border with the Gaza Strip. Occasionally a ruined bunker tilts into the sand, a single blind eye exposed to the sky. This coastal road was taken by the Israeli army in 1967. Egypt won it back with diplomacy, but the landscape still nurses its wounds. Every few miles there's an Egyptian police barricade, just to remind you you're approaching a war zone. But not an all-out war;

just the daily abrasions of a people, the Palestinians, who feel under siege from the Israelis, who feel under siege from the Arabs, who feel under siege from the United States. It's a kind of Russian 'Matryoshka' doll of pain.

The flames may leap highest now in Iraq, but, approaching Gaza, you have a sense that this is the epicentre of the storm. And that the Palestinians and Israelis may still be at war long after the Iraqis regain control of their own country. The customs and immigration hall at Rafah is packed with Palestinians, their possessions piled in precarious mountains on trolleys, heads-carved or fully swathed women crouching on the floor to mix powdered milk for babies in old tins, men in all states of traditional or modern dress, in flowing robes or sweaty T-shirts; the walkie-talkies of the white-uniformed Egyptian police crackling incessantly like insects.

On one level, the Palestinians are ordinary world citizens. They have smart green Palestinian Authority passports. They are travelling abroad to visit relatives, or to work or study, or in search of better medical care. But on another level, they are deeply traumatised. You ask a question, the answer comes normally at first, then disintegrates into either tears or fury. A woman says she is sick in her stomach from the Israeli shelling. Another says she wants to live in peace with the Israelis, but on equal terms, for her children to have what their children have. 'Now we've lost everything,' she shouts. 'The trees have been bulldozed, the school is damaged, all we've got left is our roof, and soon they'll destroy that over us.'

None of the Palestinians here believes the Israelis will withdraw next year. 'It's just another trick to make us fight against one another, fight over the rubble they've left us,' says one man. Then the anger subsides, and there are moments of gentleness and that infectious laughter common to large families the world over.

Just down the road from the border gate is Egyptian Rafah, a small town compared to the vast refugee camp of Rafah across the fortified border. A Star of David flag flutters from the side of a huge Israeli security tower, which overlooks the border like a medieval siege engine. In the shops in its shadow you can buy local olive oil, almonds, plastic bags of dried hibiscus flowers and even bars of soap from Israel. The local people are Bedouins, loyal to their tribes rather than to the Egyptian or Israeli state. For a moment one of those rare chinks in the curtain of the current conflict opens through which one sees the indigenous people of the planet, living and trading and dying much as they always have, more or less disturbed by the latest occu-piers.

Back in El-Arish, you can wash away the dust of human suffering in the hot sea. The women here bathe fully dressed, the black chador floating around them in the white surf like jellyfish. I bought postcards which bore the caption 'Sinai from Space' and lie here on the beach, on this end-of-summer night, contemplating space from Sinai.

The Americas

1
Days of Excess

Stephen Jessel

Valentine's Day is a big occasion in the United States. Hundreds of millions of dollars are spent on it. And that's just one of the big annual occasions celebrated by Americans every year. (17 February 1990)

I saw a Valentine's tree last week. A Valentine's tree is very much like a Christmas tree, or at least many American Christmas trees, in that it is decorated, made of plastic and therefore reusable year after year. But instead of tinsel and angels and shiny globes, this one was decorated with red and white hearts. I'm not sure why I should have been taken aback; after all, in the eternity that separates Christmas from Easter some occasion has to be found around which public excitement and commercial promotion can coalesce, and Valentine's Day falls very handily.

It was still mid-January when the supermarkets started clearing space for their Valentine promotions. Whole aisles full of cards, not just for that special loved one, but for friends, families, acquaintances with every nuance of relationship; cards from and for the dog or the baby-sitter or Grandpa. Cards with Barbie Doll themes or exploiting the perplexing cult of Teenage Mutant Ninja Turtles. Add not only an astounding array of sweets and chocolates, but candles and soft toys, colouring books and ashtrays, paper plates and decorations, flowers, of course, and lingerie.

Americans send 900 million Valentines a year or about four for every man, woman and child. They spend an estimated £450 million on presents. By last Wednesday the whole thing was out of control. The price of flowers had soared; work in schools had been suspended so that the children could make cards for their classmates and teachers, not to mention snacks and drinks for the Valentine's party that was to replace afternoon classes. As for restaurant dinner reservations, forget about it. It all seemed to owe rather more to cupidity than to Cupid; just as many shops seem to be holding sales that blend into a permanent year-long sale, so one event relentlessly succeeds another. If it is not a real event, one is manufactured.

Take the Superbowl, the equivalent of the Cup Final for American football, which took place last month. Now, American football is televised for large chunks of every Saturday and Sunday and on Monday evenings. During these endless games, each of which takes three or four hours to complete, millions of Americans sit at home in front of their television sets nibbling and drinking whatever takes their fancy. On the eve of the Superbowl these items are suddenly repackaged and promoted as indispensable Superbowl snacks and drinks, without which the Superbowl parties everybody is supposed to be attending will be humiliating social disasters.

But it is at Halloween that real excess sets in. There are signs that the trick-or-treat custom, according to which waifs in Batman outfits ring your doorbell and demand handfuls of teeth-rotting sweets, is being imported to Britain. Beware is all I would say. Not until you have been blackmailed into procuring useless pumpkins to turn into lanterns, found yourself buying artificial fog and worried whether your neighbours are putting razorblades in the sweets they are handing out to the importunate infants at their door – not until then can you appreciate the full horror of All Hallow's Eve. Wise parents follow their offspring at a discreet distance. In some places the police forbid the practice altogether. And indeed Halloween has become increasingly an adult's occasion. Besides spending about £600 million on sweets for children, they laid out another £200 million on costumes for fancy-dress parties to mark the occasion.

Still, Halloween is months away. The Easter baskets and bunnies and eggs and chocolates are already in the supermarkets and drugstores. The card manufacturers are hard at work printing cards for Mother's Day and Father's Day and Secretary's Day and, for all I know, Grandfather's and Grandmother's Day. And further down the road there are the celebrations for the Fourth of July to be prepared for and, later on, there's Thanksgiving. But the problem is in the short term. Between now and Easter some eight weeks have to be traversed. In a tone that I imagined to be heavy with irony, I asked how it was going to be possible to fill this dreadful void. There was, somebody said, no problem at all. Did I not realise that the 17th of March was St Patrick's Day?

2

Neighbourhood Grim Reapers

Alex Kirby

Heads of state and government from around the globe had travelled to Rio de Janeiro to discuss world poverty and ecology at the Earth Summit. (8 June 1992)

The very name Brazil is evocative. Flying down to Rio, my mind was full of the exotic associations learnt in childhood: of parrots, mahogany and anacondas, overlaid with more recent imagery of a uniquely rich environment facing an unprecedented threat. But behind all of these was another picture. Brazil is a country where they kill children. And if the same thing happens in other parts of Latin America, it happens often enough in Brazil to suggest it has the consent of a number of influential people.

Figures tell part of the story. In Pernambuco, in north-east Brazil, an average of three children a week were being killed by the death squads in early 1988. And a campaigner I met, Ivanir dos Santos, who lived on the streets himself till the age of four, says the number of children killed in the state of Rio de Janeiro alone last year was 443, more than one a day.

Rio is a violent city: two friends of mine were robbed at knife-point during the Earth Summit. Most of the children who die are killed on suspicion of involvement in a crime. If they are criminals, it is not too surprising. Brazil has perhaps the greatest disparity of any country between rich and poor. More than half the national income goes to the richest ten per cent of Brazilians. The poorest ten per cent eke out among themselves less than one per cent of the country's wealth. With the economy rocking on its heels, savage inflation and an immense foreign debt, the poor in Brazil are very poor, which helps to explain why seven million children have to fend for themselves on the streets.

The children are the prime targets for the death squads, though not the only ones. I met two poor but upright mothers whose children were in a group abducted by the police almost two years ago. None of the children has been seen again: to be young, poor and black in Brazil is to ask for trouble. Most of the killing is thought to be the work of serving or former police officers and of private security guards, usually paid by shopkeepers to deter crime by eliminating those thought to be either actual or potential criminals.

I wanted to meet some of the killers. Not surprisingly, I was not able to. But the distinguished Brazilian film-maker Otavio Bezerra has interviewed some of them and he let me listen to his tapes. My abiding memory is of men who not only show no trace of remorse for what they do – one remarked that he felt not a drop of pity – but are convinced that they are doing society a favour. They see themselves, quite simply, as pest-control officers. Several believe they are, in fact, doing their victims a favour, too. Better die now in childhood, they argue, almost in so many words, than live to be an adult criminal ten years hence. Had I not been in Brazil for the Earth Summit, I might have found it easier to write off the killers as the psychopathic products of a horribly warped society. In fact, I find it hard to condemn them. They, at least, are straightforward about what they do. And they care enough about their society to do something, even if the thing they do plumbs depths we thought were behind us.

The summit was about environment and development. But more and more it seemed to me that I was watching two summits. The one that discussed the environment, although it could have done much more, did carve out some essential toeholds for future progress. But the development summit, so far as I could see, did very little. It failed to agree on a more rapid increase in overseas aid, the most elementary step possible for reducing poverty. It certainly did not agree to reduce the poorest countries' debts, or to change the rules of international trade in a way that would give them a better chance of earning their own living. And it did not agree that the rich countries should limit their own overconsumption.

The industrial world has learnt to worry about the environment, and it has also learnt to live with poverty; the wretched of the earth are part of the familiar backdrop of life. They are wallpaper. They will not go away. They do not need to because nothing they can do or be could ever threaten us. Statistics can often simply numb the mind. But every now and then you come across a formula which will not leave you, some set of digits which casts a new light on the scene. The reality of poverty is summed up, for me, in the recollection that every day 40,000 children aged under five die of preventable causes: hunger or easily treated diseases like measles. A friend puts it a different way: the daily 40,000 he visualises as a jumbo jet crashing every fifteen minutes, with the loss of everybody on board.

This is not news, it is the way things are – reality. And the Earth Summit failed to decide, in any way I could discern, to change reality. Perhaps it is unreasonable to have hoped otherwise. Perhaps it would be reasonable, instead, to accept the summit's promises that some time, after the recession, after we have sorted out Eastern Europe, when things pick up, we will get around to tackling poverty. George Bernard Shaw thought there was a place for unreason. He wrote: 'The reasonable man adapts himself to the world. The unreasonable man persists in trying to adapt the world to himself. Therefore all progress depends upon the unreasonable man.'

How do the Brazilian death squads fit into all this? Reasonably enough, I think, they act deliberately to achieve a result the world achieves on a far grander scale despite itself. They hardly merit condemnation for that. And in a steadily more crowded world, there will be all the more need for pest-control men, for the neighbourhood grim reapers. We should be giving them medals.

3
Jerry Goes to Hollywood

John Peel

The death of an overweight middle-aged rock star doesn't normally make the headlines. But when Jerry Garcia, the Grateful Dead's co-founder, lead guitarist and personification of hippiedom, died there was an outpouring of grief around the world. (22 August 1995)

In the mid-1960s, I lived in California. Not in the seriously groovy north of the state, San Francisco, Berkeley, nor in tough and trashy Los Angeles, but in an area known to listeners to KMEN, the radio station for which I worked, as the Inland Empire. Our world was bounded by Fontana, San Bernardino and Riverside, small towns where, one felt, anything that was going to happen had already happened. Travellers to the north would come back with fantastic tales of love-ins, be-ins and happenings, but we knew that the Inland Empire wasn't ready for that sort of thing and probably never would be. Mind you, at least we had some great bands: Northside Moss, the Mystics (every town had a band called the Mystics) and, best of them all, the Misunderstood and we were close enough to go and see bands in Los Angeles. At Pandora's Box, the Whisky a Go-Go and such places we saw Love, the Doors, and even, on one unforgettable night in Hollywood, Captain Beefheart and his Magic Band.

But Los Angeles wasn't San Francisco, and a lot of us felt bad about that. In San Francisco, it seemed, life was already all about sex and drugs and rock 'n' roll. I had a girlfriend called Landa, a woman so mysterious that I was never permitted to know where she lived. We met for what the tabloids call 'love romps' on the edge of an orange grove; but San Francisco, we had heard, promised unlimited casual sex for even the most ill-favoured of us. We rather tentatively smoked some of the grass that friends of friends brought up from Mexico to sell. In San Francisco, the story went, everyone from the mayor down was out of their heads on drugs one hundred times more exciting than marijuana.

And San Francisco had the Grateful Dead. They were, we heard, a community band. 'Wow!' we went, not sure what a community band was. They played for hours and hours and hours. 'Gosh!' we went, not entirely sure that we thought that was a particularly good idea. And they had this guitarist called Jerry Garcia, who was just, well, you know, Jerry Garcia, we said to each other. Later, with other friends, we would talk about Jerry Garcia as though we kinda knew him. 'Yeah, he's great,' these other friends would say. I don't suppose any of us had ever heard him, or the Grateful Dead, play.

I never heard Jerry Garcia until the first Grateful Dead LP, drably entitled *Grateful Dead*, came to Britain, to which I had returned early in 1967, on import. It was, frankly, rather disappointing, although no one at the time would have dared to say so, being an unconvincing mix of white blues and jug band stuff. It wasn't until the *Live Dead* LP of 1969 that we finally understood what Jerry Garcia was all about.

Confirmation that his reputation was truly deserved came at a time when my own disenchantment with hippiedom was considerable. What good, I wanted to know, was a philosophy based on dropping out of society that took no account of those who had not yet had the good fortune to drop in? Our community musicians, notably the Pink Floyd, were on their way to being stars. Jimi Hendrix was on the way to being dead, and those of the beautiful people whose parents were able and prepared to indulge them were on the way to delightful, detached, freehold properties in picturesque rural settings, from which they would subsequently venture forth to sell each other badly made and overpriced leather goods at horse fairs. Some, of course, didn't get as far as stardom or giggling rusticity, having fried their brains with acid or become addicted to heroin. This was the fate that befell Jerry Garcia, of course, and led to his early death.

But in 1970, when the Grateful Dead played Hollywood, this time the small village of that name in the West Midlands, we hippies still believed ourselves immortal. And, living with Sheila, subsequently the mother of our four children, in the back of a Land Rover and marvelling at Garcia's seemingly endless ability to conjure up flowing, lyrical, throbbing music from his guitar, it did seem impossible that anything so wonderful could come to an end.

For the band's most dedicated followers, styled Deadheads – even US presidential candidate Al Gore was, at one time, a Dead fan – the dream did last for another twenty-five years, kept alive, despite personnel changes punctuated with the occasional death, by the Dead's determination to remain as true to their original ethic as possible. From the start, the band encouraged fans to record their concerts and did what they could to keep ticket prices down. As the band toured and toured and toured, their fan base never diminished, with people unborn when the band came together taking the place of those who grew weary of the repetition and moved on to other things.

I moved on myself in 1976, when punk arrived; but last week I went to find my copy of that Grateful Dead LP *Live Dead*, excited at the thought that I might recapture the feelings I had when the band played the Hollywood festival. Unfortunately, my copy of the record has vanished. Perhaps it is better that way.

4

Two Armies

Bridget Kendall

Thousands of Americans, seeking better lives for themselves away from the big cities, were flocking to the wide-open spaces bordering the Rocky Mountains. But if the small communities of Montana were havens of peace and prosperity, they were also divided places, where people were increasingly unsure of America's future. (30 November 1995)

Every morning fifty-five-year-old Chuck Lorensen gets up early and sits down with his teenage son to read the Bible for two hours. It takes four months to read the good book from cover to cover. This October he finished it for the twenty-seventh time. Since he returned to Montana from Alaska, a few years ago, to take up a job as a carpenter in his old home town Kalispell, this is how Chuck Lorensen has ordered his life.

Chuck is a fundamentalist Christian, a member of the National Rifle Association and a staunch conservative, a convert who believes America is in a moral crisis. For too long, he says, liberals like President Bill Clinton have been allowed to get away with too much. Their attempts to control guns are just plain silly. It's not guns that cause crime, he told me, but the absence of morality and the lack of God in people's lives.

Every day Chuck sends his fourteen-year-old son to Kalispell's Christian school, secure in the knowledge his lad will get an education free from the lax values of America's government-run schools. Instead of lessons to celebrate gay and lesbian history month, Kalispell's Christian school launches the day with a revivalist assembly, biology classes that teach creationism and reject Darwin's Theory of Evolution and chemistry lessons where the first question asked by the teacher is: 'What does the atomic table tell us about God and Jesus?'

In this quiet little town in the foothills of the Rocky Mountains, such God-fearing devotion might seem admirable or quaint, the old-fashioned moves of conservative small-town America. And it's true, in among the gingham-curtained cafés and saloon bars decorated with moose heads, there does seem to be a white church with a steeple on almost every street corner. And every person you meet turns out to be either a fundamentalist believer or else will tell you their father, or younger sister, or ex-wife is one instead. But probe a little deeper and you soon sense that Kalispell is a deeply divided community, and you begin to suspect that the fight between right and left in America is being played out in every small town, right across the nation.

Once or twice a week in Kalispell, outside the only full-time abortion clinic, Chuck and other anti-abortion protesters march up and down the kerb, waving placards proclaiming the local abortion doctor a baby killer. Denise Cofer, another convert and head of the local Christian Coalition movement, is there, too. Anyone who aborts an unborn foetus, she believes, is a murderer. Inside the clinic Dr Armstrong and his loyal assistant Susan Cahill admit these days they feel under siege. What's more interesting is that they document the tide turning against them, starting, they say, in the 1980s when Ronald Reagan was president.

First Dr Armstrong, an elder in the Presbyterian Church, was asked by the local school to stop coming to give his sex education talks. Then he was ousted from the School Board. Slowly, as the religious right gained in strength, abortion supporters found themselves ostracised and the abortion providers realised what they needed most urgently was lawyers, to fight the new laws being passed in the state capital, Helena, to stop them working.

'I'm not sure now I'd reveal to anyone I didn't know real well that I support abortion,' one woman told me quietly. And Susan Cahill, the abortion doctor's assistant, has begun to worry her young son could become the target of playground taunts, his mother's job has become so controversial.

The two sides line up on a variety of issues: sit in on the local Christian Coalition meeting and you'll find Chuck and Denise and their friends all support the same causes: their enemies are not just the abortion doctors, but 'greenies', environmentalists who care more for grizzly bears and spotted owls than they do for humans. They suspect gay activists, who, according to Montana law, are felons who practise illegal sodomy. They keep their distance from feminists, who, they worry, are turning upside down family values. And if you slip in to observe the local abortion support group or the human rights network, you'll find their opponents all there, lined up against them. Two armies, fighting for the political soul of America.

There's further disquiet, though. Kalispell isn't only troubled by political animosity and suspicion. There's also the threat of violence hanging over the community. Not surprising, perhaps, in a place where every man boasts of his hunting guns, and many women, if pressed, will admit they carry a pistol hidden in their handbag, and where gun shows are part of the local entertainment. But it's not the occasional saloon-bar shoot-out that worries people here, it's more the political violence. A year ago the abortion clinic was fire-bombed. No one claimed responsibility. Last month the school on the local Indian reservation was closed for a day or two after another bomb threat. Again, no one knows where it came from.

At the local sheriff's office, a special team is kept on round-the-clock alert, in case of trouble from Montana's militia groups or other recluses who've taken to the hills and forests with their families, convinced the American government has turned against the people. 'There's a plot to disarm America and turn it over to the United Nations' is the refrain you'll hear from the young men in camouflage gear at the gun shows, or from the 'Freemen' who refuse to pay their taxes.

If you believe these self-declared outlaws of Montana, America's days are numbered. Soviet Communism may have been vanquished, but there's a new enemy out there, the world government of the United Nations. And unless Americans arm themselves to defend their homeland from new foreign foes, then the UN will take over and America and Americans will disappear for ever. It may sound far-fetched, but it's a conspiracy theory with remarkably wide appeal at a time when no one else, no statesman-like politician, is reassuring ordinary Americans as to where their country is heading.

5

Trout Crazy

Rob Watson

It isn't just the wide open spaces that draw tourists to Montana. Its pristine rivers and much-prized trout have made it a mecca for fishing enthusiasts from all over America and the world. (24 August 1996)

Most Americans I know associate Montana with what they describe as a bunch of crazy weirdos living in the mountains, thinking up ways to blow up the federal government. As a correspondent working at the UN, I had heard and read a great deal about the infamous Montana militia and its strange fear that the United Nations, armed with black helicopters, was about to take over America and install a world government. But, having just returned from the state, I now know what's really strange about Montana, and it's not a distaste for government whether federal, world or any other kind. It's an all-embracing, deep-seated, possibly psychotic and, as far as I can make out, state-wide obsession with trout.

Catching them, talking about them, writing about them, painting them – in fact, anything you can name that might have some kind of connection, however tenuous, to trout, you'll find an interest in it in Montana. I say this, you must understand, as a lifelong and dedicated fly fisherman myself, who regards the pursuit of trout as one of the sanest things a man or woman could indulge in. But in Montana it appears to have got out of hand.

The signs of this fishy-fanaticism are obvious as soon as you arrive. The state's largest airport, in Billings, is festooned with pictures of trout, suggestions as to where you might find them, and plane-loads of normally suit-wearing city-dwellers, mainly from the east coast, kitted out with cowboy hats and thousands of dollars-worth of trout-catching equipment. But while the airport provides a hint of what's to come, it's not until you start talking to the locals that the extent of trout mania becomes apparent.

On hearing that I was from New York, the first native Montanan I met told me he'd often thought about visiting the city, but had always put off the journey because he was worried about the lack of trout there and that he couldn't bear to be away from the fishing and the mountains for too long.

It's a view, I discovered, that's held by most Montanans of both sexes. One woman I met shortly after arriving in the state told me she had her own favourite fishing hole that she visited every summer, which she was willing to share with me. Though, with a strange glint in her eye, she recommended I take a gun with me, as she always did, to take care of the rattlesnakes and added that her husband had to blow a rattler's head off only last summer.

The addiction also appears to start at an early age. In one small town young boys who couldn't have been much older than five were discussing with great sagacity and seriousness the merits of various fishing techniques; while in another town a local schoolboy told me he drove sixty miles after lessons every day to his favourite stream.

Even so you might be saying to yourself that this is just hearsay and not conclusive proof of a state-wide madness. That's what I thought. But the longer I stayed in Montana the more the evidence mounted. As I always do when I'm travelling outside New York, I picked up the regional papers to get some feel for local concerns. In particular I was curious to see how Montana's papers would report the opening of the Republican party's convention, given the state's reputation as a gun-toting bastion of anti-liberal attitudes. Much to my surprise there was no mention of it on the front page of the state's largest newspaper. Instead it was dominated by a huge picture of two men standing in a river, you guessed it, trout fishing.

I presumed something extraordinary had happened to them. But the caption read: 'Two visitors enjoy a day's fishing though the trout weren't biting.' The following day I decided to try a different paper. The result was similar. Instead of any discussion of Bob Dole's tax-cutting pledge, there was a front page editorial on trout which contained a passionately put case for the idea that trout should enjoy certain fundamental rights such as the right to live in clean water.

But what really convinced me that trout were perhaps taking over the state of Montana was driving into the two-horse town that was to be the base for my fishing activities. 'Welcome to the town of Ennis', the road sign said. 'Population 660, trout 11,000,000.' The town itself, which essentially consists of one main street, contains enough fishing tackle shops to equip pretty much the entire population of Britain and an array of boutiques selling such vital memorabilia as trout book-ends, trout-patterned curtains and cushions and, of course, carved trout.

Overwhelmed by all this troutery, I decided to duck into the local diner, but there was no escape. The waitress pulled out a menu in the shape of a trout and the men's room had a fly rod on the wall. Then it was time to check into my motel, the Rainbow, named, of course, after a particular species of you know what. I thought I'd try out my English sense of humour, so with a perfectly straight face I asked whether there was any fishing in the area. I quickly discovered you don't joke about trout in Montana.

So what effect did it all have on me? It made me crazier about trout fishing than ever, and for two weeks I thought of little else and did little else. And if there were any trout in Manhattan, I think I'd go out and try catch me one right now.

6

The Real America

Gavin Esler

What's America really like? And what will you miss about it? Questions our chief North America correspondent tried to answer as he packed his bags after eight years in Washington and prepared for a new BBC job in London. (31 May 1997)

A chill wind blows off the snow-covered peaks of the Rocky Mountains, stinging your face as you walk along Main Street in the town of Cody, Wyoming. It is the kind of place where you look odd unless you are wearing a cowboy hat, boots and jeans. Named after Buffalo Bill, Cody is the American West as advertised, not as wild as it was a hundred years ago, but surrounded by wide open spaces filled with Pronghorn Antelope and coyotes which yowl at the moon. Here men on horses still lasso cattle as part of their daily business. And this is the America, from the deserts of Arizona when the Saguaro Cactus is in bloom, to the Indian pueblos of New Mexico, the buffalo herds of South Dakota, to the forests and lakes of the Rockies, that I will miss above all; not a country, but a continent full of open minds and open welcomes in open spaces.

In Cody no one wears six-shooters on their hips any more, but pick-up trucks often have space for a gun rack, and you learn the rules. A gun is considered as normal and unthreatening as a briefcase to a London commuter. And you never ask how many head of cattle a local rancher has, because it is as rude as demanding to know how much money he has in the bank.

Oscar Wilde famously observed that Britain and America are two nations divided by a common language. Perhaps. But as I leave the United States after eight years of residence, I think we are more certainly divided by peculiar prejudices about one another, prejudices which are resistant to change because Britons and Americans often mistakenly think they understand one another. The British are obsessed with America, though we hate to admit it. America is our food and drink, literally and figuratively: Coca-Cola, Corn Flakes, hamburgers, pizza, plus Hollywood movies, TV shows, rock and roll, satellite technology and aeroplanes. We sometimes forget such things have American roots or sniffily dismiss their vulgarity, but imagine stripping away everything with an American accent: the result would be a profound emptiness.

And, though again we may resent it, America is news: NATO, Bosnia, Ireland, the Middle East, arms control, drugs, the Americanisation of our culture. Yet the favour is rarely reciprocated. To many Americans outside the intellectual elite, news about Britain would be that Margaret Thatcher is not prime minister. Most Americans would not recognise Tony Blair or John Major if they fell over them on the street, though there is a general American affection for the British and an antiquated obsession with the royal family as a fairy tale or soap opera.

This I will not miss: America's narrow lack of interest, knowledge or consideration for the world beyond the borders of the United States. At its worst, America is the world's biggest remote island, a blinkered, parochial society astonished that foreigners are as patriotic about their countries as Americans are about the United States, though show it in a different way. Isolated America cannot comprehend, for example, that not all Muslims are fundamentalists, or that murderers are not executed in Europe, or that most of the world considers the bizarre ritual of death in the electric chair utterly barbaric. Or that the United States has a routine level of violence that the rest of the world considers terrifying and disgusting.

I lived in Belfast during the worst of the Troubles, and it is a perpetual puzzle to me that I was statistically far less likely to be murdered in Northern Ireland than I am now in Washington. Yet for some reason Belfast gets American peace envoys rather than the other way around. In the America that I will not miss, there is a baseball 'World Series' which involves none of the world outside North America. And there is television 'World News' which mostly means news about the United States punctuated by infrequent references to countries far away of which most Americans know nothing. In such a large continent perhaps it is inevitable that to a Texan 'foreign parts' might mean Arkansas, the 'Far East' is New York, while Canada is a type of dry ginger ale, but I regret it nevertheless.

Among the most wrong-headed British prejudices, therefore, is the daft notion that Americans are deeply interested in Northern Ireland. President Clinton does care. So does a minority of hyphenated Irish-Americans in Boston, New York and the usual places. But here in Cody, Wyoming, what happens in Belfast is as interesting as news from Jupiter. Roughly forty million Americans have some Irish roots. But among my many friends who fall into this category, Northern Ireland is not a cause. It is just another sad tribal conflict like Rwanda, Bosnia or the Middle East, and it is curious that British newspapers often proclaim the vital importance of the Irish-American vote except during elections when, mysteriously, the green legions somehow never seem to have any significant impact on the result.

In truth, most Americans with Irish roots also may have English, Scottish, French, German or even African and Jewish ancestors. They are as interested in Irish politics as most English people, descended from Normans, Saxons and Jutes, are interested in the politics of Normandy, Saxony and Jutland.

American prejudices about Britain are equally peculiar and seem to date from the Second World War. We British, apparently, live in draughty homes which we do not heat. In cold rooms we drink warm beer and eat over-cooked food, especially boiled cabbage. Our teeth are rotten and frequently misshapen, our dentists incapable, our hygiene questionable, our showers useless. They are correct, of course, about the showers. Americans also credit the British with far more intelligence than we possess. I have witnessed the hypnotic effects of upper-class British accents talking nonsense to American audiences and yet, somehow, not being rumbled as stupid fraudsters. Americans also have undiminished faith that the British are polite and honest. Would that we were. Americans strike me as just as polite and at least as honest. They are more on target when they note that the British are embarrassed about personal matters yet obsessed with lavatory jokes and bodily functions.

All of these stereotypes underline what is best in America and what I will miss most: the people themselves. In Wyoming, in one of the restaurants on Cody's Main Street, I sat among cowboys who were tucking into fat steaks, ready to order dinner, with a producer who had flown in from London on his first trip to the American West. He was a vegetarian, and vegetarians are as common in Wyoming as buffalo herds in Piccadilly Circus.

'Excuse me,' the producer said to the waitress, stereotypically polite as heads turned to listen to his British accent, 'excuse me, what do you recommend for someone who does not eat red meat?' 'Why, honey,' the waitress replied deadpan, 'I recommend you leave Wyoming.' The restaurant shook to cowboy laughter. And suddenly – it happens all over America – two strangers had twenty friends who wanted to show us the town, the mountains, welcome us to their ranches, share a beer. To my regret I have been unable to capture this extraordinary strength of the warm-hearted American character. I also regret that often the United States that I have reported upon is not the United States in which I live. American news is of a nation dominated by corrupt politicians, religious fanatics, racist bigots, discontented minorities, sickening criminals and New Age weirdos preparing for a rendezvous with the Hale-Bopp Comet. All these exist, of course. And they do make news. But they are not what makes America 'America'.

My friends from Arizona to Cape Cod, Florida to New York, are boringly normal. Not movie stars, not in militias or religious cults. Not super-rich or super-indulgent, not intolerant. They are in the best American tradition: hardworking, proud of their country, yet deeply suspicious of their government. They remind me of my first taste of America, as a ten-year-old growing up in Scotland.

Filled with my own stereotypes, I thought I knew Americans from western movies and TV cops and robbers. Then I met the sons and daughters of US Air Force officers stationed near my home outside Edinburgh. One was called Hans. He had a German father and an Austrian mother, and I could never quite understand how that made him an American. But there is nothing more American than being from somewhere else. On my first visit to his home Hans's parents offered to make me a sandwich and I expected the usual British delight: soggy white bread parted by transparent meat. But this was an American sandwich: inch-thick ham plus cheese, tomatoes and lettuce, mayonnaise and half a dozen other ingredients, so big I could barely stuff it into my ten-year-old hungry mouth.

America has always been a variation on this sandwich: bigger and better than expected, more wonderful and colourful, the triumph of generosity and the human imagination, a mouthful of glorious excess. I will miss it all. The energy of Manhattan, the car factories of Ohio, the openness of Wyoming or Iowa. Hiking the red earth of Canyon de Chelly in Arizona, moose in the Tetons or bears gorging salmon on the beaches of Alaska.

I will miss the sense that nothing is impossible, that ordinary people can achieve extraordinary things, that every man is a king, or could be; the very un-European attitude that it does not matter what your father did or how posh his accent was. What matters is what you can do, how grandly you can dream. Europeans will frown at such naivety. That last word, 'dream', is responsible for a lot of trouble; Hitler, Napoleon and Stalin being among Europe's great dreamers. Yet there is still an American Dream, unfashionable and battered since my first American friend handed me that sandwich in a Cold War outpost of the American empire.

For some the American Dream often sounds like the ambition to do half as much work for twice the pay. For others it remains what it always was. Not a soppy belief that everything will end happily ever after, but the hope that despite the brutal and greedy things we do to one another, humans are the only species capable of making things forever better; that we are reasonable creatures and our good natures will eventually overcome our worst vices. In that sense, I am optimistically leaving America, knowing that part of America will never leave me.

7

Massacre in New Venice

Nick Caistor

*Suspected right-wing gunmen had killed more than sixty people in fishing
communities in the north of the country. It was one of the worst attacks on
civilians during the civil war in Colombia, which had claimed the lives of tens of
thousands of civilians. (9 December 2000)*

The Cienaga Grande has an unfortunate name, it means the 'Great Swamp',
but to me it's one of the most beautiful places on the planet. Cienaga is
a network of salt-water lagoons on Colombia's northern coast, just inland
from the Caribbean Sea. The lagoons are a few feet deep at the most, but they
create a world of air and water and silky green mangroves that seems to float
magically between the earth and the sky. In the middle of these lagoons are
villages of wooden huts raised on stilts that are home to a tightly knit community of fishermen and their families. The main village is called Nueva
Venecia, New Venice, which, like its European counterpart, rises out of the
water like an enchanted mirage.

I first saw Nueva Venecia a few years ago when I was making a programme
about environmental problems in Latin America. Early one morning I found
myself in a boat skimming across a Cienaga lagoon towards the village.
Nueva Venecia loomed up out of the mist and looked as if it was hanging
miraculously somewhere between lake and sky. I met and spent the day
with the fishermen of Nueva Venecia. As so often when meeting people
like them, what most impressed me was the harmony they enjoyed with
their extraordinary surroundings, and the ease with which they accepted
my presence.

As far as they were concerned, I could have dropped from the moon, but
they welcomed me into their canoes, and before long we were gliding out
through the mangroves, skimming over the surface of the world. As with all

fishermen, theirs was a world of silence and patience. They paddled noise-lessly along, in straw hats and smoking hand-rolled cigars, until we reached the spot where they thought there should be fish. When we arrived, they got out their nets and tridents and began fishing, their every action as simple and effective as if it had been bred in the bone. Despite their skill, the fishermen ended the day empty-handed. This was the story that had brought me to Nueva Venecia: how the environment of the lagoons had been changed with the building of a new coastal highway, which blocked the free flow of sea water in and out of the Cienaga. This had caused the salt levels in the water to build up to such an extent that both the fish and the mangroves were dying.

Back in the Colombian capital, Bogotá, the environment minister of the day explained that yes, mistakes had been made in the past, but that all this would soon be put right; scientific studies were being carried out, new blue-prints were being drawn up, and the path to progress was clear. I doubted it at the time, and it seems that in the past few years little progress has been made. The fishermen have had less and less opportunity to earn their liveli-hood, and the lagoons have continued their slow agony.

Then last week I read a few lines in a Spanish newspaper. It told the story of how a dozen of the fishermen from Nueva Venecia had been intercepted by a group of armed men. These paramilitaries had forced them to return to the village. All the men of Nueva Venecia were herded into the small church on stilts and then taken out and shot one by one in the back of the head. The paramilitaries fired on anyone else coming towards the village and then went round in their motor launches shooting at other villages in their path. The newspaper reported that more than sixty people had met their deaths in this way. The armed men's excuse for these killings? They said the fisher-men had been helping the left-wing guerrillas, who are also strong in that region of Colombia.

The death of sixty fishermen in Colombia's civil war barely made the news internationally. In Colombia it was noted as the worst massacre of civilians this year, but was little more than another gruesome statistic in a country where those killed in an ongoing civil war are numbered in the tens of thousands. Perhaps deaths like these have little impact internationally because people in Colombia are not killed for their race or their religion. They're caught up in an absurd war in which any idea of right and wrong has long since become irrelevant. The paramilitaries who killed the fish-ermen are defending their privileges, their land and the money they earn from the illegal drugs trade. The guerrilla groups opposing them lost any coherent ideology long ago.

The Colombian government has just put in place a plan which calls for more than a billion and a half dollars to be spent trying to eradicate the menace of drugs and the war surrounding their production and export. Critics say this will just mean more money spent on weapons, to kill more people. In short, like many thousands of other ordinary Colombians, the fishermen were killed out of greed and stupidity. One of the most beautiful places on the planet has been destroyed, its population almost entirely wiped out. The whole of Colombia is now a *cienaga grande*, a great swamp, where hope, decency and respect for human life are being swallowed up.

Everybody Wanted to Get Out

Jane Beresford

Jane Beresford was in New York making a radio documentary on 11 September 2001, the day two hijacked aircraft were flown into the World Trade Centre.
(13 September 2001)

It was the brightest, bluest day on Manhattan's harbour. A friend of mine has just moved to New York and on this perfect late summer's day I was envying her luck. Within ten minutes the scene was to be transformed into everyone's worst nightmare. It was so unreal, it was as if it was happening to someone else. It started with a thump. The hot-dog vendor said it was construction work and the smoke billowing out of World Trade Centre Tower One did seem like construction dust. And then I saw the plane. It was big and low, bigger than you ever normally see in the skies of Manhattan, and it was heading straight towards me across the harbour.

It seemed so low that I felt I could touch it. I could only see its white underbelly like a shark's. By now there was a lot of smoke and my first thought was that the plane was off-course; it was heading straight for the World Trade Centre, it was going to swerve, it was going to do anything to miss that building. But with pin-point accuracy it seemed to speed up, and with a loud bang it hit the tower and burst into flames. Suddenly the whole place stank of aviation fuel and people started screaming and screaming. 'My mum is in there,' one young woman cried. I felt like I was in a movie. It was Armageddon meets *Independence Day*. The police started to force us towards Brooklyn Bridge, that great landmark of New York.

We were in a snowstorm of dust. Motorbikes were tearing past. We later learnt that people were offering big money to get off the island. Hundreds of us were walking slowly towards the bridge to get across the river, to get out. Everybody wanted to leave Manhattan. If this could happen, nowhere was safe. Someone said they're going to take out the bridge, and for a moment there was panic and crying. We looked back and saw the first tower slowly collapse amid a cloud of dust and continued our long, hot tramp across the bridge. When we reached the other side, one young man with his shirt tied across his face to try and keep out the dust, started cheering. 'Asshole,' someone shouted out. It wasn't the moment to rejoice in your own safe passage out of Manhattan.

Later that day I spoke to a friend who'd been on the 83rd floor of Tower One. The worst part, he told me, had been seeing the aviation fuel streaming down the windows. 'When we saw that,' he said, 'we thought the whole place was going to go up. I went down two flights of stairs touching the handles of the exit doors to see if they were hot. We'd been taught to do that to tell if there was fire behind them.'

He and his small company of just fifteen people made their way to the stairwell. 'It seemed like we were waiting there for ever,' he said. 'People kept inching forward, then it speeded up and there was hope, hope that you were going to get out soon, and then people from further down the stairs would call back: "Hang on, hang on, there's a bottleneck down here, don't push, don't push." They were worried they were going to get crushed.'

'As we were going down, firemen were coming up with oxygen tanks and hoses. My first thought was: how are they carrying that heavy stuff up the stairs. My second thought was that they were going to their deaths. The hardest part was the waiting to get out. Just ten minutes waiting, just ten minutes seemed like hours. The worst place to have been must have been in one of those planes that hit the towers, but, after that, it was the waiting in the stairwell.'

As he reached the bottom, the emergency staff called out: 'Don't look, don't look, just keep going, just keep going,' and he ran. 'I just wanted to get the hell out of there,' he said. It was the day that everybody wanted to get out of Manhattan.

9
American Drive

David Willis

The United States was in deep shock after the attacks of 9/11, when our correspondent hired a car in Los Angeles and set out across the country to gauge the mood of middle America. (6 October 2001)

The car rental salesman seemed perplexed. 'So you're saying you don't know where or when you'll be returning this vehicle?' 'Perhaps Denver. Friday.' He dutifully filled in the details. 'Or maybe New York.' The form was suddenly torn from its pad, screwed up and thrown on the floor. Then, like errant schoolchildren, we were sent outside to unload the sporty little number he'd originally allocated us and transfer our luggage to a considerably less glamorous Ford mini-van. It was to be our home for nearly three weeks.

New York's twin towers had just collapsed and we were embarking on a macabre odyssey, a journey which would take us to the heart of a grieving nation. Ordinarily, it would have been so very pleasant: bumping through dusty desert towns dotted along the famous Route 66, speeding across the Rocky Mountains and the great plains of the old Wild West, coasting past snow-capped mountains and deep desert valleys; meandering our way from California to Colorado, Kansas to Arkansas, Oklahoma to Tennessee and finally to New York City itself, a journey through seventeen states and three different time zones.

Instead it began to feel like an intrusion into private grief. As our mini-van struggled on its way, reaction to the atrocity unfolded like the road ahead; the nation's grim mood twisting and turning like bends on our map, as grief gave way to anger, anger to vengeance. The country was still in shock, almost denial, when we reached Barstow, a one-horse town close to the California–Nevada border.

The tiny community hospital was bursting at the seams, people spilling across the cramped corridors waiting patiently to give blood – keen to do something, anything, to help those suffering in New York. A photographer from the local newspaper, *The Desert Dispatch*, hovered among them, shooting occasional glances at a television set in the corner where pictures of the disaster were repeated time after time. Across town, the tiny Barstow fire service was desperately trying to work out how best to help their colleagues in New York. The chief told a handful of men he was seeking permission to travel there and assist in the rescue operation, who was willing to go? Everybody in the room raised a hand.

By the time we reached Salt Lake City the mood had changed. Shock was subsiding, grief was taking its place. A middle-aged woman, tears rolling down her cheeks, stepped up to the microphone at a hastily arranged prayer service in a city centre parking lot. 'Thank you, Jesus, for our family. Thank you for sparing the lives that you spared.' Around her people of all faiths bowed their heads. Acknowledgement of a sense of vulnerability had suddenly gripped the nation; even those thousands of miles from the attacks counted themselves lucky to be alive. Then the famous Mormon Tabernacle choir sang the 'The Star Spangled Banner' with such dignity and such grace. They had barely reached 'Land of the Free and Home of the Brave' before I had to leave the room.

I cried more during the first few days of this trip than I have in my entire life. Of course, I tried to steel myself, to keep it private, but there were times when I suddenly found myself engulfed by sadness. In Oklahoma, a city still recovering from a terrorist attack which killed 168 people, I met a woman who should have been crying but was not. Cindy Rice lost friends in that blast and had just learnt that her son David was on the 104th floor of the World Trade Centre on the fateful morning. Shortly after watching the attacks on television, she received a phone call confirming that he was dead. Yet when I called she was making tea and fussing over neighbours and friends who had turned up to offer their condolences. Her detachment was unnerving. During our interview I was the only one to shed a tear. Only later did I realise she was still in shock: it was a tragedy too enormous to contemplate; the truth had yet to sink in.

And then came the backlash. We arrived in Ohio three days later on the morning a man drove his car at full speed through the front doors of the central mosque in Cleveland. The lower part of the building was destroyed, but mercifully no one was hurt. When the leader of the local mosque played me some of the messages on his answerphone, I got a far greater sense of what the Muslim community was up against. I heard a barrage of crude insults and anti-Islamic slurs interspersed with venomous messages which culminated in threats, the most chilling from a woman who calmly declared her intention to kill at least ten Muslims.

A light rain was falling when we finally arrived in New York and gazed at the spot where the twin towers once stood. Their ruins were still smouldering. Behind me a lone violinist launched into a wailing lament, and for a moment it seemed as though everything stood still, frozen in time amid the dust and devastation of Ground Zero. And I stared across the rubble, once again blinking back tears. I was thinking not just of those who had lost their lives, but the many, many people who'd been touched by this disaster whom we met along the way.

10
Knitting in Peru

Susie Emmett

Wherever you travel in Peru, from Lima and the other cities to the peaks of the high Andes, you will find women knitting. Some do it commercially, for a wage, but most are knitting to provide clothes for their family, or simply because they like it. (16 March 2002)

I blame Bin Laden. If it wasn't for him and his followers, then I would still be able to ease the boredom of long-haul flights with my favourite companion, my knitting. And don't think that I could get round airline restrictions by taking plastic rather than metal needles. As any knitter knows, using plastic is about as easy as riding a skateboard without wheels. And to arrive without my knitting in Peru, where so many women are at it, is like arriving naked at a knitting convention: in the markets, in the streets, on the buses, in the fields and of course at home, deft, quick, stitch by stitch, the country's clothed or jumpered.

As I travel by train in the central mountains, there's a sudden jolt and a terrible grating sound. The last coach has come off the rails. From my window, I watch as a work-gang is summoned from houses along the track to place boulders under the carriage and lever the wheels. Eventually, the shouting and shunting back and forth achieve the desired effect and we are back on track. I measure how long this takes by observing the clicking needles of two onlookers standing on a mound of earth. Thirty rows of a dainty, cabled, blue front-side of a cardigan and about three centimetres on to a hot-pink jumper for a child, and we are away.

Up in the mountains, walking between villages enveloped by cloud, I come across a woman watching her flock of wether lambs. She wears the traditional fine-woven, huge-brimmed hat and her gathered black skirt sways as she guides the sheep through the pasture in a circuit back to the village for the night. She is suckling her infant at her breast and, of course, knitting. How's that for multi-tasking?

For some women in Peru, knitting is a living. In a suburb of the capital, Lima, in an upstairs room, I meet some of the country's professional knitters. No machine can yet match their skill. Four master craftswomen are working on incredibly intricate jackets, jumpers and waistcoats destined to grace the shoulders and impress the friends of affluent women in Europe and North America. Every garment is unique.

They are shy and understandably suspicious of my questions about their lives, but my genuine appreciation of the skills at their fingertips breaks the nervous tension between us. Not only is knitting these women's living, it's an escape. Fifty-seven-year-old Anatolia, her complexion etched with years of worry, looks up from the delicate Pima cotton jacket taking shape on her lap. She tells me that she knits eight hours in the day and three or four more in the evening, if she can, as she needs the money.

'But to knit this is extraordinarily difficult,' I say. 'If you feel tense or unhappy, surely it will show?' She doesn't take her eyes away from mine as she waits for the translation and then her face breaks into a smile. 'I set all my troubles aside. I escape from them, then I knit. That's the secret.' In truth, some women have to knit in secret. If their partners were to discover their new income, they would stop contributing anything to household expenses. So the women lie about where they are going. Saying they are going to a meeting or to visit a sick friend, they sneak away for a few hours to work at their needles in a safe house.

Some partners reluctantly accept the constant gentle click, click, click. Twenty-seven-year-old Margarita is working on another equally complex creation. 'My husband tells me I pay more attention to my knitting than either him or our children. But the only work he has is washing cars in the street. He can be days without money. My knitting gives us everything we have.'

One evening in the north, in the region of Cajamarca, the clouds roll back up the high pine-forested sides of deep valleys. In this, the wet season, when the sun breaks through the dazzling depth of colour and detail in the land-scape is revealed. Below in the crazy-paved grazing, studded with farm-steads, gentle cows stand in the meadows for the evening's hand-milking. It's the speed and sound of the river that hold my attention, so at first I don't see the women coming towards me along the same path.

A grandmother, her daughter and her young child are all knitting as they walk. We greet and exchange queries about where we're heading. But it is the little girl's two rows of unsteady stitches that remind me I learnt to knit from my grandmother, too. I am invited to join them as they sit at the riverside. After days of research and interviews, this time I feel no need to ask more questions. It is enough to sit in silence together, sharing what we have in common.

11
Dance of Shattered Dreams

Peter Day

The hard times for Argentina were showing no signs of ending. A deep economic crisis had led to growing unemployment and poverty. There were street protests in the capital, Buenos Aires, and in the provinces food was in short supply and people were dying from malnutrition. But, despite the difficulties, Argentines were still dancing. (23 January 2003)

Pretty uncritically, I like most of the places I encounter whizzing round the world, reporting on global business. But not Argentina. Argentina I love. I am sitting on a terrace in one of the cultural centres of Buenos Aires, with a flawless midsummer sky stretching far over the sailing boats on the Plate estuary into Uruguay on the other side of the river. Far below, festive streets light up the lobbies of exclusive air-conditioned apartments. This is the Ricoleto, home of the famous society cemetery, with its modest tomb containing the earthly remains of that legend Evita Peron. On Sunday afternoon, there's a busy crafts market in the park below. Yesterday I went to a noisy fair at the riding club, where dozens of startlingly handsome designers were selling clothes and trinkets to crowds of bargain hunters.

In the restaurants, diners are still tucking into gargantuan plates of the best meat in the world, and there is spectacular art to be seen, including a huge metallic flower which opens and closes as dawn passes to dusk in one of the parks below me. Sitting high above it all, it's hard to imagine that Argentina is passing through what everyone says is the worst economic crisis that this country has experienced in the cumulative chaos of the past eighty years. But so it is.

At the end of 2001, the government abandoned the one peso to one American dollar exchange rate link that had been a formidable weapon against hyper-inflation when it was introduced twelve years ago. Argentina plunged into chaos last Christmas, as the peso plunged in international value, and a panicky presidential decree froze bank accounts and turned the dollars in them into shrunken local currency. Chaos followed: huge street demonstrations, five presidents drummed in and out of office in less than five weeks, leaps in unemployment, rising poverty. The peso settled at two-thirds of its dollar-linked international value, making this country one of the world's great travel bargains.

A series of debt defaults reduced proud Argentina to basket-case status among the international financial community. As a result, there's begging everywhere, soup kitchens have been set up in provincial towns to fight the deaths from malnutrition which are making daily headlines in the papers and on the garish local TV news stations. At the end of the working day, the streets of Buenos Aires are busy with whole families, including tiny children, furiously sorting rubbish into different piles, from speciality paper to plastic, ready for sale to the recyclers, for a few pesos. The *cartoneros*, as they're called, have shocked the affluent; Third World poverty in a city which always prided itself on being European.

Waiting for me to finish an interview in an admittedly dodgy part of town, my driver was robbed of his watch at gun-point by teenagers as he dozed in the car. For some help in decoding this extraordinary atmosphere of crisis I turned, as do so many visitors, to music: that speciality of Buenos Aires, the tango. This was a country founded on hope, as European immigrants crowded into the New World in the nineteenth century. Some time near the end of the century, from mixed parentage like so many other things here, the tango emerged as a joyful expression of sexual anticipation, danced in the cafés and brothels on the edge of the city by immigrant workers and bar girls.

But Argentina's economic vitality peaked in the 1920s, and some time after that, the tango developed a new sensuous melancholy. This insight was given to me one afternoon by the eminent cultural critic Ernesto Schoo, deep in his book-lined apartment.

Later that evening I watched couples dancing intently at a local *milonga*, where enthusiasts of all ages gather to tango into the night. The participants do it for themselves – not the noisy, show-off, athletic version of the tango that enthrals the crowds at the tourist haunts, but a more haunting, suggestive version of the dance. The sadness reflects, says Ernesto Schoo, the shattered dreams of the immigrants who came into the country after the 1920s, when the pre-eminence of Buenos Aires among the cities of Latin America was already in relentless decline.

Before their gig at the design fair, the rising pop group Miranda told me how their music of boy meets girl, boy loses girl, reflected an essential Argentine mixture of emotions: our audiences laugh and then they cry, they said. And that is why I think that Argentina is too headstrong to be likeable. With its ravishing women and its world-weary men; its galloping gauchos, even here in the streets of the capital; its buildings ornate with faded glory; its vast interior; its incipient corruption; its natural wonders, Argentina is a place for a love affair. Just don't expect it to be easy.

12
Maria's Hundred-dollar Bill

Jeremy McDermott

Among the stories aired about the civil conflict in Colombia was one about Maria, a woman displaced by the violence, whose husband was murdered by right-wing paramilitaries. She now feeds her five children by sifting through other people's rubbish, with little help from the state. A listener in Austria was so moved by the tale that she sent our correspondent in Colombia a hundred-dollar bill to give to Maria. (1 February 2003)

The fear was that I would not be able to find Maria again, her shack lost in the midst of Ciudad Bolivar's slums, or that if I did manage to find the place again, she would have gone. Hers is an extreme case in a country wracked with violence, but not isolated. One of the 350,000 people displaced in Colombia last year, Maria was driven from her small plot of land in the southern province of Meta after right-wing paramilitaries knocked on the door of her house in the middle of the night, thrashed her husband in front of the whole family, then took him away. She found his corpse later not far from the small farm they worked together. He had been tortured and then executed. The paramilitaries accused him of being a guerrilla sympathiser. There was no right of reply or appeal, just the single shot of the executioner.

She was told to take her family and leave. She packed up what she could carry and ushered her children on to a bus to Bogotá. Home became a one-room shack with two rough beds made of planks where the family sleeps, and it was here we found her last year, newly arrived, sifting through rubbish to feed her five children.

Enlisting the help of Blanca Pineda, one of the community leaders in the slum, who had accompanied me last year, we went in search of the hardy little peasant woman. Blanca was not only there to guide me, but to ensure

I was not robbed as soon as I appeared in the streets of this, the most dangerous part of the capital. The word went out immediately that there was a foreigner in the area as locals appeared at the doors of their houses or peered suspiciously from windows. I shrank closer to Blanca, a well-known face in the slum, who waved and greeted the hard-looking men and women who stalk the muddy lanes of this part of the city, largely abandoned by the state. Police are too afraid to patrol here; further up the hill left-wing guerrillas control the area, whilst in a neighbouring slum right-wing paramilitaries are the law. This is an urban jungle, every bit as dangerous as the real jungle Maria fled last year.

But, sure enough, the shack was still there, nestling between two brick buildings, the wood and corrugated iron creating a shelter against the cold and wet of this city set high in the Andes mountains. When we knocked on the gate, a tiny girl peered through the gap in the fence, her broad indigenous face spreading in a huge beautiful smile. This was Maria's youngest daughter, aged five, obviously remembering the foreigner who had visited before. Maria seemed unsurprised to see us, but then her tired face seldom registers much emotion. She was hanging out the family's laundry. Her two girls were dressed in borrowed clothes, waiting for their own to dry.

I tried to explain why we were back, but she did not know where Europe was or how an Irish lady living in Austria could have heard about her or wanted to give her money. All she knew was that it was a blessing from God, the answer to her long prayers. I had changed the dollar bill into the local currency, pesos, and put the bundle of notes into her hands. It was more than she had seen since her flight from her farm and it disappeared into the folds of the rags she was wearing.

Little had changed since our last visit a year ago. She was still cooking on a wood stove she had built; the kids were scavenging around as school was an expensive luxury belonging to a different world to the one in which she lived. One of her sons was sick, but he was just having to fight his way through it; there was no money to go to a clinic and, with a peasant's toughness, he would have to rough it out.

We tried to talk a little about her life and the current situation. But Maria was unaware of what was going on in the world around her; with no television or radio in the house and unable to read, she picked up titbits of information along with the food scraps she recovered during the day. I dared to ask if she had any hope for the future and she looked at me as if I were mad.

'Of course I do. God will provide; he has up till now.' I was humbled that someone who had challenges each day that would crush most people was able to get up each morning with hope and tackle another day. Everyone should have a Maria in their lives, as I never complain about anything now. I don't have the right and have been twice humbled, first by Maria's fortitude and second by a far-off listener who cared enough to send money.

13

A Dog's Life

Stephen Evans

Severe winter weather in New York spells bad news for the city's homeless; but for its canine population, it's an opportunity to dress up. (31 January 2004)

At the top end of Union Square, in Manhattan, there are often two competing charity stalls. On one side of the Barnes and Noble bookstore on 18th Street is a trestle table with pamphlets outlining the needs of dogs in this hard city. On the other is a stall seeking support for humans. Sad to say, it is the human cause that loses out. Sympathisers flock to show interest in orphaned dogs seeking homes, while New Yorkers rush past the stall seeking cash for the homeless, homeless humans that is.

Volunteers for the United Homeless Organisation sit behind the upturned plastic water-cooler urn and chant: 'One penny, one dime, one dollar; one penny, one dime, one dollar; help make a difference.' But, it has to be said, the clink of coins in the bottle is not deafening. The begging chant is a vain cry to the wind. And it is a bitter wind in New York, these days, with temperatures of 20 and 30 degrees below freezing and a wind rushing in from the Arctic via the Hudson and East rivers.

These are not good times to be homeless in New York. They sit like zombies round midnight on the benches in the subway below Penn Station, or in bundles of rags in carriages of the A trains. One of the longest routes on the network, it offers the longest period of warmth without disturbance.

The Police Department has what it calls a Homeless Outreach Unit whose officers tour the city, looking for people who need shelter. But in this coldest of times, most people get off the freezing streets under their own steam, if that is the right word. They either get to the shelters in their thousands, or find the nooks, crannies and havens of free heat on the subway system. All in contrast to the dogs of New York.

For the trendier parts, like the East Village where I live, cold weather is an opportunity to parade your pet. It is your walking fashion accessory, dressed in exotic winter clothes. I have seen a tiny puppy carried in a papoose, a sling for babies, on the chest of one young male fashionista. Puppies wear knitted coats, coats made of special insulated, wet-suit material. They even wear hats and booties.

New York is without doubt the dog capital of the world. It is pooch city. No doubt, they like dogs in Paris, but there they seem to belong to ladies of a certain age who need elegant, if canine, companionship at dinner. In Britain, a dog is for walking in the country. But in New York, it is as much a part of the young fashion scene as a tattoo on your shoulder blade. Only in New York, it seems to me, are dogs owned by young, single people with very small apartments indeed.

The city's Department of Health keeps records of the dog population: 530,000 mutts at the latest count. It seems that twenty per cent of New Yorkers aged eighteen to twenty-four are registered as dog-owners. Furthermore, the city authorities can tell you who owns what kind of dog and where. There are few surprises.

Chihuahuas are favourite in zip code 10029, Spanish Harlem. Rottweilers are the preferred choice in 10473, the South Bronx, where the people are tough. And in zip code 10021, the rich and chi-chi Upper East Side, it is the shitzu, those tiny, fluffy toy dogs that are paraded in pink ribbons and bows on the sidewalks outside the Metropolitan Museum.

One thing the cold weather has put a stop to is the habit of humans using their dogs as a means of meeting members of the opposite sex. The parks of New York have what are called dog-runs, enclosed areas where dogs are allowed to run free and do what dogs do. It is also where single New Yorkers can go and do what single New Yorkers do: meet other single New Yorkers. The ritual is well-documented: dog meets dog, with a bit of sniffing. Human pulls leash back apologetically. Humans compare their respective dogs and conversation ensues. Love blossoms.

The New York Times quotes one vet, and I swear this is true, who advises that the best way of striking up a conversation with a potential partner is to get a three-legged animal, a real talking point on the dog-run.

But canine-assisted courtship will have to wait until the winds abate and the air warms up. In the meantime, the dogs are either paraded fleetingly in their garb or cooped up in the average apartment, in which there is not enough room to swing, well, a cat. It is baffling how animal lovers can care so little about the object of their love that they confine them in the tiniest spaces. Every weekend in my block, I can hear a dog howling upstairs while its owners are away.

Not that it is much better for humans. This winter, many have had to live in the usual cramped conditions, but also without heating. The city authorities have logged nearly 4,000 complaints from people saying their landlords are not providing heating or hot water. In New York, then, it can be a dog's life – at least if you are human and poor or homeless.

14
A Navy with No Sea

Elliott Gotkine

Bolivia used to have its own coastline until neighbouring Chile seized it after triumphing in a nineteenth-century war. But for Bolivians getting their beach back was a matter of great importance, not just for those who wanted to bathe in the blue Pacific, but, more significantly, for the country's navy which has been exposed to ridicule for having no sea on which to sail its ships. (14 August 2004)

Bolivia lost its access to the sea 125 years ago. But its sense of injustice remains, and nowhere more so than in the Bolivian navy. The Bolivian navy! But how can it have a navy when it doesn't have access to the sea? Fair point. Yet, in a triumph of nationalism over adversity, Bolivia's armada instead makes do with the chilly ice-blue waters of Lake Titicaca, which is where I spent a swashbuckling day with hundreds of Bolivia's most able seamen.

My first port of call was Tiquina, home of the Bolivian navy's main base on the shores of the world's highest navigable lake, 3,810 metres above sea level, where the cold winds are often so biting that they leave teeth marks. The grey-haired Commander Jose Luis Cabas was supposed to have been our guide for the day. But, as he hobbled down the stairs of his house on crutches, it became clear that this wasn't to be. He'd snapped his Achilles tendon playing football and he wouldn't be able to get his hands on deck for up to three months. Nor would he be giving us an interview, as previously agreed. We were later told that Commander Cabas had had a bitter experience with Chile's *El Mercurio* newspaper, which had apparently used its day out with Bolivia's navy to poke fun at its sea-less neighbour. 'Bolivia can't breathe without the sea,' he told me. 'It's like having no lungs.'

We left the commander to his convalescence and were led on a tour of the sprawling base by Captain Reme de la Barra Caceres. The dark-skinned, moustachioed captain, dapper in his black and gold-trim uniform, bent over backwards to show my cameraman and me everything he could. Best of all, he took us on one of his ageing patrol boats, which ferried us up and down the devastatingly beautiful deep-blue abyss. 'Isn't it strange being in a navy which doesn't have a sea?' I asked him. 'Bolivia's navy,' he told me, 'is as old as the republic.' One hundred and seventy-nine years old, to be precise. But then, in 1879, the War of the Pacific broke out with Chile. The fighting was over the mining of *guano*, that's bird poo to you and me, valuable for use as a fertiliser. Bolivia was trounced by Chile. Ever since then, on 23 March, Bolivia has marked the Day of the Sea with sombre ceremonies across the country. It doesn't seem to matter that Bolivia signed the inappropriately named Treaty of Peace and Friendship with Chile one hundred years ago, ratifying Santiago's dominion over its neighbour's former lands.

Being shut-off from the sea 'causes us deep pain', a wistful Captain Reme told me as we headed back to port. He added, however, that Bolivia's navy also operated in the rivers in the east of the country and that it had training arrangements with the sea-faring states of Argentina, Brazil, Peru and Venezuela. 'This,' he told me, was 'to help them prepare for the day, not too far away, when Bolivia gets its sea back.' And, to help speed things along at a faster rate of knots, Bolivia is trying to use its vast natural gas reserves as a bargaining chip with Chile. You give us sovereign access to the sea and we'll sell you, not give you, mind, the gas you so desperately need.

But just in case that doesn't work, Bolivia's navy has a song it sings every day. Soon after we stepped back on to dry land, I was treated to a surreal spectacle: trumpets were blown, drums were rolled and dozens of young seamen stood stiffly by the lakeside in their sailors' hats and navy uniforms, chests inflated. The song went something like this:

> We'll get back our sea.
> We'll get back our coastline
> After this century of injustice.
> It's worth tolerating death
> To recover our coastline and the wide sea.

So far, there's little sign of Bolivia doing so. To the gas offer, Chile's answer is unequivocal: 'No way, Commander Jose.' Besides, says Chile, Bolivia already has access to the sea via Chilean ports like Arica, through which Bolivia exports everything from zinc to soya. And in summertime, I'm told, you can't find a parasol for love nor money when Bolivians invade the beaches of northern Chile.

For now, diplomacy looks like the best bet for a solution and the two countries are talking, I was told by Bolivia's foreign minister, who I was intrigued to learn was actually born in Chile to a Chilean mother. But don't be surprised if in another hundred years Bolivia is still a landlocked country; its navy still chugs forlornly around Lake Titicaca; and young cadets still sing a song in the fervent belief that one day Bolivia will get its beach back.

15

FOOC for Bush

Justin Webb

Two months before the US presidential election which saw George Bush defeat his Democratic rival John Kerry to win a second term, his party, the Republicans, held their convention in New York. The Republicans, it became clear, had borrowed the considerable moral weight of From Our Own Correspondent *to make their point. (4 September 2004)*

It is two o'clock in the morning and I have escaped. Out from the basement of Madison Square Garden, an oddly unglamorous concrete bunker plonked in the seedy streets of midtown Manhattan. Out past the police, past the grey-suited secret service men with those wiggly wires in their ears, past the paramilitary SWAT teams with automatic weapons and army helmets, out into the heat of the New York night. Two blocks away, I pass a parked car where a man is screaming, screaming into a mobile phone. 'I have just had sex with your sister,' he bellows. 'What are you going to do about it?' Actually he uses a terser phrase than that, but you get the drift. The sister, I assume it was she, was looking bored and filing her nails.

What can the Republicans make of this place?

When you talk to them they are polite in a glassy-eyed kind of way. But it is an odd paradox that the Republicans chose to show their solidarity with people who regard them with contempt at best. Most New Yorkers are Democrats, but, more importantly, most New Yorkers are cross and busy. I stood on a Manhattan corner this week as the president passed. The police hemmed us in, batons drawn. The helicopters buzzed overhead and the sirens blared. Now on most corners of most cities in the US, the passing of the presidential motorcade would occasion some interest. People would clap, would boo, would do something. But New Yorkers did not even look. They read their papers, they glanced at their watches, they barked into their phones. And when the presidential ambulance and the outriders finally brought up the rear of the convoy and the police withdrew, New Yorkers just surged across the street, slightly crosser but otherwise unmoved. And these folks, as the president would say, are the ones who are about to be incinerated if John Kerry gets in and the French take over the defence of the US. Such ungratefulness!

But the delegates did not need to focus too heavily on the hostile environment of Seventh Avenue. Inside the convention centre they had created the kind of jolly, triumphant bubble which political parties manage even in desperate times, and for the Republicans these are interesting, but not desperate, times. The secret of their ability to stay in business in spite of all that has gone wrong? Discipline. And genuine enthusiasm for the party message, which, judging by their behaviour when the speeches stopped and the television cameras were turned off, the Democrats' party faithful just did not have in Boston in July.

There, after the speeches, you could wander like a beachcomber among the detritus on the floor and come up with some wonderful souvenir tat. Not quite 'Pretty Girls for Nixon', my favourite dated poster, but some nice Kerry/Edwards endorsement which my children might one day like to have. But, at the end of the Republican speeches, delegates fold up their posters and take them home. They love Bush and Cheney and they want them on their walls.

Of those two traits, discipline and enthusiasm, it is the former which really impresses: the steely way in which the Republican party is capable of using anything to its advantage.

Senator Kerry has discovered that words uttered in the past can be brought to life and used as the party sees fit. But he is a politician of thirty years' standing. As a foreigner of no consequence to anyone here except my family, I was somewhat surprised to find my own words used by the Republicans to make a buck and make a point. A year or so ago on this programme, I said: 'Nobody spends more time on his knees than George W. Bush.'

It was intended as a faintly ironic comment on the president's religiosity. Imagine my surprise when I came across a copy of the DVD *George Bush: Faith in the White House*. On the back, among the glowing endorsements: '"Nobody spends more time on his knees than George W. Bush," says BBC Washington correspondent, Justin Webb.' I have endorsed the president without even intending to.

At the beginning of the year, one of the president's backroom fixers is alleged to have muttered of John Kerry's military service: 'By the time we've finished with him, people won't know whose side he fought on.' At the time it seemed an implausible boast. But now, not so far-fetched. Hold on to your hats for the next two months. It is going to get tough.

Correspondents

PAUL ADAMS: BBC Diplomatic correspondent formerly in Belgrade and Jerusalem.

HILARY ANDERSSON: BBC correspondent in Johannesburg, Lagos and Jerusalem.

NATALIA ANTELAVA: BBC correspondent in Georgia and Iran.

CHLOE ARNOLD: BBC correspondent in the Caucasus based in Baku, and in Sri Lanka.

BRIAN BARRON: Works throughout the world as a BBC news correspondent.

MARTIN BELL: Worked throughout the world as a BBC news correspondent.

OWEN BENNETT-JONES: BBC correspondent in Islamabad and a presenter for BBC World Service.

JANE BERESFORD: BBC Current Affairs programme-maker.

JIM BIDDULPH: BBC Far East correspondent.

MALCOLM BILLINGS: Presenter of BBC programmes including *Today*, *Heritage* and *Seven Seas*.

COLIN BLANE: BBC Scotland correspondent who has also worked in various BBC foreign bureaux.

ELIZABETH BLUNT: BBC correspondent and Africa specialist at BBC World Service.

JEREMY BOWEN: BBC Middle East Editor, formerly in Rome.

CHRIS BOWLBY: BBC correspondent in Central Europe and BBC Current Affairs programme-maker.

ALEX BRODIE: BBC Middle East correspondent and programme presenter on Radio 4 and BBC World Service.

BEN BROWN: Works throughout the world as a BBC Special correspondent.

TIM BUTCHER: Reports for *FOOC* from Africa and the Middle East.

NICK CAISTOR: Latin America analyst and contributor to BBC programmes on Radio 4 and BBC World Service.

KATE CLARK: BBC correspondent in Kabul.

KEVIN CONNOLLY: BBC correspondent in Warsaw, Paris, Moscow and Belfast.

KIERAN COOKE: BBC correspondent in Jakarta and contributor to *FOOC* from various countries.

PETER DAY: BBC Business Editor.

ERIK DE MAUNY: BBC correspondent in Paris and Moscow.

LYSE DOUCET: BBC Middle East correspondent and BBC World Service presenter.

MARK DOYLE: BBC correspondent in East and West Africa.

FUCHSIA DUNLOP: Contributes to *FOOC* from China.

ROBERT ELPHICK: BBC correspondent in Prague.

SUSIE EMMETT: Maker of and contributor to BBC Current Affairs programmes.

GAVIN ESLER: BBC Washington correspondent and presenter of programmes including BBC2's *Newsnight*.

STEPHEN EVANS: North America Business correspondent.

MATT FREI: BBC correspondent in Hong Kong, Rome and Washington.

JONATHAN FRYER: Contributes to *FOOC* from various countries.

FRANK GARDNER: BBC Security correspondent, formerly in Cairo.

MISHA GLENNY: BBC Central Europe correspondent and historian.

DIANA GOODMAN: BBC correspondent in Bonn and Moscow.

ELLIOTT GOTKINE: BBC Buenos Aires correspondent.

DAMIAN GRAMMATICAS: BBC correspondent in Hong Kong and Moscow.

ORLA GUERIN: BBC correspondent in Rome and Jerusalem.

ANDREW HARDING: BBC correspondent in Moscow, Nairobi and Singapore.

FRANCES HARRISON: BBC correspondent in Sri Lanka and Tehran.

RED HARRISON: BBC Australia correspondent.

HUMPHREY HAWKSLEY: BBC World Affairs correspondent, formerly in Delhi and Hong Kong.

JONATHAN HEAD: BBC correspondent in Jakarta and Tokyo.

JULIET HINDELL: BBC correspondent in Tokyo.

WILLIAM HORSLEY: BBC correspondent in Tokyo and Bonn and Europe specialist at BBC World Service.

DOMINIC HUGHES: BBC correspondent in Sydney.

CATHY JENKINS: BBC East Africa correspondent.

STEPHEN JESSEL: BBC correspondent in Washington and Paris.

ALAN JOHNSTON: BBC correspondent in Kabul and Gaza.

IVOR JONES: BBC correspondent in Budapest and Delhi.

FERGAL KEANE: BBC Special correspondent, formerly in Ireland, Africa and Hong Kong.

BRIDGET KENDALL: BBC Diplomatic correspondent, formerly in Washington and Moscow.

ANDY KERSHAW: Presenter, programme-maker and contributor to *FOOC* from various countries.

THOMAS KIELINGER: London Correspondent of the German newspaper *Die Welt*.

ALEX KIRBY: BBC Environment and Religious Affairs correspondent.

EMMA JANE KIRBY: BBC Europe correspondent.

DANIEL LAK: BBC correspondent in Delhi, Kathmandu and Miami.

ANTHONY LAWRENCE: BBC Far East correspondent.

ALASTAIR LEITHEAD: BBC correspondent in Johannesburg.

ALLAN LITTLE: BBC correspondent in Johannesburg, Moscow and Paris.

TIM LLEWELLYN: BBC Middle East correspondent.

BARNABY MASON: BBC Cairo correspondent and Diplomatic correspondent at BBC World Service.

ISHBEL MATHESON: BBC correspondent in Nairobi.

ANGUS MCDERMID: BBC correspondent in Africa and the United States.

JEREMY MCDERMOTT: BBC correspondent in Bogotá.

IAN MCDOUGALL: Worked throughout the world as a BBC news correspondent.

JILL MCGIVERING: BBC correspondent in Hong Kong, Delhi and Washington.

CHRIS MORRIS: BBC correspondent in Ankara and Brussels.

KYLIE MORRIS: BBC correspondent in Kabul and Bangkok.

JIM MUIR: BBC Middle East correspondent.

ADAM MYNOTT: BBC correspondent in Delhi and Nairobi.

ROBERT PARSONS: BBC correspondent in Moscow and the Caucasus.

JOHN PEEL: Presenter of BBC programmes.

BARNABY PHILLIPS: BBC correspondent in Lagos and Johannesburg.

GERALD PRIESTLAND: BBC correspondent in Delhi and Washington and Religious Affairs correspondent.

WILLIAM REEVE: BBC correspondent in Kabul.

PAUL REYNOLDS: BBC correspondent in Washington.

JAMES ROBBINS: BBC Diplomatic and Royal correspondent, formerly in New York, Brussels and Jerusalem.

JOANNA ROBERTSON: BBC correspondent in Albania and *FOOC* contributor from various countries.

JACKY ROWLAND: BBC correspondent in Belgrade and Moscow.

STEPHEN SACKUR: BBC correspondent in Jerusalem and Washington; Europe correspondent.

HUGH SCHOFIELD: BBC Paris correspondent.

PHILIP SHORT: BBC correspondent in Paris and Tokyo.

DAVID SHUKMAN: Works throughout the world as a BBC news correspondent.

JOHN SIMPSON: BBC World Affairs Editor.

CLIVE SMALL: BBC correspondent in Washington.

JANE STANDLEY: BBC correspondent in Nairobi, Johannesburg and New York.

DOUGLAS STUART: BBC Middle East correspondent.

JOHN SWEENEY: BBC news correspondent and programme presenter.

HUGH SYKES: Works throughout the world as a BBC news correspondent.

NICK THORPE: BBC Central Europe correspondent.

MARK TULLY: BBC Delhi correspondent and programme presenter.

JEREMY VINE: BBC correspondent in Johannesburg, BBC Political correspondent and programme presenter.

ROB WATSON: BBC correspondent in New York and Washington.

JUSTIN WEBB: BBC correspondent in Brussels, Washington and programme presenter.

CHARLES WHEELER: Worked throughout the world as a BBC news correspondent.

TIM WHEWELL: BBC Current Affairs programme-maker and presenter.

MONICA WHITLOCK: BBC correspondent in Central Asia.

DAVID WILLEY: BBC correspondent in Rome.

RICHARD WILLIAMS: BBC correspondent in Africa.

DAVID WILLIS: BBC correspondent in Los Angeles.

RUPERT WINGFIELD-HAYES: BBC correspondent in Beijing.

PAUL WOOD: BBC Diplomatic correspondent, formerly in Cairo.

MIKE WOOLDRIDGE: BBC World Affairs correspondent.

CAROLINE WYATT: BBC correspondent in Paris and Moscow.